The Magical Jewel of Devotion in Kashmir Shaivism

Stava Cintāmaṇi of Bhaṭṭa Nārāyaṇa

Revealed by
Swami Lakshmanjoo

WITH ORIGINAL AUDIO

John Hughes, Editor

Lakshmanjoo Academy

Published by:

Lakshmanjoo Academy

First printing 2018

Printed in the United States of America

For information, address:
Lakshmanjoo Academy
www.lakshmanjooacademy.org

ISBN 978-1-947241-05-3 (paperback)
ISBN 978-1-947241-04-6 (hardcover)
ISBN 978-1-947241-06-0 (ebook)

This sacred text is dedicated to Swami Lakshmanjoo,
our beloved teacher and spiritual father
who has given us everything.
Glory be to Thee!

Table of Contents

Guide to Pronunciation vii
Preface ix
Introduction xi
Acknowledgements xxix
Swami Lakshmanjoo xxxiii

Stava Cintāmaṇi

Introductory Verses of Kṣemarāja 1 to 8
Stava Cintāmaṇi of Bhaṭṭa Nārāyaṇa 9 to 142
Concluding Verses of Kṣemarāja 143 to 145

Appendix

1. *Spanda* (vibrationless-vibration) 147
2. *Vimarśa* (the Self Reflective light of consciousness) 149
3. *Upāyas* (the "means" or "ways") 150
4. *Praṇava mantra, auṁ* (*oṁ*) 151
5. *Svatāntrya* (absolute freedom) 154
6. The Six-fold Proofs (*pramāṇas*) 157
7. *Turya* and *Turyātīta* 161
8. The Three Impurities (*malas*) 163

Bibliography 166
Index 171
Published works 180
Instructions to download audio 182

Guide to Pronunciation

The following English words exemplify the pronunciation of selected Saṅskṛit vowels and consonants. The Romanized Saṅskṛit vowel or consonant is first listed and then an English word is given to aid you in its proper pronunciation.

a	as	a in ***A***merica.
ā	as	a in f***a***ther.
i	as	i in f***i***ll, l***i***ly.
ī	as	i in pol***i***ce.
u	as	u in f***u***ll.
ū	as	u in r***u***de.
ṛi	as	ri in mer***ri***ly.
ṛī	as	ri in ma***ri***ne.
e	as	e in pr***e***y.
ai	as	ai in ***ai***sle.
o	as	o in st***o***ne.
au	as	ou in h***ou***se
ś	as	s in ***s***ure.
ṣ	as	sh in ***sh***un, bu***sh***
s	as	s in ***s***aint, ***s***un

Preface

Devotional hymns have always held an important place in the history of the Monistic teachings of Kashmir Shaivism. The recitation of such devotional hymns is a common part of the daily spiritual practice for many Shaiva aspirants.

Stava Cintāmaṇi, The Magical Jewel of Devotion in Kashmir Shaivism, is a sublime and unique hymn addressed to Lord Shiva, whom the author, Bhaṭṭa Nārāyaṇa, clearly holds as the Supreme Reality. Though highly devotional, these hymns are at the same time practical and deeply philosophical.

The Sanskrit text of the *Stava Cintāmaṇi* with Kṣemarāja's commentary was first published in the *Kashmir Series of Texts and Studies*, Volume X, in Kashmir (1918). This was the text used by Swami Lakshmanjoo in his translation and commentary of this present publication.

Swamiji's love for devotional hymns is evidenced by the fact that he translated and commented upon the *Stava Cintāmaṇi* on three occasions. The first, in 1978, was recorded by John Hughes and forms the basis of this present publication. Then, in 1990, he gave an impromptu translation during which time Denise Hughes compiled extensive hand written notes.[1] Lastly, a recording of Swamiji's recitation of the verses along with a brief translation of selected verses was recorded in Los Angeles in 1991.

To facilitate the reader, these last two renderings have been incorporated as footnotes and are indicated as *Stava Cintāmaṇi* (1990) and *Stava Cintāmaṇi* (1991), respectively. All footnotes, unless otherwise indicated, are by the editors. An appendix has been added to further assist the reader.

Lakshmanjoo Academy
9th May, 2018

---

1 This edition was not recorded.

Introduction

"God and the individual are one.
To realize this is the essence of
Kashmir Shaivism."

The author – Bhaṭṭa Nārāyaṇa

Swami Lakshmanjoo tells us that Bhaṭṭa Nārāyaṇa was one of the most important Kashmir Shaivite masters and that he lived approximately one century before the illustrious Abhinavagupta (924-1020 CE).[1]

This places Bhaṭṭa Nārāyaṇa's time-frame somewhere between the time of Vasugupta[2] and Somānanda.[3] Together these highly revered masters disseminated the foundational texts of a system of philosophy that would later become known exclusively as Kashmir Shaivism.

Thus, the ninth century was a significant period in the history of Shaiva philosophy, which Somānanda tells us had its origins almost 4,000 years earlier, at the beginning of the

---

1 Contemporary scholars generally place Abhinavagupta from 950 to 1020 CE. Drawing from the oral tradition, Swami Lakshmanjoo confirmed that Abhinavagupta lived to the age of ninety six.
2 Vasugupta (800-850CE) was the renowned Shaiva Saint who received the Shiva Sutras directly from Lord Shiva. See: Swami Lakshmanjoo, *Shiva Sutras–The Supreme Awakening*, ed. John Hughes (Lakshmanjoo Academy, Los Angeles, 2002), Introduction.
3 Somānanda (875-925) was the author of the *Śivadṛṣṭi* and the teacher of Utpaladeva, who expanded on the *Śivadṛṣṭi* and in doing so established the Pratyabhijñā school of Kashmir Shaivism.

present era of Hindu chronology known as Kaliyuga.[4] At that time, out of compassion for humanity, Lord Shiva appeared to the sage Durvasa Rishi and entrusted him with the preservation and propagation of the three branches of Shaiva Philosophy: monistic (non-dualistic), mono-dualistic, and dualistic.[5] Over the next 4,000 years, the dualistic teachings, based mainly upon external practices, and the mono-dualistic teachings, based upon meditation and contemplation in combination with formal rituals, remained largely intact. However, the non-dual monistic school of the Bhairava Tantras, having their basis in the direct comprehension and experience of consciousness,[6] waxed and waned to the extent that a few generations before Bhaṭṭa Nārāyana their importance had all but disappeared from the mainstream of Shaiva teachings.

At that time, again out of compassion for humanity, Lord Shiva appeared in a dream to the sage Vasugupta and duly instructed him to seek out a large rock nestled on the side of a stream in the sacred Valley of Harvan.[7] "Inscribed on the underside of that rock," He told the sage, "you will find My *sūtras*." Following the Lord's instructions, Vasugupta located that place and upon touching the rock it miraculously lifted out of the water and exposed the engravings of the *Shiva Sūtras*. These sūtras became the foundation-stone of what would later be known as the Monistic Philosophy of Kashmir

4 Somānada gives a brief recount of the history of Shaiva Philosophy at the end of his *Śivadṛṣṭi*. See: Swami Lakshmanjoo, *Kashmir Shaivism–The Secret Supreme*, ed. John Hughes (LJA, Los Angeles), Chapter 13, *Birth of the Tantras*, pp87-93.

5 These are known as the Bhairava, Rudra and Shiva Tantras respectively.

6 The non-dualistic Bhairava Tantras lay emphasis on both *bauddha jñāna* (intellectual knowledge) and *puruṣa jñāna* (the direct experience of the Self).

7 This rock, known as Śaṅkaropal, is located in the Harvan Valley, about 11 kilometres from Srinagar, at the foot of the sacred Mahādev Mountain.

Shaivism.

In the wake of this revival of non-dual Shaivism, Bhaṭṭa Nārāyaṇa composed his *Stava Cintāmaṇi*. Little is known about the author's life, as he hardly mentions himself in his writings, but we read in Kṣemarāja's commentary that the name of his grandfather was Parameśvara, his father Aparājita, his mother Śrī Daya, and his eldest brother Śaṁkara.[8]

Taking into account the spiritual climate of that generation, with the majority of the population being en-trenched in dualistic and mono-dualistic practices,[9] one could easily assume that he had composed his devotional hymn with the underlying intention of making available a *liṅgoddhāra* text,[10] something that was needed to educate sincere spiritual aspirants in the 'non-dual-monistic' way of thought and practice. Since his commentators indicate that the *Stava Cintāmaṇi* was well received and highly influential, it is more than likely that Bhaṭṭa Nārāyaṇa achieved that goal.

That the author endeavored to enlighten his audience in the direction of non-dual Shaivism is evident in the inclusion of his interpretation of the ancient and highly revered Gāyatri mantra,[11] where he says:

---

8 Commentary of verse 3.

9 Following in the tenets of Buddhists and Shaiva Siddhāntins.

10 Literally, the removal (*uddhāra*) of the order (*liṅga*) of a religious student. *Liṅgoddhāra* is a form of purification, which is a prerequisite to entering the path of monistic Shaivism. The master has to purify the student by removing the misunderstandings of the religious order that they have been following. Only then can the initiation into Shaivism be effective. This process, called *liṅgo-ddhāra*, is found only in the non-dual tradition of Kashmir Shaivism.

11 The Gāyatrī *mantra* has its origins in the *Ṛg Veda*, and is mentioned in many classic Hindu scriptures. Its recitation has been an essential part of daily Hindu practice since ancient times.

> "I don't care to possess that effulgent light (*tat savitur varenyam*) of the three worlds (*bhuḥ*, *bhuvaḥ*, and *svaḥ*),[12] and I don't need my intellect elevated to the state of universal understanding (*dhiyo yo naḥ pracodayāt*); I want only for that effulgent light to direct me on the path of Shaivism–that is all I long for–and that is the only favor I ask of Gāyatrī."[13]

For those sincere aspirants caught in the snare of dualistic disciplines,[14] who were attempting to remove the obstacles to their spiritual progress and who were oblivious to the fact that such ascetic disciplines often serve to develop a distaste for the world, which, from a dualistic point of view, is declared to be an illusion (*moha*) and unreal (*māyā*), it must have been like a stream of nectar to hear Bhaṭṭa Nārāyaṇa boldly declare:

> "*Jayanti*...! Glory be to those divine drops of knowledge which are existing in the cycle of Śaiva Yoga . . . and which have the ability of destroying and washing off all of the three impurities (*malas*)."[15]

With these words, Bhaṭṭa Nārāyaṇa is clearly refuting the long-held notion that ignorance is some kind of physical substance that requires a physical means for its removal. In the wake of this revival of non-dual Shaivism, it is not surprising that Bhaṭṭa Nārāyaṇa's contemporary, Somānanda, begins his *Śivadṛṣṭi* with a verse carrying the same spirit of Shaiva monism:

---

12 *Bhūḥ* is earth; *bhuvaḥ* is the intermediate region of stars and planets; and *svah* means heaven. See also verse 78.

13 Verse 78.

14 It was an entrenched belief amongst the Shaiva Siddhantas that the strict adherence to daily observances, which included various rituals and ascetic yoga practices, was the only means for the attainment of liberation (*mokṣa*).

15 Verse 77. See appendix 8 for an understanding of the three *malas*: *āṇavamala*, *māyīyamala* and *kārmamala*.

> "Let Siva, who is my own nature, bow down to his real nature, Universal Śiva, through His own Śakti, for the removal of bondage and limitation which is none other than Śiva."[16]

Despite the efforts of these spiritual pioneers to propagate a new revelation of non-dual Shaivism, the overall spiritual atmosphere of Kashmir continued to labor under the influence of the long-established dualistic traditions. This is evidenced by the fact that several generations after Vasugupta, Bhaṭṭa Nārāyaṇa, and Somānanda, the illustrious master, Abhinavagupta, found it necessary to continue in the spirit of his predecessors by writing a commentary on the Bhagavad Gītā, and a recension on Ādiśeṣa's (Patañjali) Paramārthasāra, both of which were clearly *liṅgoddhāra* teachings. One can only assume that these two commentaries were not well received by the strict Vaiṣṇava and Vedāntin communities because, under the pen of Abhinavagupta, the Supreme Being, who was originally nominated as Lord Viṣṇu, was now replaced by Lord Shiva.

Though this present publication is concerned solely with Stava Cintāmaṇi, The Magical Jewel of Devotion, it will not be out of place to consider the similarities between Bhaṭṭa Nārāyaṇa and Abhinavagupta.

A prolific commentator and composer,[17] Abhinavagupta was relentless in spreading the non-dual message of Kashmir Shaivism. This he did on the basis of the teachings he had received directly from his lineage (sampradāya) of Shaiva masters, which he substantiated by his own spiritual experience. That he held Bhaṭṭa Nārāyaṇa's words in high

---

16 Somānanda's *Śivadṛṣṭi* 1.1: "*asmad rūpa samāviṣṭaḥ svātmanātmanivāraṇe śivaḥ karotu nijayā namaḥ śaktyā tatātmane.*"

17 Abhinavagupta published more than 40 individual works on Kashmir Shaivism.

esteem can be seen in his famous hymn, the *Bhairava Stava*,[18] where he clearly reflects on verse 77 of the *Stava Cintāmaṇi*:

> "It is said that through ritual bath and the practices of penance, the troubles of worldly existence subside, but even more than this, by remembrance of the sacred *śāstra*s and Your words alone, the current of immortality, like a stream of peace, enters my heart."[19]

> And:

> "O Lord Bhairava, I have perceived You in the unique sacrifice of oneness, which otherwise is not possible though performing mountains of rituals."[20]

There is no doubt that Abhinavagupta's words were well received by sincere aspirants, who, by the grace of Lord Śiva, were eager to understand and embrace these inspiring revelations that exposed the subtle and secret truths,[21] which hitherto lay hidden in the ancient scriptures. Though many of Abhinavagupta's contemporaries saw in him the signs of a *yogin* who had achieved the state of *rudra śakti samāveśa*,[22] there were others who were not so ready to accept his new

---

18 A hymn (*stava*) to Bhairava (Lord Shiva), more commonly known as the *Bhairava Stotra*, which today is recited regularly by Kashmiri pandits and westerners alike.

19 *śaṅkara satyam idaṁ vrata dāna snāna tapo bhava tāpa vināśi / tāvaka śāstra parāmṛita cintā syandati cetasi nirvṛitti dhārā* //8//

20 *Bhairava Stotra*, verse 9.

21 According to Abhinavagutpa, these subtle truths of the non-dual monistic teachings (*bhairava āgama*s) were understood and subsequently revealed only by the masters and disciples who were in the direct line of the oral tradition, the master-disciple (*guru-śiṣya*) tradition (*sampradāya*).

22 1) Unswerving devotional attachment to Lord Shiva. 2) Full attainment of Mantra Siddhi. 3) Attainment of controlling power over the five elements. 4) Capacity to accomplish the desired end. 5) Mastery over the whole science of rhetoric and poetics. 6) The sudden dawning of knowledge of all of the *śāstra*s (scriptures).

interpretations of the established teachings.

Fortunately, in the kingdom of monistic thought, there is no room for criticism because, after all, there is only one Being, so who is to blame? Bhaṭṭa Nārāyaṇa follows this line of thought by explaining that the misunderstanding of the detractors is due to Lord Shiva's play of 'concealing' and 'revealing':[23]

> "O Lord Śiva, You conceal the joy of the knowledge of oneness for those who are ignorant, and You reveal the joy of the knowledge of oneness for those who deserve. So, in both ways You create misunderstanding and You destroy misunderstanding."[24]

Abhinavagupta is more specific when addressing his detractors:

> "These teachers," he says, "were not capable of understanding the subtle import of the non-dual Shaiva teachings, as they were disconnected from the teacher-disciple (*guru-śiṣya*) tradition (*sampradāya*) of masters.[25]

He also cautioned that:

> "The chief indication of being concealed (*tirodhāna śakti*) is showing external signs of spirituality, but not having spirituality inside."[26]

Out of concern for these concealed teachers caught in the

---

23 Concealing (*tirodhāna*) and revealing (*anugraha*).

24 Verse 72.

25 This *guru-śiṣya sampradāya*, based on the oral tradition of master-disciple, is the fundamental principal behind the teaching of Kashmir Shaivism. See: *Tantrāloka* 1.19 and *Bhagavad Gītā* 4.24 commentary.

26 The subject of *tirodhāna śakti* (the energy of concealing) is addressed in the 13th and 14th chapters of Abhinavagupta's *Tantrāloka*.

grip of their own *tirodhāna śakti*, Bhaṭṭa Nārāyaṇa shines a ray of hope when he says that devotion to Lord Shiva is so great that it can even overcome spiritual pretense:

> "If anybody who develops Your devotion, even if it is artificial and not real devotion, still, the greatness of Your devotion is–because it is Your devotion–it will divert him towards that un-artificial devotion in the end."[27]

And for those solely devoted to Shiva's external form, he adds:

> "O Lord Śiva, this is a great wonder to me that although You are beyond the imagination of one's mind . . . the wonder is that if somebody sees Your figure on some picture, or on some painting, the greatness is that You bestow upon him the supreme fruit of God consciousness."[28]

And then:

> Just the recitation of the *mantra*, "*Śivāya namaḥ namaḥ, śivāya namo namaḥ, śivāya namo namaḥ*," those people who are reciting this *mantra* in continuity . . . they are fortunate and they are just likely to get entry in *śāmbhava samāveśa*.[29]

Through their hymns and writings, both Bhaṭṭa Nārāyaṇa and Abhinavagupta were attempting to uplift the Shaiva adherents and, at the same time, educate the non-dualists to a deeper understanding of the principals of Shaiva monism. These teachings instill an awareness that all practice, whether

27 Verse 109.

28 Ibid., 97.

29 Ibid., 20. "When you put your mind, when you meditate, on nothingness, absolute nothingness . . . that is the *śāmbhava* state." Swami Lakshmanjoo, *Vijñāna Bhairava, The Manual for Self Realization* (with original audio), ed. John Hughes (Lakshmanjoo Academy, Los Angeles, 2007), verse 107, commentary.

internal, external, or a combination of both, can be understood and experienced[30] as the expression of that one universal consciousness, Paramaśiva, in the playful act of creating, maintaining, destroying, concealing, and revealing the universe.[31]

Viewed in this light, no action, whether it be meditation, formal ritual, or the mundane daily routine of life, is seen as separate from consciousness, because all such activities are simply the expressions of consciousness flowing out into the world through the avenue of the senses.

Still, these elevated concepts would have been difficult for the dualist to assimilate, especially those who were steeped in the centuries-old habit of worshipping a pantheon of gods and goddesses with the hope of receiving their worldly blessings and favors.

Bhaṭṭanārāyana puts this in perspective when he says:

> "I bow to that creeper of energy of Lord Śiva, where Brahmā, Viṣṇu, Rudra, Īśvara, and Sadāśiva, along with the five states of consciousness and the seven states of the perceivers, everything, whatever exists in this universe, all of these are just blossoms (*puṣpitā*) of That creeper."[32]

Kṣemarāja adds while commenting on the above verse:

> "I bow to that Śiva, who is *bodhābdhim*, a great ocean where the all-knowing and all-acting Brahma, Viṣṇu, Rudra, Īśvara, and Sadāśiva, all of these five gods are seen just like bubbles in that great ocean of God

---

30 Understood (viz., *bauddha jñāna*), and experienced (viz., *pauruṣa jñāna*).

31 These are the five universal activities of creation (*sṛṣṭi*), protection (*sthiti*), destruction (*saṁhāra*), concealing (*tirodhāna*), and revealing (*anugraha*-grace).

32 Verse 34.

consciousness."[33]

Abhinavagupta adds his unique perspective on the practice of worshipping the gods and goddesses in his hymn on the '*Universal Wheel of Energies in one's own Body*':

> "I bow collectively to all the divine gods and goddesses who are always present and always shining in the temple of one's own body. Vibrating as the essence of one's experience, all the gathering of gods and goddesses can be perceived, can be achieved, and can be known directly by your own intellectual way of understanding."[34]

Longing for this experience, the author sings:

> "O Lord Śiva, let me merge in Your nature of God consciousness everywhere, so whatever I do in the dreaming state, whatever I say in this daily routine of life, good or bad, let that become divine, and let that be reflected in the mirror of God consciousness always. Let me merge in God consciousness in each and every respect of the daily routine of life, not only at the time of meditation."[35]

In his hymn, Bhaṭṭa Nārāyaṇa not only addresses this flow of consciousness into the world, but also Its flowing back from the world to its origin, the state of God consciousness. This he seeks to achieve in the simple act of bowing, which to him is not only the ultimate expression of one's knowledge of God, but

---

33 Ibid., commentary.
34 "Abhinavagupta composed these fifteen verses to help the sincere *sādhaka* (aspirant) understand that their body is divine, it is not something bad. Your own body is divine, so you should always worship your body with good things." Swami Lakshmanjoo, *Dehastha-devatā-cakra-stotram of Abhinavagupta*, translation and commentary, (original audio recording, LJA archives, Los Angeles, 1980), verse 15.
35 Verse 104.

more importantly, the ultimate expression of one's love and devotion towards God. The constant theme that runs like a thread through the one hundred and twenty verses (*ślokas*) of the *Stava Cintāmaṇi* is that love and devotion for God are everything. It is why Bhaṭṭa Nārāyaṇa declares:

> "Even if you are already drowned in this cycle of the ocean of repeated births and deaths, when you once find attachment (love) and devotion for Lord Śiva, then you have found that *cintāmaṇi* jewel."[36]

Interestingly, when given the choice between the light of the candle of knowledge (*bodha dīpika*) and the light of the candle of devotion (*bhakti dīpika*), Bhaṭṭa Nārāyaṇa chooses the candle of devotion, because:

> ". . . with knowledge there is still some darkness, in the sense that there is always something more to know, but with love and devotion, what else does one need?"[37]

Also, when he addresses Lord Śiva as the bestower of all treasures in this universe, he humbly requests:

> "Although there are so many things existing in Your treasury of God consciousness, I ask only that you give me devotion for You, that is all."[38]

Finally, when the impurity of ignorance (*māyīyamala*) has covered his eyes and made him blind, Bhaṭṭa Nārāyaṇa asks only for the medicine (*añjana*) of devotion (*bhakti*) to clear his eyesight.[39]

Here we find the greatness of Śiva's devotees in that they sow the seeds of their devotion in the body of Lord Śiva purely

36 Ibid., 26.
37 Ibid., 59.
38 Ibid., 100.
39 Ibid., 89.

out of love, just to please Him, without desiring anything in return.[40]

But in order to understand the special significance of this *Stava Cintāmaṇi* hymn, we must first understand what the author actually means by the word devotion (*bhakti*). The first hint is given when Bhaṭṭa Nārāyaṇa, after addressing Lord Śiva as the supreme bestower of liberation, goes on to declare:

> "Real devotees don't bow to Lord Śiva, instead, they bow to the bowing of Lord Śiva's devotees. In other words, real devotees worship that bowing, not Lord Śiva."[41]

This verse, in a subtle yet illustrative way, sheds light on the inner meaning of devotion in Kashmir Shaivism. The author elaborates further when he says:

> "In this drama of the three worlds, it is only Lord Śiva who can produce this sprout of *bhakti*."[42]

Then, in this same verse, he adds:

> "In wakefulness I must not ignore You, in the dreaming state I must not ignore You, and in the dreamless state I must not be away from You."[43]

Traditionally, the three worlds, as previously mentioned in the Gāyatrī *mantra*, are understood as earth (*bhuḥ*), sky (*bhuvaḥ*) and heaven (*svaḥ*), but according to the masters of the oral tradition of Kashmir Shaivism the three worlds also convey a second meaning. For the Shaivas, the outer objective world of earth, sky, and heaven, are symbolic of the three states of waking, dreaming, and deep sleep, respectively, which represent the inner subjective pathway on which the

---

40 Ibid., 43.
41 Ibid., 25.
42 Ibid., 60.
43 Ibid.

spiritual aspirant has to tread on the journey from ignorance to enlightenment.[44]

This is the essence of the spiritual path, the real pathways of Shiva, as understood and propagated by the masters of the oral tradition of Kashmir Shaivism.

Lord Shiva alludes to this subjective pathway in a number of places in His Shiva Sutras, and Bhaṭṭa Nārāyaṇa clearly states the importance of this inner path when he says, "The only favor I ask of Gāyatrī, and the only thing I long for, is that the effulgent Light should direct me on the path of Shaivism."

In the final verse of his hymn, Bhaṭṭa Nārāyaṇa praises the *cintāmaṇi ratna* (the jewel of the mind), which he says exists in heaven:

> "It is such a jewel that, while holding It in your hand, whatever you think, wish, or desire, you'll get it."[45]

He adds that his *Stava Cintāmaṇi* is the "magical jewel of devotion for Lord Śiva" and by singing this hymn one achieves everything one desires.

Abhinavagupta's concluding verse of his *Bhairava Stotra* conveys the same sentiment:

> "O compassionate Lord, under the influence of Your glory, and for the benefit of Your worshippers, I, Abhinavagupta, have composed this hymn. By meditation and recitation of this hymn, within a moment, that merciful Lord Bhairava destroys the torments and sufferings springing from this wilderness of *samsāra*."[46]

---

44 The importance of viewing these three states of consciousness as expressions of the fourth state (*turya*) is emphasized frequently by Lord Shiva in His Shiva Sutras.
45 Verse 121.
46 *Bhairava Stotra*, verse 10.

The commentator - Keṣmarāja

In his concluding verses (*maṅgala ślokas*), Kṣemarāja lists three reasons why he embarked upon his commentary of the *Stava Cintāmaṇi*. Firstly, he says:

> "Although Bhaṭṭa Nārāyaṇa was not my *guru*, what he had experienced in his heart was a vast ocean of knowledge, and the knowledge which came out from his lips was this book. But actually, Bhaṭṭa Nārāyaṇa was more than that, and this *Stava Cintāmaṇi* was just one tide of his vast ocean."[47]

Kṣemarāja also admits that he had one friend, Śūrāditya, who admired him for the fact that he was a direct disciple of Abhinavagupta, and that Śūrāditya had repeatedly requested him to do something with the hymns of Bhaṭṭa Nārāyaṇa.

Finally, Kṣemarāja shares the instructions which he received from his master, Abhinavagupta:

> "You should spread the message of Shaivism in such a way that everybody understands it more than you. Don't try to keep others behind, keep them ahead and you go behind, so that you can push them towards the state of Parabhairava. Then you should remain in the depth of the consciousness of Parabhairava."[48]

Heeding Abhinavagupta's instructions, Kṣemarāja became one of the most prolific commentators on Shaiva philosophy. He composed some original works as well as commentaries on

---

47 "I think Bhaṭṭa Nārāyaṇa was more than Parabhairava." Swami Lakshmanjoo, *Stava Cintāmaṇi of Bhaṭṭa Nārāyaṇa*, translation and commentary, handwritten notes by Denise Hughes, Los Angeles (1990), LJA archives, verse 34.

48 Swamiji's additional comments on Kṣemarāja's concluding verses.

established texts and devotional hymns,[49] in many places correcting previous commentators, and expounding the Shaiva scriptures in the light of the non-dual monism he had learned at the feet of his master.

His style followed that of Abhinavagupta in that he avoided literal and scholarly word-by-word translations in favor of revealing the essence of the teachings which had been handed down from teacher to disciple (*guru-ṣiśya*) through the oral transmission of the Shaiva lineage (*sampradāya*).

The present author – Swami Lakshmanjoo

In a span of six decades of teaching,[50] Swami Lakshmanjoo always held a special place for the devotional hymns of Kashmir Shaivism.[51] Upholding the long standing Kashmiri tradition, Swamiji would encourage his disciples to recite these devotional hymns regularly as they embodied the essence of Lord Shiva's message of liberation for all mankind.

Swamiji's understanding of devotion was in keeping with his predecessors, and whether he was translating philosophical

---

49 Kṣemarāja wrote commentaries on the *Vijñāna Bhairava Tantra*, and Vasugupta's *Shiva Sūtras* and *Spanda Kārikā*. He wrote commentaries on the *Svacchanda* and *Netra Tantras*. His original works include: *Pratyabhijñā Hṛdayaṁ*, *Parāpraveśikā*, and *Spanda Saṅdoha*. His commentaries on devotional hymns include: Samba's *Sambapañcaśika*, Utpaladeva's *Śivastotrāvali*, and Bhaṭṭa Nārāyaṇa's *Stava Cintāmaṇi*.

50 Swamiji taught from the age of 26 (1933), till he left this world at the age of 84 (1991). He taught free of charge to whomever had a sincere desire to learn. As the last living master of the oral tradition of Kashmir Shaivism, he shared many of the secrets of his *guru-ṣiśya sampradāya* through his teachings.

51 He translated and commented on the *Sambapañcāśika, Pañcastavi, Stutikusmāñjali, Śivastotravāli* and *Stava Cintāmaṇi*. Swamiji also translated a number of devotional hymns of Abhinavagupta.

texts or devotional hymns, he would always emphasize that meditation was the essence of devotional practice. He taught that this inward journey of consciousness through the practice of meditation was the key to traveling on the spiritual path, and like Bhaṭṭa Nārāyaṇa, he also revealed that real devotion was embodied in the deeper understanding of the act of 'bowing':

> *Namaḥ*[52]–What does it mean to say, "I bow to Bhairava?" Real bowing is to drive this physical body, this whole universe, which is existing in the outside world, into the internal world, which is also a body, the subtle body, the body governing the dreaming state.[53] Then, in turn, this subtle dreaming state must be pushed into that subtler and more refined state, the body of dreamless sleep. And ultimately, all these bodies are driven inside the body of consciousness. This is real bowing, and this is the meaning of *namaskāra*.[54]

As mentioned previously, Somānanda expresses the same in the first hymn of his *Śivadṛṣṭi* when he says, "Let Shiva, who is my own nature, bow down to His real nature, Universal

---

52 The literal meaning of the word *namaḥ* is 'salutation', 'to bend', or 'to bow down'.

53 Known as the *puryaṣṭaka*, lit., the city of eight, which is comprised of the mind (*manas*), ego (*ahaṁkāra*), and intellect (*buddhi*), along with the five *tanmātras* (the five sensations).
"*Puryaṣṭaka* is the body existing in dreaming state . . . it carries the impressions again and again, [from one life to the next]. Otherwise if *puryaṣṭaka* is not existing at the time of death, you'll be united with God automatically without doing anything. *Puryaṣṭaka* is the trouble maker." Swami Lakshmanjoo, *Parātrīśikā Vivaraṇa with the commentary of Abhinavagupta*, translation and commentary (original audio recording, LJA archives, Los Angeles, 1982-85).

54 *Deha-prāṇa-sukhādīnā nyag-bhāvād-bhaktasaṁ-hateḥ, yā cidātmani viśrāntir-namaḥ śabdena socyate.* Swami Lakshmanjoo, *Aṁṛteśvara Bhairava puja,* LJA audio archives, (1984). This verse is from an unknown source.

Shiva, through His own Sakti,[55] for the removal of bondage and limitation, which is none other than Śiva."[56] Here lies the fundamental principal of Self Recognition[57] in Kashmir Shaivism.

It was clear that when translating any devotional texts, Swami Lakshmanjoo would often enter a state where he completely identified (*samāveśa*) with the composer of the text. This phenomena was witnessed many times by those who were fortunate to be in his audience. And even now, when listening to his original recordings, one can't help but notice the subtle change in his tone when he is obviously overcome by the devotional words of these ancient masters of his cherished oral tradition.

Oṁ Namaḥ Śivāya . . . !

---

55 In verse 20 of the *Vijñāna Bhairava Tantra* it is explained that, "Śakti (energy) is the real pathway on which one has to tread."

56 See footnote 16 of this introduction.

57 In the path of Self Recognition (*pratyabhijñā*) there is no practice, and therefore the act of *bowing* is simply the spontaneous recognition of one's own true nature.

Acknowledgements

First of all, I would like to thank our team of associate editors: Viresh Hughes, George Barselaar, Denise Hughes, and Stephen Benson. They took the raw unedited audio transcript and transformed it into a polished document ready for publication. Being closely attuned to Swamiji's vision, they were able to lightly edit the manuscript without tarnishing the flow and original voice of the narrative. Recognizing that these revelations were meant to aid the student in gaining an understanding of the philosophy and practices of Kashmir Shaivism, additional footnotes and an appendix have been added to facilitate this quest. Lastly, I would like to thank Michael Van Winkle, our audio engineer who enhanced the original audio, Claudia Dose, our creative director who was responsible for the formatting and creation of the overall design of this book, and Shanna Hughes, who tirelessly coordinated this project.

Swami Lakshmanjoo

Swami Lakshmanjoo

Swami Lakshmanjoo was born in Srinagar, Kashmir, on May 9, 1907. He was the most recent and the greatest of the long line of saints and masters of the Kashmir Shaiva tradition. From a young age, Swami Lakshmanjoo spent his life studying and practicing the teachings of this unique and sacred tradition. Having a complete intellectual and spiritual understanding of the philosophy and practice of Kashmir Shaivism, he was a true master in every respect.

Being born with a photographic memory, learning was always easy for him. In addition to possessing a complete knowledge of Kashmir Shaivism, he had a vast knowledge of the traditional religious and philosophical schools and texts of India. Swamiji would freely draw upon other texts to clarify, expand, and substantiate his lectures. He could recall an entire text by simply remembering the first few words of a verse.

In time, his reputation as a learned philosopher and spiritual adept spread. Spiritual leaders and scholars journeyed from all over the world to receive his blessings and to ask questions about various aspects of Kashmir Shaiva philosophy. He gained renown as a humble devotee of Lord Shiva and as an accomplished master (*siddha*) of the non-dual tradition of Kashmir Shaivism.

Throughout his life, Swamiji taught his disciples and devotees the ways of devotion and awareness. He shunned fame and all forms of recognition. He knew Kashmir Shaivism was the most precious jewel and that, by God's grace, those who desired supreme knowledge would be attracted to its teachings. He taught freely, never asking anything in return, except that his students, young and old, should do their utmost to assimilate the teachings of his cherished tradition. His earnest wish for Kashmir Shaivism was for it to be preserved and made available to all humankind.

On the 27th of September, 1991, Swami Lakshmanjoo left his physical body and attained *mahāsamādhi*, the great liberation.

Swami Lakshmanjoo

Stava Cintāmaṇi
of
Bhaṭṭa Nārāyaṇa

KṢEMARĀJA'S INTRODUCTORY VERSES:

Audio 1 (00:00)

ॐ नमः स्वात्मामृतवपुषे परमशिवाय ॥
अथ स्तवचिन्तामणिः श्रीभट्टनारायणविरचितः
श्रीक्षेमराजकृतविवृत्युपेतः

oṁ namaḥ svātmāmṛtavapuṣe paramaśivāya / /
atha stavacintāmaṇiḥ śrībhaṭṭanārāyaṇaviracitaḥ
śrīkṣemarājakṛtavivṛtyupetaḥ

First, Kṣemarāja's commentary *ślokas* of glory:

प्रकाशमाने परमार्थभानौ नश्यत्यविद्यातिमिरे समस्ते ।
तदा बुधा निर्मलदृष्टयोऽपि किंचिन्न पश्यन्ति भवप्रपञ्चम् ॥ १ ॥

prakāśamāne paramārthabhānau
naśyatyavidyātimire samaste /
tadā budhā nirmaladṛṣṭayo'pi
kiṁcinna paśyanti bhavaprapañcam / /1/ /[1]

---

1 "When the *surya* (sun) of Parabhairava has risen, and when all darkness of ignorance has ended, at that moment, those *jñānis* (intellectuals) who have achieved the knowledge of Parabhairava, although their eyes are wide open, they do not see any of the objective world before them." *Stava Cintāmaṇi* (1990).
"When, while he is doing this practice, he realizes the Sun of Supreme Knowledge, and when his ignorance is ended and he becomes a

This *śloka* is composed by Kṣemarāja. This, too, also:

नमः शिवाय सततं पञ्चकृत्यविधायिने ।
चिदानन्दघनस्वात्मपरमार्थावभासने ॥ २ ॥

namaḥ śivāya satataṁ pañcakṛtyavidhāyine /
cidānandaghanasvātmaparamārthāvabhāsine //2//[2]

अन्तः स्पन्दान्दोलनानन्दसंपद्-
बाह्यस्पन्दामन्दसंदोहनीभिः ।
संविद्धाराधोरणीभिः समन्तात्
सिञ्चन् विश्व स्वात्मशंभुर्नमस्यः ॥ ३ ॥

antaḥ spandāndolanānandasaṁpad -
bāhyaspandāmandasaṁdohinībhiḥ /
saṁviddhārādhoraṇībhiḥ samantāt
siñcan viśvaṁ svātmaśaṁbhurnamasyaḥ //3//[3]

---

realized soul, then no matter whatever he does he is soaked in God consciousness everywhere and he has attained eternal *samādhi.*" Swami Lakshmanjoo, *Special Verses on Practice*, (original audio/video recording, LJA archives, Los Angeles, 1988).

2 "I bow to Lord Śiva, not one, two, or three times, I just go on bowing to Lord Śiva always. He is conducting His five great acts of creation, destruction, protection, concealing, and revealing–this is His nature. And also what is His behaviour in doing actions? The essence of His real nature of God consciousness is always being revealed to anybody who comes before Him." *Stava Cintāmaṇi* (1990).

3 "Lord Śiva, who is not separate from your nature, and who from all sides waters the whole universe and soaks it with the water of the unstoppable flow of the streams of God consciousness, is worth adoring. He soaks the whole universe so that it will be as great as Lord Bhairava. The internal *spanda* and the external *spanda*, after uniting the internal and the external, both are mixed and the whole universe is soaked with God consciousness. That Lord Śiva is worth adoring." Ibid. See Appendix 1 for an explanation of *spanda*.

These are Kṣemarāja's *śloka*s.

Kṣemarāja's another *śloka*, the 4th *śloka* in the *maṅgala ācaraṇa*:[4] "Why I have commentated upon Bhaṭṭa Nārāyaṇa, as Nārāyaṇa was not my *guru*," but he says, "Nārāyaṇa was a great master."

Audio 1 (02:12)

नारायणः स्वहृदयाम्बुनिधेर्विवेक-
भूभृद्विमर्दरभसोच्छलितं यदेतत् ।
श्रीशंकरस्तुतिरसायनमाचकर्ष
तच्चर्वणादिह बुधा विबुधा भवन्तु ॥४॥

nārāyaṇaḥ svahṛdayāmbunidherviveka -
bhūbhṛdvimardarabhasocchalitaṁ yadetat /
śrīśaṃkarastutirasāyanamācakarṣa
taccarvaṇādiha budhā vibudhā bhavantu //4//[5]

About Bhaṭṭa Nārāyaṇa he says, "Bhaṭṭa Nārāyaṇa, although he was not my *guru*, but whatever he had experienced in his heart, that experience in his heart was knowledge just like an ocean, an ocean-like knowledge, vast knowledge. That is this book! That knowledge is, in other words, this book, this book which has come out from Bhaṭṭa Nārāyaṇa's, from his lips.

But Bhaṭṭa Nārāyaṇa was more than that, and this was one tide of his ocean.[6] This *Stava Cintāmaṇi* was one tide of his

---

4 A benediction or prayer for success in one's undertaking.

5 "Bhaṭṭa Nārāyaṇa has exposed this nectar of singing the glory of Lord Śiva. That nectar he has taken out from his heart. His heart is not a flesh heart, his heart is this whole philosophy of Śaivism, which resides in his heart like a great ocean. And from that ocean, he has taken out all of the good points and has placed them before us. And by tasting that new recovery of that nectar, those who are fully unaware become aware of That." Ibid.

6 While commenting on verse 34 of this text, Swamiji added, "I think Bhaṭṭa Nārāyaṇa was more than Parabhairava." *Stava Cintāmaṇi* (1990).

ocean, and I have gone into the depth of that [ocean] to churn it; to get from that [ocean of] milk, the cream, the butter.[7] My *ṭīkā* (my commentary) of Bhaṭṭa Nārāyaṇa will be the butter of that. And if you taste it, if anybody tastes this, if you are [even] in one way awakened, you'll be one hundred times awakened. For this [reason] I have [under]taken this [work], because it was my duty, I have been told by my master, immediate master, Abhinavagupta: "You should spread this. This message you should spread in such a way that everybody will understand more than you have understood. Don't try to keep them behind, try to keep them ahead, and then you go behind so that you push them towards Parabhairava. And then you [will] remain in the depth of the consciousness of Parabhairava." So, I have to do that. This *udyoga* (this effort) was my [duty] because of my Bhagavan's *upadeśa*.[8]

Audio 1 (04:52)

Stava Cintāmaṇi is the work of Bhaṭṭa Nārāyaṇa. Bhaṭṭa Nārāyaṇa is one of the most important Shaivite masters–Bhaṭṭa Nārāyaṇa. And he was, maybe he was, one century elder to Abhinavagupta.[9]

JOHN: What does the title mean?

SWAMIJI: *Stava Cintāmaṇi* means–you want the meaning? –*Stava Cintāmaṇi* means, *cintāmaṇi*, a jewel. The *cintāmaṇi* jewel is that kind of jewel [by which] whatever you wish, it will come. It is the giver of, the bestower of, all your boons, all your desires. All of your desires are fulfilled by that *cintāmaṇi*, that jewel, and this is the jewelry of that *Cintāmaṇi of Hymns* to Lord Śiva–it purifies all of your desires and wishes.

JOHN: So we are starting at the beginning here?

---

7 A reference to the episode in which the gods and demons had churned Kṣīrasāgara (the milky ocean) to obtain *amṛta*, the divine nectar. For more on this episode, see Swamiji's commentary on verse 4, next page.

8 Here Kṣemarāja is referring to the instruction (*upadeśa*) of Abhinavagupta whom he refers to as his lord (Bhagavan).

9 Abhinavagupta (924-1020CE).

SWAMIJI: Yes, one *śloka* of Kṣemarāja first.[10]

Audio 1 (06:15)

नारायणः स्वहृदयाम्बुनिधेर्विवेक-
भूभृद्विमर्दरभसोच्छलितं यदेतत् ।
श्रीशंकरस्तुतिरसायनमाचकर्ष
तच्चर्वणादिह बुधा विबुधा भवन्तु ॥४॥

nārāyaṇa svahṛdayāmbunidherviveka-
bhūbhṛdvimardarabhasocchalitaṁ yadetat /
śrīśaṅkarastutirasāyanamācakarṣa
taccarvaṇādiha budhā vibudhā bhavantu //4//
(*verse repeated*)

Now, Bhaṭṭa Nārāyaṇa is the author of these hymns. He has composed these hymns. What are these hymns?

Svahṛdayāmbunidher viveka, in other words, you must understand that these are not actually hymns. This is just churning the great *kṣīrasāgara* of God consciousness.

Kṣīrasāgara is the milky ocean. The ocean of milk is Kṣīrasāgara and it belonged to Lord Śiva. Once all of the gods went to Lord Śiva and requested Him if they could [have permission to] churn it. [They said,] "We want to churn this Ocean of Kṣīrasāgara, this milky ocean, and whatever substance will come out, it will be ours. Please accept [to offer] this boon to us." He said, "Alright, go on and churn it. You take whatever comes out from this by churning."

And this was a great ocean. This great Ocean of Kṣīrasāgara was churned by the gods and the demons. On one side the gods were gathered and on the other side the

10 Kṣemarāja, the chief disciple of Abhinavagupta, was the commentator of this *Stava Cintāmaṇi*.

demons were gathered. And they got for a churner, as a churner, [who could] churn it, *Mandara Parvata*, the Great Mountain. The Great Mountain, it is called *Mandara Parvata*.[11] This Great Mountain was put as the churner in this [ocean], and Vāsuki, that serpent, was put for . . .

DENISE: a rope.

SWAMIJI: . . . as the rope. And one end was held by the gods and another end of this Vāsuki was held by the demons, and they began to churn it, this Kṣīrasāgara. When they were churning it, it went down, this mountain went down it went down [and was sinking] by-and-by. Then they were confused what to do because it would sink altogether in the ocean of Kṣīrasāgara. Then they prayed to Lord Śiva: "Please help us. We can't do it. We can't churn it [because] it goes down and down. How can we churn it?"

Then Lord Śiva told them, "Tell Nārāyaṇa[12] to take the incarnation of a . . . crocodile?

DEVOTEES: Crocodile.

SWAMIJI: ". . . a crocodile, a big crocodile."[13] And a big crocodile, Nārāyaṇa became a big crocodile at the bottom of that mountain, and he held the bottom of the mountain on his back. [With the mountain] on his back, they began to churn it, and He . . .

ERNIE: Supported it.

SWAMIJI: . . . He held it, He held it with His power . . .

ERNIE: So it wouldn't sink.

---

11 The legend of *Mandara Mountain* and the churning of the milky ocean appears in the *Samudra manthana* episode in the Hindu Purāṇas.

12 An appellation of Lord Viṣṇu.

13 In the ancient story of the churning of the milky ocean, Nārāyana actually took the incarnation of a tortoise. This mistake is merely the result of Swamiji's occasional difficulty with the English language.

SWAMIJI: . . . so it wouldn't sink. Now they churned it. This is the example.

He [Kṣemarāja] puts the same example: Nārāyaṇa, Bhaṭṭa Nārāyaṇa (Nārāyaṇa is the author of this book), *svahṛdaya-ambu-nidher*, he wanted to churn his heart, the ocean of his heart, the milky ocean of his heart. He has churned the milky ocean of his own heart. Who?

DEVOTEES: Nārāyaṇa.

SWAMIJI: Nārāyaṇa, the author of this book. He has churned the milky ocean of his heart, *svahṛdaya-ambuja-nidheḥ viveka bhūbhṛt*, and he has put the mountain of awareness to churn it.

[Kṣemarāja] has put, instead of the *Mandara Mountain*, he has put the mountain of [Bhaṭṭa Nārāyaṇa's] awareness–by awareness he churns it, [by] *viveka bhrumat.*[14] *Yadetat śrī-śaṅkara stuti rasāyana*, and then nectar has appeared from that churning. From that ocean, nectar has appeared, eternal nectar that will make you immortal for centuries and centuries. And that important nectar is this book. *Tat carvaṇāt*, so, you [can] taste this. By tasting this nectar, which he has brought before us by churning with his awareness the ocean of his heart, *tat carvaṇāt*, by tasting this nectar, *iha budhā vibudhā*, let the enlightened become more enlightened (because this is meant for enlightened people). Let enlightened people become more enlightened by tasting this nectar.

---

14 Swamiji often instructed his disciples to maintain awareness (*viveka*) between the two eyebrows (*bhrumat*). "In this very world of the milky ocean (this world is considered to be a milky ocean, Kṣīrasāgara), if you have extracted the nectar of God consciousness from this ocean of the world, and if you taste that nectar by churning the *mandara* of breath, then the attainment of the Śiva state is cent-percent sure to you–*niścitam vaḥ śivatvam*." Swami Lakshmanjoo, translation and commentary, *Janma Maraṇa Vicāra* of Bhaṭṭa Vāmadeva, LJA archives, paraphrased excerpt.

STAVA CINTĀMAṆI
By Bhaṭṭa Nārāyaṇa

Now, the first *śloka* of Bhaṭṭa Nārāyaṇa. Now, this is the text:

Audio 1 (12:38)

सुगिरा चित्तहारिण्या पश्यन्त्या दृश्यमानया ।
जयत्युज्ज्ञासितानन्द महिमा परमेश्वरः ॥ १ ॥

sugirā cittahāriṇyā paśyantyā dṛśyamānayā /
jayatyullāsitānanda-mahimā parameśvaraḥ //1//

This is first the prostration before Lord Śiva. He prostrates before Lord Śiva, [he] does *namaskāra*: "*Jai Guru Deva, Jai Śiva.*" *Sugirā citta hāriṇyā*, when He produces His word, His supreme word (*sugirā* means, that supreme and beautiful word, His one word), and that word which is *citta hāriṇyā*, which carries away your mind along with its thought–His one word carries away your mind along with all its thoughts, all its notions (*paśyantyā*)–and *dṛśyamānayā*, and by looking at you with grace, He creates unlimited cycles and cycles of ecstasy in you. And that kind of Lord Śiva, [let] that Lord Śiva be victorious. Let that Lord Śiva be victorious, by whose word your mind is finished along with its notions, and by whose graceful look, all of your worries are gone.

JOHN: What is that first sound?

SWAMIJI: That sound is the embodiment of awareness.

JOHN: I mean, is it an actual sound like some *mantra* or is it just . . . ?

SWAMIJI: No, it is not. It is . . .

JOHN: *Spanda* or . . . ?

ERNIE: Silent sound.

SWAMIJI: *Spanda*, silent sound.[1] This is the first *śloka*. The next *śloka*:

Audio 1 (14:34)

यः स्फीतः श्रीदयाबोधपरमानन्दसंपदा ।
विद्याद्द्श्यातितमाहात्म्यः स जयत्यपराजितः ॥२॥

yaḥ sphītaḥ śrīdayābodha-paramānandasaṁpadā /
vidyoddyotitamāhātmyaḥ sa jayatyaparājitaḥ //2//

Let that Lord Śiva be victorious, be always victorious, who is clearly found by the glory of [*śrī dayā bodha param-ānanda*], . . .

Śrī means, the wealth of consciousness; *dayā* means, kindness.

. . . by kindness, by the wealth of consciousness, by kindness, great kindness, by God consciousness (*bodha*), *paramānanda*, and by perfect ecstasy. He who is glorified by these, Lord Śiva, let Lord Śiva be victorious, who is glorified by the wealth of God consciousness, by *dayā* (grace, pity, kindness always; He is kind, always kind, compassionate), and *bodha*, knowledge, and *paramānanda*, supreme ecstasy. *Vidyoddayotitamāhātmya*, and whose glory is enlightened, whose glory is put to strength, whose glory is put to strength by *vidyā*, by *śuddhavidyā*, by supreme pure knowledge, let that God consciousness be victorious all round, everywhere.

Bas,[2] these are two *śloka*s which are just a prayer to Lord Śiva. Now, [Bhaṭṭa Nārāyaṇa] will start these hymns of devotion, and these we will do on Saturday. Good? We won't do the commentary.

---

1 Swamiji defines *spanda* as "movementless movement," which is synonymous with *vimarśa śakti*, the supreme energy of Self-awareness, and *svātantrya śakti*, the supreme energy of Lord Śiva's absolute freedom. See Appendix 1 for an explanation of *spanda*.

2 Hindi for "enough." Swamiji often uses this expression throughout the text.

Audio 1 (17:08)

प्रसरद्बिन्दुनादाय शुद्धामृतमयात्मने ।
नमोऽनन्तप्रकाशाय शंकरक्षीरसिन्धवे ॥ ३ ॥

prasaradbindunādāya śuddhāmṛtamayātmane /
namo'nantaprakāśāya śaṅkarakṣīrasindhave //3//

I bow to that Śaṅkara,[3] who is just like the ocean of milk, a milk ocean. I bow to that Śaṅkara who is just like a milk ocean, a vast milk ocean, and *prasarat bindu nādāya*, where there are flows, two-fold flows, of *bindu* and *nāda*.

Bindu is *prakāśa* and *nāda* is [*vimarśa*].[4] *Bindu* is I-consciousness; *nāda* is to observe I-consciousness.[5] Consciousness is *bindu*; "I am consciousness, I am God consciousness," this is *nāda*.

For instance, this *prakāśa* of *sūrya* (sun), the *prakāśa* of the light of the moon, [the *prakāśa* of] the light of fire, it is *bindu*, but there is no *nāda* in it, there is no understanding power of that *prakāśa*. There is *prakāśa* in the sun, but [the sun] does not know that, "I am *prakāśa*." He is just a [star].[6] He does not understand that, "I am filled with this *prakāśa*."

When there is understanding power, the understanding

---

3 Lord Śiva.
4 "In the world of Shaivite philosophy, Lord Śiva is seen as being filled with light. But more than this, Lord Śiva is the embodiment of light and this light is different than the light of the sun, of the moon, or of fire. It is light (*prakāśa*) with consciousness (*vimarśa*), and this light with consciousness is the nature of that supreme consciousness, Lord Śiva." *Self Realization in Kashmir Shaivism–The Oral Teachings of Swami Lakshmanjoo*, ed. John Hughes (State University of New York Press, Albany, 1995), 3.56-57. See Appendix 2 for an explanation of *vimarśa*.
5 That is, to be Self-aware.
6 That is, insentient (*jaḍa*).

that, "I am this *prakāśa*," that is *nāda*. *Bindu* and *nāda* are both found in God consciousness. In other lights, only *bindu* is found, not *nāda*. *Nāda* is understanding.

Fire is burning but it does not know that, "I am burning." In the same way, the light of the moon, the light of the sun, they are absolutely unaware of their nature. So there must be, there is, *bindu* and *nāda* both in God consciousness.

In the same way, *prakāśa* and *vimarśa* is *bindu* and *nāda* according to the *śāmbhava* state. According to *śāktopāya*, *jñāna* and *kriyā* (knowledge and action) will be *bindu* and *nāda*. According to *āṇavopāya*, breathing in and breathing out, in-going breath and out-coming breath, will be *bindu* and *nāda*.[7] [*Bindu* and *nāda* are] inhaling and exhaling from the *āṇavopāya* viewpoint, and knowledge and action from *śāktopāya*, and *prakāśa* and *vimarśa* from *śāmbhavopāya*.[8] You understand? It is very easy.

Prasarat bindu nādāya, so I bow to that Lord Śiva who is filled with *bindu* and *nāda*.

The flows of *prakāśa* and *vimarśa* [are] always there according to the *śāmbhava* state, according to the *śākta* state, and according to the *āṇava* state. [In the] *āṇava* state, what is *bindu* and *nāda*?

ERNIE: In-breath and out-breath.

SWAMIJI: Inhale . . . , yes. And *śāktopāya*?

DENISE: Action and knowledge.

SWAMIJI: Action and knowledge. And *śāmbhavopāya*?

ERNIE: *Prakāśa* . . .

---

7 *Bindu* (*prakāśa*) arises from the internal turning point of breath in the heart, while *nāda* (*visarga*) arises from the external turning point of the breath, which is twelve finger spaces outside the body.
8 See Appendix 3 for an explanation of the three means (*upāya*s): *śāmbhavopāya*, *śāktopāya*, and *āṇavopāya*.

SWAMIJI: *Prakāśa* and *vimarśa*. *Suddhāmṛtamayātmane*, and this is the embodiment of nectar, pure nectar. The purest nectar you will find only in God consciousness. Other nectars you will find in the gods. They have become immortal by that. By using that nectar, they have become immortal in heaven, but immortal only for some particular period. *Kṣīṇe puṇye martya lokaṁ viśanti*,[9] after some [time], say one billion years, they come down again. That nectar, the effect of that nectar, is vanished, is gone. But this nectar, which you find in the state of God consciousness, Lord Śiva, it is immortal nectar. It is real, pure nectar. It will never fade, it will never vanish. That nectar is always remaining, residing, eternal. That is meant by "*śuddha amṛta mayātmane*." And *namo ananta prakāśāya*, and He is the light of all lights, He is the light of all darknesses (all ignorance of light). All absence of light and the presence of light have come out from That light. *Śaṅkara-kṣīra-sindhave*, and I bow to that Śaṅkara[10] who is just like a milky ocean.

Next:

Audio 1 (22:12)

द्विष्मस्त्वां त्वां स्तुमस्तुभ्यं मन्त्रयामोऽम्बिकापते ॥
अतिवाल्लभ्यतः साधु विश्वङ्गो धृतवानसि ॥४॥

dviṣmastvāṁ tvāṁ stumastubhyaṁ mantrayāmo'mbikāpate /
ativāllabhyataḥ sādhu viśvaṅno dhṛtavānasi //4//

Ambikā pate ho, O Husband of my universal Mother (the universal Mother is Pārvatī), O Husband of the universal Mother, O Lord Śiva, I love You. *Ativāllabhyataḥ*, I have got the greatest love for You, the greatest attachment for You. Because of that greatest attachment, I hate You sometimes!

DEVOTEES: (laughter)

---

9 Swami Lakshmanjoo, *Bhagavad Gītā In the Light of Kashmir Shaivism* (with original video), ed. John Hughes (Lakshmanjoo Academy, Los Angeles, 2013), 9.21.
10 Lord Śiva.

SWAMIJI: [Although] I hate You sometimes, You should not care for that. I will praise You sometimes (*stumas-tubhyaṁ*). I will praise You sometimes because of love, too much love. I love You very much, so I hate You. I love You very much, so I praise You. *Mantrayāma*, I recite Your *mantra* because I love You. *Ativāllabhyataḥ*, because I have no one, I have no one to handle except You. Whom I will hate? I will hate You! I have nobody [else] to hate because *viśvaṁno dhṛtavānasi*, I perceive You everywhere. I perceive You everywhere, so I have got the greatest love for You, I will hate You, I will praise You, I will hit You, I will kick You, I will embrace You, I will do everything, I will do everything to You.

Bas, this is the meaning of this *śloka*.

Audio 1 (23:44)

संहृतस्पर्शयोगाय संपूर्णामृतसूतये
वियन्मायास्वरूपाय विभवे शंभवे नमः ॥ ५ ॥

saṁhṛtasparśayogāya saṁpūrṇāmṛtasūtaye /
viyanmāyāsvarūpāya vibhave śaṁbhave namaḥ //5//

I bow to Lord Śiva, *saṁhṛta sparśa yogāya*, who is beyond attachment to touch. He does not touch. He is beyond the sensation of touching.

Because, whenever you touch some beautiful thing, what do you get?

DENISE: Pleasure.

SWAMIJI: You get pleasure.

You are beyond that touching, You have gone above the cycle of touching. And, at the same time, *saṁpūrṇāmṛta*, You are filled with pleasure! But it is a unique thing found only in You that without touching, You are filled with joy. Without touch, you can't be filled with joy, but Lord Śiva is joyous without touching; *saṁhṛta sparśa yogāya*, without touching, *saṁpūrṇ-āmṛta*, and with full *amṛta*.[11] *Viyat māyā svarūpāya vibhave*

11 "You are not [coming into] union with Your *śakti*, but without

śambhave namaḥ, *māyā svarūpāya*, the illusive energy of Lord Śiva is fading there in Your body–*māyā svarūpāya* is *viyat* (*viyat* is, fading). *Vibhave śambhave*, and He is all-pervading–Lord Śiva. I bow to that Lord Śiva.

Audio 1 (25:20)

भिन्नेष्वपि न भिन्नं यच्छिन्नेष्वच्छिन्नमेव च ।
नमामः सर्वसामान्यं रूपं तत्पारमेश्वरम् ॥ ६ ॥

bhinneṣvapi na bhinnaṁ yacchinneṣvacchinnameva ca /
namāmaḥ sarvasāmānyaṁ rūpaṁ tatpārameśvaram //6//

I bow to that formation of Lord Śiva who is *sarva sāmānya*, who is seen in sameness everywhere.

For instance, there is a body, He has become a body. You cut that body into pieces–He is cut. You will see Lord Śiva cut, as cut pieces. [Or] you will burn that body: You will see Lord Śiva, burnt Lord Śiva.

Bhinneṣvapi, if He is separated in separated things, [although] He is separated, He is not [separated]. In one form, He is in this, another form in this book, another form in [spectacles], and is separately found everywhere. In separation (*bhinneṣvapi*), in separation [He] is one, in separated things [He] is one. *Chineṣu acchinnam eva ca*, in those things which are cut into pieces, in those things, He is *abhinnaṁ*, He is not cut–He is not cut, He is there. So, His formation, of Lord Śiva's formation, is *sarva sāmānya*, He is the same everywhere. So He won't be burnt, he won't get any change. He is changeless in changes, all changes.[12]

---

union, You create the world. This is Your power that, without union, everything is born. By Your mere will, everything is born. What is born? *Amṛta* (nectar)." Swami Lakshmanjoo, *Stava Cintāmaṇi of Bhaṭṭa Nārāyaṇa*, translation and commentary (original audio recording, Los Angeles, 1991), Lakshmanjoo Academy archives.

12 "In broken, He is not broken; in bad, He is good; in effort, He is effortless; in sleep, He is awake–He is the opposites. I bow to that *rūpa* [form] of Parameśvara (Lord Śiva). This is the statement of Bhaṭṭa Nārāyaṇa." Ibid.

Audio 1 (27:10)

प्रणवोर्ध्वार्धमात्रातोऽप्यणवे महते पुनः ॥
ब्रह्माण्डादपि नैर्गुण्यगुणाय स्थाणवे नमः ॥७॥

praṇavo'rdhvārdhamātrāto'pyaṇave mahate punaḥ /
brahmāṇḍādapi nairguṇya-guṇāya sthāṇave namaḥ //7//

I bow to that Lord Śiva who is a big ancient log, an ancient log; an ancient log, and a rotten log inside.[13] *Praṇavo urdhva urdhva ardha mātrāto'pi aṇave*, and That log is very subtle, subtler than the subtle.

Which is the subtlest? The subtlest is . . . there is *praṇava*. *Praṇava* is the name of Lord Śiva–*oṁ*. *Oṁ*–you have already known that *Oṁ* is the name of Lord Śiva.

Oṁ is classified in twelve sections: *Akāraśca ukāraśca makāro bindureva ca*: *a-kāraśca* ('*a*'), *u-kāraśca* ('*u*'), *ma-kāro* (and '*ma*'), *bindureva ca* (and '*aṁ*')–"*auṁ*". *Akāraśca ukāraśca makāraśca bindureva*, it is *Oṁ*.

You have not to recite only '*oṁ*' there. '*Oṁ*' is not the complete *praṇava*. *Oṁ-kāra*, '*oṁ*', is only a gross *mantra*. Beyond that [recitation of] '*oṁ*' you have to [recite] '*oooooooṁṁṁ*', then that goes in the depth of that subtle Word inside, internal.

And the twelfth is *unmanā*. *Akāraśca ukāraśca* . . . *a-kāra* ('*a*') is the first. The first flow of *oṁ-kāra* is '*a*', the second is *u-kāra*, the third is *ma-kāra*, the fourth is *bindu* ('*aṁ*'), *ardhacandra* is the fifth,[14] *nirodhi* is the sixth,[15] *nāda* is

13 "All thunders have fallen on It, all ups and downs have come, and It is still a log, because *śāśvata*, Lord Śiva cannot be destroyed. It is very old and very strong–eternal–that's what is meant by "log". "Rotten" means, very old. I didn't mean "rotten" in that sense [of being decayed]." Ibid.

14 "The pervasion of *mantra* begins from *ardhacandra*, it does not

> the seventh,[16] *nādānta* is the eighth,[17] *śakti* is the ninth,[18] *vyāpinī* is the tenth,[19] *samanā* is the eleventh,[20] and *unmanā* is the twelfth.[21] *Unmanā* is where there is no approach of the mind, beyond the mind–super-mind.[22]

He says that the stage of *praṇava*, which is residing in the state of the super-mind state, that twelfth step, Lord Śiva's consciousness is subtler than that. *Praṇavo urdhva ardha mātrato'pi aṇave*, It is subtler than that state of *praṇava*.[23]

Which state? The twelfth, *unmanā*. So, It is very subtle. You can't understand It, you can't perceive It. You can't understand It and you can't perceive It in *samādhi*.

And, on the other side, you know His wideness. *Brahmāṇḍāt api nairguṇya-guṇāya, brahmāṇḍa*, He is more gross than the one hundred and eighteen worlds.[24] He is, on the other

---

begin from *a-kāra*, it does not begin from *u-kāra*, *ma-kāra*, or *bindu*. It begins from *ardhacandra* where nothing is to be recited." Swami Lakshmanjoo, *Parātrīśikā Vivaraṇa with the commentary of Abhinavagupta*, translation and commentary (original audio recording, LJA archives, Los Angeles, 1982-85), audio 359a (27:42).

15 "*Nirodha*, the stoppage of breath, and you go in." Swami Lakshmanjoo, *Stava Cintāmaṇi of Bhaṭṭa Nārāyaṇa*, translation and commentary (based on handwritten notes by Denise Hughes (Nepal 1990), LJA archives.

16 "Unstruck sound." Ibid.

17 "More than un-struck sound." Ibid.

18 "The electric power of *samādhi*." Ibid.

19 "Pervasion." Ibid.

20 "Complete appeasement. Subtler." Ibid.

21 "You are That, subtler than the subtlest." Ibid.

22 See Appendix 4 for a complete understanding of the twelve phases of the *praṇava mantra*, '*oṁ*'.

23 "After *unmanā*, you enter in the state of Śiva." Swami Lakshmanjoo, *Vijñāna Bhairava–The Manual for Self Realization*, ed. John Hughes (Lakshmanjoo Academy, Los Angeles, 2007), verse 42, commentary.

24 *Brahmāṇḍa* is the first of five [egg shaped] circles (*aṇḍas*) that contain the thirty-six elements (*tattvas*) that, in turn, makes up the one hundred and eighteen worlds. For an explanation of the one

side, more gross than the one hundred and eighteen worlds. He is gross and subtle also. I bow to that Lord Śiva.

Audio 1 (31:06)

ब्रह्माण्डगर्भिणीं व्योमव्यापिनः सर्वतोगतेः ।
परमेश्वरहंसस्य शक्तिं हंसीमिव स्तुमः ॥८॥

brahmāṇḍagarbhiṇīṁ vyoma-vyāpinaḥ sarvatogateḥ /
parameśvarahaṁsasya śaktiṁ haṁsīmiva stumaḥ //8//

I bow to that *haṁsī* of Parameśvara.[25]

He has nominated Śiva as *haṁsa*, a swan. And He has a wife, a misses, that is *haṁsī*. His *svātantrya śakti* is, the energy of *svātantrya śakti*[26] is, *haṁsī*, His wife.

And this *haṁsī* is already pregnant–pregnant with what?– *brahmāṇḍa garbhiṇī*, pregnant with the one hundred and eighteen worlds. The one hundred and eighteen worlds are there in Her womb–one hundred and eighteen worlds.[27] And *sarvatogateḥ . . . parameśvara-haṁsasya śaktiṁ haṁsī*, the *haṁsa* (the swan) who is Parameśvara, His *śakti*, His energy, is Mrs. Swan, who has kept the one hundred and eighteen worlds in Her womb, I bow to that *śakti* of Parameśvara.

Audio 1 (32:28)

निरुपादानासांभारमाभित्तावेव तन्वते ।
जगच्चित्रं नमस्तस्मै कलाश्लाघ्याय शूलिने ॥९॥

---

hundred and eighteen worlds, see Swami Lakshmanjoo, *Kashmir Shaivism–The Secret Supreme*, ed. John Hughes (Lakshmanjoo Academy, Los Angeles, 1985-2015), chapter 2, *Ṣaḍadhvan*, The Sixfold Path of the Universe.

25 A name of Lord Śiva.

26 See Appendix 5 for an explanation of *svātantrya śakti*.

27 "All of the *kalā*s (circles) containing the 118 worlds are existing in Her womb, and they will come out now, and this whole universe will shine with the offshoots of Parabhairava." *Stava Cintāmaṇi* (1990).

nirupādānasaṁbhāram-abhittāveva tanvate /
jagaccitraṁ namastasmai kalāślāghyāya śūline //9//

I bow to that Lord Śiva who holds a *triśūla* (His weapon). The *triśūla* is three-fold, that [trident].[28] I bow to that Lord Śiva. And He is the greatest artist. Who is Lord Śiva? Lord Śiva is the greatest artist I have ever seen, I have ever come to know, because He is such an artist that, *nirupādāna saṁbhāram*, He creates this art of the one hundred and eighteen worlds on no basis. There is no paper on which He draws this map of the one hundred and eighteen worlds–*nirupādāna saṁbhāram*. And *abhittau eva tanvate*, and without a pen, there is no pen for Him to draw this sketch of the one hundred and eighteen worlds. He draws this sketch of the one hundred and eighteen worlds without any basis, without any paper, without any pen, without any ink, without any colors, without any of these . . .

ERNIE: Crayons.

DEVOTEES: Pencils.

SWAMIJI: Yes, pencils. *Abhittau eva tanvate jagat citraṁ, jagat citraṁ*,[29] the one hundred and eighteen worlds are created by Him without a basis. And *kalāślāghyāya*, and He has such an art, He is such an artist, who has this kind of art that He can wind up this map at once. At the time of destruction, total destruction, He can wind up this art. No, he has not to roll it [up]. He just vanishes it in one second at the time of total destruction. And I bow to that greatest artist, Lord Śiva.

Audio 1 (34:50)

मायाजलोदरात्सम्यगुद्धृत्य विमलीकृतम् ।
शिवज्ञानं स्वतो दुग्धं देह्येहि हरहंसः नः ॥ १० ॥

---

28 "*Triśūla* is *parā śakti*, three energies, triple energies: *icchā* (will), *jñāna* (knowledge), and *kriyā* (action)." *Parātrīśikā Vivaraṇa*, LJA archives.
29 Lit., the variations (*citraṁ*) of the world/universe (*jagat*).

māyājalodarātsamyak-uddhṛtya vimalīkṛtam /
śivajñānaṁ svato dugdhaṁ dehyehi harahaṁsaḥ naḥ / / 10

O Lord Śiva, You are the greatest swan! And that swan already has the power to separate milk from water.

Have you ever heard that?

DENISE: I think I have heard something.

SWAMIJI: He separates this: milk and water he can separate. If you have got a swan at home, at the time of purchasing milk, you can understand how much water they have put in that if you have that swan. He will suck only the milk and throw it in another pot, not the water if water is also mixed in it. This is the art of that swan.

And You are also a great swan! O Lord Śiva, You are also [a great swan]. I can't perceive the ways and processes of un-minding my mind, which is already existing in this world. There are ways and *upāya*s (means)[30] to un-mind one's mind. They are existing in this *jaloddhāra*, in this ocean of *māyā*, *māyā śakti*.

Māyā, he has kept [described] as an ocean, an ocean of water and milk.

And there is milk also! In *māyā*, the one hundred and eighteen worlds (this is the expansion of *māyā*), in that there is water and milk. What is water? Water is ignorance. Milk is knowledge. And knowledge I cannot find in this, in this cycle of *māyā*, in this cycle of the world, I cannot find knowledge. I have to ask for some swan who will separate this milk from this water. So, from this ocean of *māyā*, please, for my sake, *uddhṛtya*, take it out, *uddhṛtya vimalīkṛtam*, take it out and purify it, take it out, this *śiva-jñānam*, the knowledge of Śiva,

30 "The meaning of the Sanskrit word "*upāya*" is "means". The word "*upāya*" in Kashmir Śaivism is used to indicate the means to enter into Universal God Consciousness from individual consciousness." *Kashmir Shaivism, The Secret Supreme*, 5.33. See also Appendix 3 for an explanation of *upāyas*.

which is milk, pure milk. Please take out this know-ledge of *śiva-jñāna*, which is milk, from this ignorance, the field of ignorance, and please give it, offer it, to me. I want to have it, and please come to me for my rescue.

BRUCE H: Swamiji, isn't "*haṁsaḥ*" "*so'ham*"?

SWAMIJI: That is *mantra vargaḥ*, yes, according to *mantras*. And you have to recite that *mantra*. We call it "*haṁsaḥ*".

Audio 1 (38:18)

षट्प्रमाणीपरिच्छेदभेदयोगेऽप्यभेदिने ।
परमार्थैकभावाय बलिं यामो भवाय ते ॥ ११ ॥

ṣaṭpramāṇīpariccheda-bhedayoge'pyabhedine /
paramārthaikabhāvāya baliṁ yāmo bhavāya te //11//

I want to surrender my whole body to You, O Lord Śiva, because You are filled with truth. You are one in the differentiated world of the six-fold proofs.[31]

This is, in the *śloka* he says, *ṣaṭ pramāṇī paricched abheda yoge api abhedine*, in these six-fold proofs, in these six-fold classes of proofs, Lord Śiva is One, Lord Śiva is unchanging. So, there is no way, there is no space, for proofs. Lord Śiva does not need *pratyakṣa pramāṇa*.[32] Lord Śiva does not need *anumāna*.[33] Lord Śiva is existing without proofs. On the contrary, Lord Śiva gives life to proofs. So, He is the reality of all proofs.

I surrender my body, my soul, and my mind, to Him.[34]

---

31 See Appendix 6 for a complete explanation of the 'six-fold proofs'.

32 The proof (*pramāṇa*) that comes from direct perception (*pratyakṣa*).

33 Inference.

34 "He needs no proof for His existence. Although You are not seen by anybody, You are seen by everyone. I want to sacrifice my life to You just as one who has surrendered his life for the well-being of his father; like when a father has a terminal disease, which cannot be cured, and someone with a strong will surrenders his life for him. I

Another *śloka:*

Audio 1 (39:42)

अपि पश्येम गम्भीरां परेण ज्योतिषाभितः ।
उन्मृष्टतमसं रम्यामन्तर्भव भवद्गुहाम् ॥ १२ ॥

api paśyema gambhīrāṁ pareṇa jyotiṣābhitaḥ /
unmṛṣṭatamasaṁ ramyām-antarbhava bhavadguhām //12 //
(verse repeated)

Will that day come sometime when I will, O Lord Śiva, I will see, inside my own body, Your cave, Your cave in which You exist, in which You are situated, that cave, the cave in my heart? Will that be possible for me in this life that I will ever experience the glamour of that cave inside my heart, which is *gambhīrām*, very deep (that cave is very deep, it is very long; you go inside, inside, and there is no end–*gambhīrām*). *Pareṇa jyotiṣa abhitaḥ*, in that cave which is deep, there is no light. In a deep cave, generally you won't find any light, it is dark, but this cave, this deep cave of Lord Śiva, is *pareṇa jyotiṣābhitaḥ unmṛṣṭa-tamasaṁ*, there you will get all of the darkness vanished, there in that cave, by the supreme light of consciousness. And a deep cave is always terrible, terrific (not terrific; it is frightful). A deep cave is already frightening to people, but this cave [of Lord Śiva] is *ramyāma*, very beautiful. "Will that day come that I will see that cave, I will perceive that cave, in my life time," he asks Lord Śiva.

Audio 1 (42:05)

नमस्तेभ्योऽपि ये सोम कलाकलितशेखरम् ।
नाथं स्वप्नेऽपि पश्यन्ति परमानन्ददायिनम् ॥ १३ ॥

namastebhyo'pi ye soma-kalākalitaśekharam /
nāthaṁ svapne'pi paśyanti paramānandadāyinam //13//

---

mean, I want to surrender my limited being to be consumed in the unlimited state of Bhairava." *Stava Cintāmaṇi* (1990).

I bow to those people also (*namastebhyo'pi*, I bow to those people also), who experience, who perceive, Lord Śiva in the dreaming state, in the dreaming state also (in dreams, not in wakefulness). In the dreaming state, [those] who perceive Lord Śiva with *soma kalākalita śekharam*, whose forehead is beautified by that crescent moon (on the forehead), *param-ānanda-dāyinam*, who is the bestower of all peace and ecstasy to those who perceive Him, those persons who perceive Him in the dreaming state also, I bow to those people. They are also blessed. What to speak of perceiving Him in wakefulness? That is wonderful! But those people also who perceives Him in the dreaming state, I bow to them. They are also blessed.[35]

Audio 1 (43:29)

भगवन्भव भावत्कं भावं भावयितुं रुचिः ।
पुनर्भवभयोच्छेददक्षा कस्मै न रोचते ॥ १४ ॥

bhagavanbhava bhāvatkaṁ bhāvaṁ bhāvayituṁ ruciḥ /
punarbhavabhayocchedadakṣā kasmai na rocate / / 14 / /

O Lord Śiva (*bhagavan*, O Lord Śiva), *bhāvatkaṁ bhāvayitum ruciḥ, kasmai na rocate*, who cannot own, who will not like to own, the desire for perceiving Your nature? Who will

35 "In the dreaming state also, You bless them with supreme bliss up to the end of their lives. They become *jīvan mukta* then." Ibid. "I told my master, 'I have achieved this power [of freedom] in the dreaming state by this practice', and he said, 'I will only believe that you have achieved this power when you go in the dreaming state and wish to see Lord Śiva in His full glory in His body, 'in *sākāra*,' with *triśūla* (trident), with *candrika* (crescent moon), [and] if that comes true, then it is perfect *svapna svātantrya* (freedom in the dreaming state).'" Swami Lakshmanjoo, *The Mystery of Vibrationless-Vibration in Kashmir Shaivism–Vasugupta's Spanda Kārikā and Kṣemarāja's Spanda Sandoha*, ed. John Hughes, Lakshmanjoo Academy, Los Angeles, 2016, (3.2 commentary). This was an account of Swamiji's experience after he had been initiated by his master, Swami Mahatab Kāk.

not like to perceive, who will not like to have, the desire for perceiving Your nature? And that desire, the power of that desire, is *punar-bhava-bhayoccheda-dakṣā*, it is efficient, it is completely efficient, to destroy, to vanish, the fear of the cycle of repeated births and deaths. The fear of repeated births and deaths, the cycle of repeated births and deaths, the fear of that is vanished in a moment, in an instant, instantaneously. By which? By this desire. Who will not own this desire in this world? Everybody would like to have this desire.

So:

Audio 1 (45:07)

यावज्जीवं जगन्नाथ कर्तव्यमिदमस्तु नः ।
त्वत्प्रसादात्त्वदेकाग्रमनस्कत्वेन या स्थितिः ॥ १५ ॥

yāvajjīvaṁ jagannātha kartavyamidamastu naḥ /
tvatprasādāttvadekāgra-manaskatvena yā sthitiḥ / / 15 / /

O ruler of the one hundred and eighteen worlds,[36] Lord Śiva, *yāvat jīvam*, as long as I am living in this world, my only work and my only desire is this [world]–not by my efficiency, I am not efficient to have that desire–. . .

Which desire?

STEPHANIE: To perceive Lord Śiva?

SWAMIJI: No.

. . . *tvad ekāgra manas katvena yā sthitiḥ*, just centralizing my mind in one-pointedness of God consciousness–this kind of desire. This kind of desire, I want to have this desire, but I don't deserve this desire, I don't deserve this desire. By Your grace, if You like to bestow that desire to me, then I would like to have that desire. Not by my efficiency, I am not efficient, I am not fit, for [obtaining] that desire. As long as I am living in this world, this desire must come to me by Your grace, not by my efficiency.

This is what he asks in this *śloka*. Do you understand? It is very easy!

36 See fn 24 for an explanation of the 118 worlds.

Audio 1 (47:00)

शाखासहस्त्रविस्तीर्ण-वेदागममयात्मने ।
नमोऽनन्तफलोत्पाद-कल्पवृक्षाय शंभवे ॥ १६ ॥

śākhāsahasravistīrṇa-vedāgamamayātmane /
namo'nantaphalotpāda-kalpavṛkṣāya śaṁbhave //16//

In fact, Lord Śiva is existing, Lord Śiva is existing with full light and glamour. And this Lord Śiva has got thousands of offshoots of His rays. Thousands of offshoots are expanded from the effulgent light of Lord Śiva, and those offshoots are the Vedas, those offshoots are Buddhism, those offshoots are Sāṁkhya, logic (Nyāya), Vaiśeṣika, grammar, Vedānta, Śaivism, Mīmāṁsā, Pūrva-mīmāṁsā, Uttara-mīmāṁsā, Nigama. All those offshoots have come out from Him. So, there is no worry. You should not worry in which offshoot you are residing. If you are residing in the offshoot of Vedānta, never mind. If you are residing in Shaivism, that is okay. If you are residing in Vedānta, Yoga, Mīmāṁsā, Nyāya, Vaiśeṣika, that is okay, because it has come out from that Lord Śiva! It has come out from the effulgent light of Lord Śiva–all these directions have come out. Veda, Āgama, Nigamana, Purāṇa, all of those things have come out from that one light, that one effulgent light, of Lord Śiva. *Ananta phalot pāda kalpa*, so Lord Śiva is, in other words, *kalpa vṛkṣa*, the tree of the bestower of all boons.

In the Tantras, it is also said at one place:

Audio 1 (48:50)

वेदं सांख्यं पाञ्चरात्रं वामं चैव न निन्दयेत् ।
यतः शिवोद्भव सर्वे शिवधामफलप्रदाय ॥

vedaṁ sāṁkhyaṁ pāñcarātraṁ vāmaṁ caiva na nindayet /
yataḥ śivodbhava sarve śivadhāmaphalapradāya //[37]

37 *Svacchandatantra* 5.44bc-45ab, also paraphrased in *Tantrāloka* 35.36: "*sāṁhkhyaṁ yogaṁ pāñcarātraṁ vedāṁścaiva na nindayet / yataḥ śivodbhavāḥ sarva*. See also Swamiji's commentary of verse 23.

You should not discard Vedānta, you should not discard Śaiva, you should not discard Vāma *mārga*,[38] Pāñcarātra you should not discard. You should not discard, you should not hate, these systems of all these *śāstra*s. Why? *Yataḥ śivodbhāvaḥ sarve*, because they all have come out from Śiva! *Śiva dhāma phala*, they will carry you to that Śiva, in one second or in one thousand seconds.

There was one master, his name was Puṣpadanta,[39] he has also said one *śloka*:

Audio 1 (50:13)

त्रयी सांख्यं योगः पशुपतिमतं वैष्णवमिति ।
प्रभिन्ने प्रस्थाने परमिदमदः पथ्यमिति च ॥

trayī sāṁkhyaṁ yogaḥ paśupatimataṁ vaiṣṇavamiti
prabhinne prasthāne paramidamadhaḥ pathyamiti ca /[40]

The followers of the three Vedas, the followers of the Sāṁkhya System, the followers of Yoga *Darśana*, the followers of Paśupāti *Darśana* (that dualistic Śaivism), Vaiṣṇava (the followers of the Vaiṣṇavites), *prabhinne prasthane*, they have come out differentiated from one point. Which is that one point? Lord Śiva. But they have been differentiatedly existing in coming out.

ERNIE: In this world.

SWAMIJI: In this world. *Paramidam adhaḥ pathyam*, "This is the highest philosophy," "This is a wretched philosophy," "This is a good philosophy," "This philosophy is [the one] that I must have," *paramidam*, "This is supreme," "This is not supreme," . . .

---

38 *Mārga*: path, way.

39 Puṣpadanta was the revered composer of the *Śiva Mahimna Stotra*, a celestial hymn that sang the unending glories of Lord Śiva.

40 Kṣemarāja's commentary, verse 7a of *Śiva Mahimna Stotra*.

Audio 1 (51:25)

रुचिनां वैचित्र्याद्दजुकूटिलनानापथजुषां
नृणामेको गम्यस्त्वमसि पयसामर्णव इव ॥

rucināṁ vaicitryādṛjukūṭilanānāpathajuṣāṁ
nṛṇāmeko gamyastvamasi payasāmarṇava iva / /[41]
(not recited)

. . . *rucinām vaicitryāt*, because of their likings, the likings of those people, *ṛjukūṭilanānāpathajuṣāṁ*, some go ahead, some go astray, some go this way, some go that way, but where will their journey end? Their journey will end at that one point, that is, Lord Śiva. It may take time, but they are leading to that one point.

End of Audio 1 (51:57)

Start of Audio 2 (00:00)

वाङ्मनः कायकर्माणि विनियोज्य त्वयि प्रभो ।
त्वन्मयीभूय निर्द्वन्द्वाः कच्चित्स्यामापि कर्हिचित् ॥ १७ ॥

vāṅmanaḥ kāyakarmāṇi viniyojya tvayi prabho /
tvanmayībhūya nirdvandvāḥ kaccitsyāmāpi karhicit / / *17* / /

O Lord, O my Master, will that day ever come to me when *vāṅ manaḥ kāya karmāṇi*, I will surrender all of my activities of speech, all of my activities of mind, and all of my activities of action, I will surrender them to You? Whatever I do, whatever I speak, whatever I think, I'll surrender it to You; let it be another thought, let it be another activity, than meditation–whatever I do. Will that day ever come to me that I will surrender, I will see that I do [everything] just for You? I hate just for You, just for Your attachment, I hate You just for Your love; I scold You just for . . . because I love You; I adore You because I love You; I kick You because I love You. Whatever I do, I . . .

41 Ibid., 7b.

DENISE: . . . I do it for Your sake.

SWAMIJI: Yes. And *tvanmayī bhūya*, and in conclusion, I will become one with You. I will be the embodiment of oneness with You, *nirdvandvā*, without separation from You. Will that day ever come?

ERNIE: He really says, "I hate You, I'll kick You, . . . ?"

SWAMIJI: [He says:] "I would hate You out of love; I would kick You out of love; I will scold You, I would hate You, I would . . . ."

ERNIE: Every . . .

SWAMIJI: Yes. "Whatever I do, I want to do out of love [for You]. Will that day ever come?"

Audio 2 (02:08)

जगतां सर्गसंहार-तत्तद्धितनियुक्तिषु ।
अनन्यापेक्षसामर्थ्य-शालिने शूलिने नमः ॥१८॥

jagatāṁ sargasaṁhāra-tattaddhitaniyuktiṣu /
ananyāpekṣasāmarthya-śāline śūline namaḥ //18//

I bow to that Lord Śiva who holds the weapon *triśūla*[42] in His hand, and *ananyāpekṣya sāmarthya śāline*, and who is glorified with that supreme power, which is an unparalleled supreme power; which power is not found in any god, any other god, than You. *Jagatām sarga saṁhāra tattaddhitani yuktiṣu*, and Your power is fit, that power of Yours is fit, to give, to bestow, boons, or to curse, or to create, or to protect, or to destroy this whole universe. Your power is that power which will create the universe, which will protect the universe, which will destroy the universe, which will conceal the universe, which will reveal Your real nature,[43] and which will bestow boons to people, and which will curse people. This is the power

---

42 The trident (*triśūla*) represents Lord Śiva's threefold energies: *parā* (supreme), *parāparā* (medium), and *aparā* (inferior).

43 These are the five great acts (*pañcakṛtya*) of Lord Śiva. See *Kashmir Shaivism, The Secret Supreme*, 10.65

which You have adjusted. And Your power is *ananyāpekṣayā*, unparalleled [compared] to all other powerful gods. I bow to You, who has held in His hand the *triśūla* as His weapon.

Do you like it?

DEVOTEES: Yes.

SWAMIJI:

Audio 2 (04:00)

व्यतीतगुणयोगस्य मुख्यध्येयस्य धूर्जटेः ।
नामापि ध्यायतां ध्यानैः किमन्यालम्बनैः फलम् ॥ १९

vyatītaguṇayogasya mukhyadhyeyasya dhūrjaṭeḥ /
nāmāpi dhyāyatāṁ dhyānaiḥ kimanyālambanaiḥ phalam / / 19

Those people, those fortunate devotees, who recite the name of *dhūrjaṭa*, . . .*

Dhūrjaṭa means, that Being whose–what is that hairdo?–hairdo is not done, is undone, always.

JOHN: Unkempt hair? I mean, His hair is just matted hair?

SWAMIJI: Matted hair. It is not combed, it is not in order. That is *dhūrjaṭeḥ*. His hair is . . .

ERNIE: Unkempt.

JOHN: In disarray. Unkempt hair.

SWAMIJI: Yes.

*. . . and who is *vyatītaguṇa yogasya*, who has gone beyond the cycle of the three *guṇa*s (*sattvaguṇa*, *rajoguṇa*, and *tamoguṇa*)[44]–who is *guṇātīta*; in brief words, who is *guṇātīta*

---

44 "*Sukha* (joy) means, *satoguṇa*, *duḥkha* (suffering) means, *rajoguṇa*, and *mohamātraṁ* (illusion) is *tamoguṇa*." Swami Lakshmanjoo, *Abhinavagupta's Paramārthasāra–Essence of the Supreme Reality,* with the commentary of Yogarāja, ed. John Hughes (Lakshmanjoo Academy, Los Angeles, 2015), verse 19.
"You cannot find any living being in this gross earthly world . . . or in the heavens, who has escaped . . . who is not entangled, by the

vyatīta guṇa yogasya–and *mukhya dhyeyasya*, who is to be meditated [upon], who is to be adored, who is to be worshipped (He only is worth worshipping, He only is worth adoring, He only is worth having, owning)–*vyatītaguṇa*, *dhūrjaṭa*[45]–and those fortunate people who just think of Him, who just remember Him, what remains for them to achieve in this world? They have achieved everything. Who?

STEPHANIE: Those who remember.

SWAMIJI: Those who remember Him, remember His name only! So they don't need to catch hold of any other support. They are always with the greatest support.

Audio 2 (06:06)

नमो नमः शिवायेति मन्त्रसामर्थ्यमाश्रिताः ।
श्लाघ्यास्ते शाम्भवीं भूतिमुपभोक्तुं य उद्यताः ॥२०॥

namo namaḥ śivāyeti mantrasāmarthyamāśritāḥ /
ślāghyāste śāmbhavīṁ bhūtim upabhoktuṁ ya udyatāḥ //20//

Those people are fortunate (*ślāghyāste*, they are fortunate people), who have got, who have attained, only one power, one power in their thought, in their minds. Which is that power? Just the recitation of the *mantra*, "*Śivāya namaḥ namaḥ*, *śivāya namo namaḥ*, *śivāya namo* "–this *mantra*, those people who are reciting this *mantra*. And this *mantra*, to recite this *mantra* in continuity, is under their control, nothing else–only "*Namo namaḥ śivāya*, *śivāya namo namaḥ*." They are fortunate. *Śāmbhavīṁ bhūtim upabhoktuṁ ya udyatāḥ*, they

---

guṇas of *prakṛti*. Everybody is entangled by the *guṇas* of *prakṛti*!" *Bhagavad Gītā In the Light of Kashmir Shaivism*, 18.40.

"These three tides of the three *guṇas* are, in the real sense, one with God consciousness." Swami Lakshmanjoo, *Bhagavadgītārtha-saṁgraha of Abhinavagupta*, translation and commentary, (original audio recording, LJA archives, Los Angeles, 1978), 7.14 commentary.

45 Swamiji is restating the said quality and name of Lord Śiva: He who is *guṇātīta* (*vyatītaguṇa*), and He who is with matted locks (*dhūrjaṭa*).

are very likely to get entry in the state of *śāmbhava*, *śāmbhava samāveśa*.[46] That is *śāmbhavīm bhūtim* (*bhūtim* means, glory).

Audio 2 (07:30)

कः पन्था येन न प्राप्यः का च वाङ्नोच्यसे यया ।
किं ध्यानं येन न ध्येय: किंवा किं नासि यत्प्रभो ॥ २१ ॥

kaḥ panthā yena na prāpyaḥ kā ca vāṅnocyase yayā /
kiṁ dhyānaṁ yena na dhyeyaḥ kiṁvā kiṁ nāsi yatprabho //21

O my Master, *kaḥ panthā*, which is that path, *yena*, by which path, *na prāpya*, You are not achieved? Which is that path? Even going on the wrong path will carry him to You. So, all pathways are focused to Your point. Whatever activity you do, this is the pathway, this is the real pathway.[47] So, which is that path by which path You are not achieved, You are not attained. What is that speech (*kā ca* [*vāk*], what is that speech), *nocyase yayā*, by which You are not indicated? If I say, "bloody fool," by this speech, "bloody fool," You are [nominated].[48] So, which is that speech which does not point out Your Being? *Kim dhyānam*, which is that meditation [that does not point out Your Being? If you meditate on sexual activity, *kim dhyānam*, if you meditate on that, this is meditating on You, Sir. It is not another meditation. *Kim dhyānam yena na dhyeyaḥ*, so by that meditation, You are achieved, You are attained. What is existing in this world which is not one with You (*kim vā kim nāsi yat*)? Everything is

---

46 Absorption (*samāveśa*) in the the *śāmbhava* state. "When you put your mind, when you meditate, on nothingness, absolute nothingness, that is the *śāmbhava* state." *Vijñāna Bhairava,* verse 107, commentary.

47 "If it is a good action or a bad action, You will be achieved." *Stava Cintāmaṇi* (1990).

48 "When I say, 'Give us tea,' these words will nominate Your point. 'I will take butter and this and that,' and these words nominate Your Being. You are existing in disguise in all objects–butter, paper, tea, etc." Ibid.

You.

So, if this is a fact . . . another *śloka*:

Audio 2 (09:43)

अर्चितोऽयमयं ध्यात एष तोषित इत्ययम् ।
रसः स्त्रोतःसहस्त्रेण त्वयि मे भव वर्धताम् ॥२२॥

arcito'yamayaṁ dhyāta eṣa toṣita ityayam /
rasaḥ srotaḥsahasreṇa tvayi me bhava vardhatām //22//

O Lord Śiva, this *rasa*, this . . .

["*Rasa*" is] not exactly "taste". This is *rasa*: *rasa* is, he who has got attachment with that *rasa*, a weakness, if you have got a weakness for something, you can't leave that, that *rasa*. That means "*rasa*".

. . . this *rasa*, that *rasa*, *srotaḥ sahasreṇa*, let that *rasa* increase in my mind, increase in my brain, increase in myself, through *srotaḥ sahasreṇa*, through a hundred and thousand flows, through a hundred and thousand avenues–"avenues"?–for You. Let that *rasa*, let that weakness, flow from all sides. In one hundred and one thousand ways, let it increase in me. What is that *rasa*? What is that weakness? A weakness for what? "*Arcito ayam*, you know, I was worshipping God, I was worshipping Lord Śiva. You know, I was meditating on Lord Śiva, I was contemplating on Lord Śiva. Oh, Lord Śiva must be very pleased with me"–all of these things. A weakness for this [preoccupation with You], not a weakness for any other thing in this world. Let this weakness rise a hundred and thousand ways in me by Your grace–this weakness.

Do you understand?

DEVOTEES: Yes.

Audio 2 (12:00)

नमो निःशेषधीपत्रिमालायमयात्मने ।
नाथाय स्थाणवे तुभ्यं नागयज्ञोपवीतिने ॥२३॥

namo niḥśeṣadhīpatri-mālālayamayātmane /
nāthāya sthāṇave tubhyaṁ nāgayajñopavītine //23//

Now, in this universe, you see, there are only two things to be held. *Patri mālā*: *Patri mālā* is, you know, those birds, those kinds of birds, who fly in one line, in one line in the sky, one after another, one after another. That is *patri mālā*, the range of all of those birds. They fly only in the morning and in the evening; they fly in the mornings and in the evenings. In the morning, they fly *from* their nests. In the evening, they fly *to* their nests. In the evening, when they fly to their nests, this is the case in the world, this is the case in the world which we observe. What do we observe? *Niḥśeṣa dhī patri*, all these intellectual pathways. Your intellectual pathway is one, yours is one, yours is one, yours is one, etc. So, there are hundreds and thousands and millions of intellectual pathways. All of these intellectual pathways are just like those birds. And *niḥśeṣa dhī patri*, these have come out from That log, from That eternal log, Lord Śiva. Lord Śiva is an eternal log. That trunk of the tree is very old, ancient, and in that they make their nests. They come out from That, they come out from That log in the morning and fly in their own way, and afterwards, when they return, they return to That same log. So, all intellectual pathways are directed towards You.

So, it is said:

Audio 2 (14:35)

vedaṁ sāṁkhyaṁ pāñcarātraṁ vāmaṁ caiva na nindayet /[49]
yataḥ śivodbhavāḥ sarva . . . . .

You should not discard the Vedas, the theory of the Vedas. You should not discard the theory of Sāṁkhya. You should not discard this theory of Yoga. You should not discard the theory of other schools of thought–Mīmāṁsā, Naiyyāyika (logicians). Don't discard those. Don't discard the theory of Christ, or the theory of Mohammed, or the theory of Lord Kṛṣṇa, or Śiva, or Vaiṣṇava. You should not do that. You should not hate these

49. See also verse 16, fn 37.

theories. Why? *Yataḥ śivodbhava sarve*, they have come out from That log, and they are sentenced to That log in the end. So, nobody is out of the way, outside of That pathway.

DENISE: We are all included!

SWAMIJI: Included on That pathway. The pathway is one. And *nāga yajñopavītine*, and You have got that garland of snakes.[50] And That log also has got so many snakes and vipers there; because It is an eternal log, there you will find snakes also. In the same way, [on] the body of Lord Śiva, you will find snakes also. And from Lord Śiva, all pathways come. The pathways of intellectual pathways come out and they get entry in the same log. I bow to That log. Whose log? Lord Śiva's.[51]

Audio 2 (16:36)

अज्ञानतिमिरस्यैकमौषधं संस्मृतिस्तव ।
भव तत्तत्प्रदानेन प्रसादः क्रियतां मयि ॥२४॥

ajñānatimirasyaikam-auṣadhaṁ saṁsmṛtistava /
bhava tattatpradānena prasādaḥ kriyatāṁ mayi //24//

O Lord Śiva, I have got *timira*,[52] I have got a *timira* disease in my eyes. I can't see in an actual way.

> You know *timira*? *Timira* is *rekhā timira roga*, it is a disease in the eyes [in which a] line comes just in the center of that pupil. In the pupil, one line comes, to some

---

50 In his commentary, Kṣemarāja mentions Vāsuki, the cobra who, like a garland, adorns Lord Śiva's neck. Vāsuki is the snake with which the gods and demons churned the milky ocean.

51 In his commentary on this verse, Kṣemarāja quotes verse 97 of this same text, which Swamiji translated as follows: "If you see a photograph of Lord Śiva with great love, [by] just [seeing] that Lord Śiva is very beautiful, by that only you will get liberation. This is the power of Lord Śiva." *Stava Cintāmaṇi* (1991).

52 Literally, *timira* means an affliction of the eye, but here it is used in the sense of perceiving duality.

persons, and it is called *rekhā timira roga*. By that, you will see two, you'll see two Vireshes, two Shannas.[53] This is a kind of disease in the eyes.

Ajñāna, and this is of ignorance, this is a disease of ignorance to see that, "I am one," "Denise is another," "He is my enemy," "He is my friend," all of these things. This is the disease. This is the disease in perception. What is not the disease? To see everyone as your own Self. If you feel that, "All of the embodiment of this whole universe is my own Self," will you hate anybody? You won't hate anybody. You will love everyone. Whenever hate comes, it comes from that disease, that disease in your eyes, because you see separate, two things.

ERNIE: Duality.

SWAMIJI: Duality. And this disease has come in my perception, O Lord–*ajñāna timirasyaikam*. And there is only one medicine for this, one dose for the removal of this disease, which You have, which You could bestow to me. Otherwise, there is no hope for my cure, I will never get cured from this disease. That [dose] is *saṁsmṛtistava*, just Your memory. O Lord Śiva, give me that dose of remembering You. Do this favor to me, O Lord Śiva. I want this.[54]

This is *auṣadha*: *Auṣadham āstām*[55] is one dose of the mixture by which this disease will get vanished. Really, this is a disease, and this disease has spread, you know, in a hundred and thousand million ways (laughter), in all of the one hundred and eighteen worlds.[56]

---

53 The son and daughter of John and Denise Hughes.

54 "The dose is the constant remembrance of Your Being. This is the only medicine for this blindness of Your Being. Please, from time-to-time, bestow on me That remembrance. If something bad happens in my life sometimes, like a relative dying, please bestow me the power to remember You, not that relative, then I will feel You have blessed me from all sides." *Stava Cintāmaṇi* (1991).

55 The medicine (*auṣadham*) that will cure me of seeing two (*āstām*).

56 See fn 24 for an explanation of the 118 worlds.

DENISE: In all of the worlds it's like that?

SWAMIJI: Yes.

Audio 2 (19:47)

नम ईशाय निःशेष-पुरुषार्थप्रसाधकः ।
प्रणन्तव्यः प्रणामोऽपि यदीय इह धीमताम् ॥२५॥

nama īśāya niḥśeṣa-puruṣārthaprasādhakaḥ /
praṇantavyaḥ pramāṇo'pi yadīya iha dhīmatām //25//

I bow to Lord Śiva, who is *niḥśeṣa puruṣārtha prasādhakaḥ*, who is the adopter of supreme *puruṣārtha*,[57] supreme *mokṣaḥ*, supreme final liberation; who is the bestower of that final liberation, I bow to Lord Śiva. And that bowing before Lord Śiva is bowed [to] by real devotees of Lord Śiva. They don't bow to Lord Śiva. What do they bow to?

DENISE: To themselves?

SWAMIJI: No! The bowing.

DENISE: They bow to the bowing?

SWAMIJI: For instance, you bow to Lord Śiva. I bow to your bowing! I appreciate your bowing.

ERNIE: You celebrate her . . .

SWAMIJI: That bowing, I worship that bowing, not Lord Śiva! You will bow to Lord Śiva, and I will worship your bowing.[58] And those intellectual *yogi*s bow to that bowing. They don't bow to Lord Śiva, they bow to that bowing. When you worship Lord Śiva, those intellectual genius *yogi*s bow to that, your worship, the worshipping. They appreciate that worshipping, they bow to that worshipping, they celebrate that worshipping.

---

57 Lit., *ārtha* (the highest goal) of *puruṣa* (the individual being).

58 "Those great scholars who bow to you," Bhaṭṭa Nārāyaṇa says, "I am a slave who is bowing to *their bowing*. I am not bowing to You, I am not bowing to Your devotees. I bow to the bowing of Your devotees." *Stava Cintāmaṇi* (1991).

Audio 2 (21:48)

मग्नैर्भीमे भवाम्भोधौ निलये दुःखयादसाम् ।
भक्तिचिन्तामणिं शारवं ततः प्राप्यं न कं जितम् ॥ २६ ॥

magnairbhīme bhavāmbhodhau nilaye duḥkhayādasām /
bhakticintāmaṇiṁ śārvaṁ tataḥ prāpyaṁ na kiṁ jitam //26

In *bhavāmbhodhau*, in this ocean of the universe, in this ocean of repeated births and deaths, . . .

> This is the great ocean where we are caught, where we are entangled, in the cycle of repeated births and deaths. This is the great ocean.

. . . and in that ocean, [those] who are *magnair*, who are drowned (*magnair*), *bhīme*, in this fearful ocean, *nilaye duḥkha yādasām*, which is the residing compartment of *yādasa*, . . .

> *Yādasa* means, those beings who reside in the ocean, e.g., *magarmaccha* (crocodile) and those big fish, and all of those . . .
>
> **DENISE:** Sharks.
>
> **ERNIE:** Sharks, whales, crocodiles.
>
> **SWAMIJI:** Yes. They are so big! Some are so big that they can crash this ship in one strike.

. . . and those who are drowned in this ocean–in this ocean of what?–the cycle of repeated births and deaths, those who are drowned in that and who are caught by those beings, . . .

ERNIE: *Magarmaccha* and . . .

SWAMIJI: Yes.

. . . those beings which are *duḥkha*, of that pain, various pains,[59] . . .

> You will find, finally you will find, this is painful. In this world, you will finally [find], [although] it is joyous, [although] it is ever-joyous, you will find, in the long run, you will find, that this joy was also painful in the end.

. . . and those who are drowned in this ocean, *bhakti cintāmaṇiṁ śārvaṁ*, if once anybody drowns in this ocean and then realizes and finds the jewel, . . .

> There is a jewel also in this ocean, and that jewel is devotion for Lord Śiva. Once you get devotion for Lord Śiva, when once you are attached–[even if you are] already drowned in this cycle of repeated births and deaths (the ocean)–when you once find attachment and devotion for Lord Śiva, that is the [*cintāmaṇi*] jewel, you have found that jewel in this ocean.

. . . when once you have found that jewel, the jewel of Lord Śiva, *tataḥ prāpyaṁ na kiṁ jitam*, what is not achieved then afterwards? You can achieve everything. He is fortunate, he is the only fortunate [person] in this world.[60]

Twenty-six ending.

End of Audio 2 (25:07)

Start of Audio 3 (00:00)

निरावरणनिर्द्वन्द्वनिश्चलज्ञानसंपदाम् ।
ज्ञेयऽसो किल केऽप्येते ये त्वां जानन्ति धूर्जटे ॥२७॥

nirāvaraṇanirdvandvaniścalajñānasaṁpadām /
jñey'si kila ke'pyete ye tvāṁ jānanti dhūrjaṭe //27//

---

59 "There are many whales of various shapes of torture in the world, in the ocean of *saṁsāra*. You are never safe in this world. You have one trouble and, as soon as that is over, then another trouble comes in excess." *Stava Cintāmaṇi* (1990).

60 "If, by the grace of Your *tīvra śaktipāta*, somebody is blessed with the *cintāmaṇi* jewel of Your entire love, this is the only remedy, the only medicine, for them to get rid of all of this torture." Ibid.

"*Dhūrjaṭe*" is just a calling: "O Lord Siva, *dhūrjaṭe*, [You] whose hair is not done," . . .

JOHN: Matted hair.

SWAMIJI: Yes. "O matted hair *wallah*!"[61]

DEVOTEES: (laughter)

SWAMIJI: . . . *nirāvaraṇa-nirdvandva-niścala-jñāna-saṁpadām jñeyo'si kila*, there are some very few devotees who have the wealth of knowledge, who have achieved the wealth of knowledge, which is *nirāvaraṇa* (*nirāvaraṇa* means, exposed, all-around exposed). It doesn't remain a secret [with] them. This knowledge which they own, that knowledge they always expose to everybody. And *nirdvanda*, they have no duality, they have no differentiated perception that, "I will bestow this knowledge to that person and I won't bestow this knowledge to such and such person." This kind of differentiation does not exist in them. They just go on bestowing. Whoever may take it, whoever may not take it, they go on bestowing it. And *niścala*, and the glory of that wealth which they have, is *niścala*, is not flickering.

You know "flickering"?

DENISE: It's constant.

SWAMIJI: It is constant, always the same. And those people, in a real sense, know You, and they are very few in this world.[62]

Next:

Audio 3 (02:20)

निर्गुणोऽपि गुणज्ञानां ज्ञेय एको जयत्यजः ।
निष्कामोऽपि प्रकृत्या यः कामनानां परं फलम् ॥२८॥

---

61 "*Wallah*" is Hindi for a person concerned or involved with a specific thing or business.

62 "O Lord Śiva, Your hair is matted like a *sadhu* and You have so many energies. For instance, if you will take one lock of Lord Śiva's hair, you cannot imagine how many energies are in that one lock of hair. He has numberless energies in His matted hair." Ibid.

nirguṇo'pi guṇajñānāṁ jñeya eko jayatyajaḥ /
niṣkāmo'pi prakṛtyā yaḥ kāmanānāṁ paraṁ phalam //28//

Aja, who is never born, who never dies, that Lord Śiva who never is born and never dies, *nirguṇo api*, He is *nirguṇa* (*nirguṇa* is, without *guṇa*s, without qualifications), He has no qualifications.

> He has no *sattvaguṇa*, He has no *rajoguṇa*, and no *tamoguṇa*, these three states of intellectual existence, the intellectual cycle which we have, these three-fold states (*sattvaguṇa*, *rajoguṇa*, and *tamoguṇa*). Sometimes we have *sattvaguṇa* in our mind when this love for God is created in our minds and detachment for the world is created in our minds. At that time, you should know that we have got *sattvaguṇa*, the wave of *sattvaguṇa* is functioning in our minds. And sometimes the wave of *rajoguṇa*, when we are extremely fond of excitement, worldly excitements, that is the sign of *rajoguṇa* in us. And *tamoguṇa*, when we are fond of just sleeping, doing nothing.

These three waves work in all living beings but, in You, these waves have already vanished. *Nirguṇo'pi*, although these three-fold qualifications are not seen in You, *guṇa jñānāṁ jñeya*, but You are known by qualities, You are known by qualifications. That person who has qualifications will attain You. So this is contradictory to the states [of Universality and individuality]. If You are *nirguṇa*, then by the *guṇa*s You should not be known, but by the *guṇa*s You are known [by] those who have got *guṇa*s, qualifications.

> There are two [meanings] of "*guṇa*s": one is *sattvaguṇa*, *rajoguṇa*, and *tamoguṇa*, and the other is "qualifications." You must translate the second [instance of the] word *guṇa* as "qualifications."

If You are without *guṇa*s, but by the *guṇa*s You are

achieved, this is a wonder, this is one wonder to me.

Do you understand?

DENISE: Yes.

SWAMIJI: *Niṣkāmo'pi*, You have no desire, although You have no desire in Your nature–this is Your nature that You are without desire–but You fulfill all of the desires. You are desireless, Yourself You are desireless, but You fulfill all of the desires of people. This is another second wonder to me.

Audio 3 (06:02)

श्रीरत्नामृतलाभाय क्लिष्टं यत्र न कैः सुरैः ।
तत्क्षीरोददमैश्वर्यं तवैव सहजं विभो ॥२९॥

śrīratnāmṛtalābhāya kliṣṭaṁ yatra na kaiḥ suraiḥ /
tatkṣīrodadamaiśvaryaṁ tavaiva sahajaṁ vibho //29//

O Lord Śiva, O my Master, *śrī ratna amṛta lābhāya*, at the time of churning this milky ocean, at the time when the *deva*s and *āsura*s[63] churned this milky ocean, the purpose of churning this milky ocean was just to have the goddess of wealth from that, and *ratna* (and all jewels), and *amṛta* (and the nectar which makes you immortal). For these three things, they exhausted themselves in churning that milky ocean, that milky ocean which belongs to You, O Lord Śiva.

The milky ocean, in the real sense, is the property of Lord Śiva, and Lord Śiva gave them the order, consent, to churn that, because without His permission, they couldn't churn it.

And the purpose of churning was to attain the goddess of wealth from that, and the jewel (that is, the *cintāmiṇi* jewel). The *cintāmaṇi* jewel is that kind of jewel that whatever you desire you can have, you can achieve. If you want your body to disappear, think [of that], take that

63 The gods and demons, respectively.

> jewel in your hand, and you won't be seen by anybody. If you want to become as big as a mountain, think [of that] and you'll become like that. This is the greatness of that *cintāmaṇi* jewel. That *cintāmaṇi* jewel was longed for by these gods and demons.
>
> So they churned it after the agreement with Lord Śiva because this Kṣīrasāgara, the milky ocean, belonged to Lord Śiva.

So they exhausted themselves for finding these three things out of this milky ocean.[64] *Tat kṣīrodadam aiśvaryaṁ*, and the glory of that wealth of Kṣīrasāgara, in that milky ocean, the glory is Your own.

> And the glory of that Kṣīrasargara was known to everybody afterwards, that this whole milky ocean You bestowed on one devotee of Thee. You didn't [keep] it. Upamanyu, his name was Upamanyu. He just worshipped Lord Śiva for some particular period, and afterwards, Lord Śiva was pleased with him and He bestowed on him the whole ocean, the milky ocean, [and He told him], "This will belong to you from today."[65]

---

64 The three things were: the goddess of wealth (Lakṣmī), the *cintāmaṇi* jewel (*ratna*), and the nectar of immortality (*amṛta*).

65 The life of Upamanyu is narrated in the *Shiva Mahā Purāṇa*. As a child, Upamanyu had an insatiable desire for milk, however, his family was unable to afford it. After his mother informed him of Lord Śiva's benevolence, Upamanyu began to worship Lord Śiva and performed great penances for the purpose of receiving milk. Lord Śiva eventually granted him an entire ocean of milk.

"Upamanyu, whom Lord Śiva loved very much, addressed Lord Śiva with the words, 'You are such a great soul!' Then Lord Śiva asked him if he wanted any boons. Upamanyu replied, 'I want only You, not any boons.' Lord Śiva replied, 'No, hereafter I will give you all good things from the Ocean of Milk, including the realization of My Being.' Upamanyu replied, 'You give everything to others, and don't care to keep anything for Yourself, and then You beg from door-to-

So, this is the *aiśvarī*. *Aiśvarī* is not, the glory is not, if you have one *lakh*[66] and you will spend out of it 50,000 rupees. The glory is that you will spend the whole *lakh*. You will give the whole *lakh*, this whole property, to Your devotees. This is the glory. This glory is only seen in Lord Śiva. He keeps nothing for Himself. Whatever He has is for His devotees. That is what [Bhaṭṭa Nārāyaṇa] says: "This is the real glory, and the real glory of Your wealth."

Audio 3 (10:32)

नमो भक्त्या नृणां मुक्त्यै भवते भव तेऽवते ।
स्मृत्या नुत्या च ददते शंभवे संभवेऽभवे ॥ ३० ॥

namo bhaktyā nṛṇāṁ muktyai bhavate bhava te'vate /
smṛtyā nutyā ca dadate śaṁbhave śaṁbhave'bhave //30//

In the real sense, O Lord Śiva, *nṛṇāṁ muktyai bhavate*, You liberate those people who adore You, who love You, who adopt devotion for You. [Those] who have devotion for You, You liberate them. And not only liberate them; You always protect them (*avate* means, You always protect them). And, by remembrance, by bowing, You bestow them glory day and night, second after second, birth after birth. You bestow them glory, You go on in continuity to bestow them glory. This is Your greatness, O Lord.

Audio 3 (11:38)

सर्वज्ञःसर्वकृत्सर्वमसीति ज्ञानशालिनाम् ।
वेद्यं किं कर्म वा नाथ नानन्त्याय त्वयार्प्यते ॥ ३१ ॥

sarvajñaḥ sarvakṛtsarvam-asīti jñānaśālinām /
vedyaṁ kiṁ karma vā nātha nānantyāya tvayārpyate //31//

You are all-knowing, You are all-doing; You do everything

---

door. So, I want nothing from You, I want only to praise You.'" *Stava Cintāmaṇi* (1990).
66 100,000 rupees.

and You know everything. In this way, You are known to those persons who are glorified with real knowledge. So, for them, what is that action and what is that knowledge, which is not surrendered to You at Thy feet? They surrender all of their activities and all of whatever they know, they surrender it to You. They keep nothing for themselves.

Audio 3 (12:40)

इच्छाया एव यस्येयत् फलं लोकत्रयात्मकम् ।
तस्य ते नाथ कार्याणां को वेत्ति कियती गतिः ॥३२॥

icchāyā eva yasyetat phalaṁ lokatrayātmakam /
tasya te nātha kāryāṇāṁ ko vetti kiyatī gatiḥ //32//

Nātha, O my Master, *icchāyā eva yasyeyat phalaṁ lokatrayātmakam*, whose only desire, the fruit of [Your] desire, is just the creation of these three worlds. He just desires and these three worlds are created. This is the fruit of His desire, will. And, when He acts, that is not known–the fruit of His action, what would be the fruit of His action. When He acts, it is only by thinking, [His] thinking power makes the creation of the three worlds–just thinking only. When He acts, what will be the fruit of His action? That is not known, that is unknown to me. It will be some tremendous fruit!

Do you understand? You don't understand.

Audio 3 (14:02)

ब्रह्मादयोऽपि तद्यस्य कर्मसोपानमालया ।
उपर्युपरि धावन्ति लब्धुं धाम नमामि तम् ॥३३॥

brahmādayo'pi tadyasya karmasopānamālayā /
uparyupari dhāvanti labdhuṁ dhāma namāmi tam //33//

I bow to that state of Lord Śiva, I bow to that residence of Lord Śiva, whose residence, with the hope to achieve That residence, of Brahmā, Viṣṇu, and Rudra, all of these five great gods (god of creation, god of protection, god of destruction, god of concealing, and god of revealing) . . .

JOHN: What are those gods? Concealing and revealing is . . . ?

SWAMIJI: Brahmā, Viṣṇu, Rudra, . . . Brahmā is the god of creation, he creates this whole universe; Viṣṇu is the god of protection, he protects this universe; Rudra is the god of destruction, he destroys this universe; Īśvara is the god of concealing, he conceals this universe at the time of *pralāya*. You know "*pralāya*"?

DENISE: Voidness.

SWAMIJI: No. *Pralāya* is total destruction, when you destroy the destruction also. This whole universe is created, it is protected, and it is destroyed. When you destroy, it is only barren, all void, just space only. And that space is also destroyed. That is done by Īśvara. And, after that destruction, Your Self is revealed. That is done by Sadāśiva.

. . . all of these five gods of *pañcakṛtya*, the five great actions (actions of creation, protection, destruction, concealing, and revealing), they do all of this only with the hope, with this hope, that *karmasopāna*, by fulfilling their activities, fulfilling their duties (the duty of Brahmā is to create, the duty of Viṣṇu is to protect, and like that), all of these five gods tread on this duty just with this hope that they would find out the real residence of Lord Śiva in the end. This is the desire in them. I bow to that residence of Lord Śiva.

Audio 3 (17:02)

अयं ब्रह्मा महेन्द्रोऽयं सूर्याचन्द्रमसाविमौ ।
इति शक्तिलता यस्य पुष्पिता पात्वसौ भवः ॥३४॥

ayaṁ brahmā mahendro'yaṁ sūryācandramasāvimau /
iti śaktilatā yasya puṣpitā pātvasau bhavaḥ //34//

Let that Lord Śiva protect us (*asau bhava*; *bhavaḥ* means, Lord Śiva), let Lord Śiva protect us, whose creeper of energy . . .

You know "creeper"?

JOHN: Yes.

SWAMIJI: . . . whose creeper of energy is blossomed, blossomed in this way that you perceive that this is Brahmā, this is Viṣṇu, this is Rudra, this is Īśvara, this is Sadāśiva; this is *jāgrat* (this is wakefulness), this is the dreaming state, this is the dreamless state, this is *turya*, this is *turyātīta*;[67] this is *pralayākala*, *sakala*, *vijñānākala*; all of these three states, all of these seven states,[68] everything, whatever exists in this universe–whatever. All of these states, they are just blossoms of That creeper. You know? [All of these states are] *puṣpitā*, these are flowers of That creeper. Whose creeper? Whose is this creeper? The creeper of energy. Whose energy? Lord Śiva's energy. I bow to that Lord Śiva, whose creeper is blossomed in such and such a way in this world.

There is one *śloka*, which is composed by the commentator [Kṣemarāja] somewhere:[69]

Audio 3 (18:54)

सर्वज्ञः सर्वकर्तारो ब्रह्मद्या भुवनेश्वराः ।
यत्रैते बुधुदायन्ते बोधाब्धिं तं शिवं स्तुमः ॥

sarvajñaḥ sarvakartāro brahmādyā bhuvaneśvarāḥ /
yatraite budbudāyante bodhābdhiṁ taṁ śivaṁ stumaḥ / /

I bow to that Śiva who is just *bodhābdhim*, an ocean of consciousness. The great ocean of consciousness who is Lord Śiva, I bow to that ocean of consciousness, where, in which ocean of consciousness, the all-knowing and all-acting, . . .

JOHN: Yes, all-acting.

SWAMIJI: . . . all-acting Brahmā, Viṣṇu, Rudra, Īśvara, Sadāśiva, all of these five gods, they seem in that ocean just

67 See Appendix 7 for an explanation of *turya* and *turyātīta*.
68 See *Kashmir Shaivism–The Secret Supreme*, "The Seven States of The Seven Perceivers," (*Pramātṛin*), 8.51-56.
69 The source text of this verse is unknown.

like bubbles, where these five gods are seen just like bubbles in that ocean of God consciousness, Lord Śiva. I bow to that God consciousness.[70]

Audio 3 (19:58)

भ्रमो न लभ्यते यस्य भ्रान्तान्तःकरणैरपि ।
दूरगैरपि यस्यान्तो दुर्गमस्तं स्तुमो मृडम् ॥ ३५ ॥

bhramo na labhyate yasya bhrāntāntaḥkaraṇairapi /
dūragairapi yasyānto durgamastaṁ stumo mṛḍam //35//

Mṛdam means, Lord Śiva who bestows peace, who bestows joy. He is the bestower of joy.

Lord Śiva is, in the real sense, the bestower of joy in everybody. I bow to That bestower of joy. *Brahmo na labhyate yasya bhrāntānta karanairapi*, *bhrāntānta karanairapi*, those people who go on hiking after all of their senses to control them, . . .

You know "hiking". What is "hiking"?

DEVOTEES: Walking in the mountains.

SWAMIJI: No, hiking in the cycle of the organic field.[71] The organic field is a path of the mountain, . . .

ERNIE: A journey.

SWAMIJI: . . . a journey.

. . . and those people who are walking on that pathway just to control their senses, they are wandering, and after wandering also, they don't get the avenue, the pathway, of Lord Śiva, who is the bestower of joy to everybody–they don't get It. Go on hiking on the pathway of the mountain of the organic field, still you won't find the avenue, that pathway, of *mṛḍa*.

70 After translating this verse, Swamiji said, "I think Bhaṭṭa Nārāyaṇa was more than Parabhairava." *Stava Cintāmaṇi* (1990).
71 The organs of knowledge (*jñānendriyas*) and the organs of action (*karmendriyas*).

"*Mṛḍa*" is?

DENISE: The joy of Lord Śiva?

SWAMIJI: The bestower of joy. *Dūragairapi yasyānto*, and those people who take the journey to travel to that abode of Lord Śiva, and they go on, go on, traveling, traveling, traveling, traveling, traveling–in the end, they go on traveling, traveling–and after traveling also, they don't find the avenue of Lord Śiva, I bow to that Lord Śiva who is the bestower of joy to everybody.

So, He'll be unknown.

DENISE: He can't be reached by our efforts.

SWAMIJI: No [affirmative].

Audio 3 (22:35)

नमः स्तुतौ स्मृतौ ध्याने दर्शने स्पर्शने तथा ।
प्राप्तौ चानन्दवृन्दाय दयिताय कपर्दिने ॥३६॥

namaḥ stutau smṛtau dhyāne darśane sparśane tathā /
prāptau cānandavṛndāya dayitāya kapardine //36//

Kapardine is Mahādeva, Lord Śiva (*karpardine*, He who has got brown hair). He has got brown hair. Brown hair is said to be the beauty of the body–brown hair. He has got brown hair–Lord Śiva. Brown hair means . . . "hair" means, the totality of His energies, and the totality of His energies is "brown". "Brown" is in *pramātṛ bhava*, in the subjective [state]. [The totality of His energies] reside in the subjective cycle, they don't reside in the objective cycle or the cognitive cycle.[72] So, it is *kapardine*, His brown hair.

And that brown-haired [Lord], who is dear to me (*dayitāya* means, He is dear to me, He is very dear to me), I bow to Him. And who is that Lord Śiva? *Stutau smṛtau dhyāne darśane sparśane tathā*, *prāptau ca ānanda vṛndāya*, He who gives you a multitude of ecstasy, who gives you a multitude of . . .

You know "multitude"?

72 *Pramāṇa* (cognition), *prameya* (objectivity), *pramātṛ* (subjectivity).

STEPHANIE: Manifold.

SWAMIJI: Manifold.

. . . a multitude of ecstasy by singing (if you sing His glory, He gives you a multitude of ecstasy); *smṛtau*, if you remember Him, He will give you a multitude of ecstasy; *dhyāne*, if you meditate on Him, He will give you a multitude of ecstasy; *darśane*, if you see Him, He will give you a multitude of ecstasy; [*sparśane*], and if you touch Him, He will give you a multitude of ecstasy. *Stuti*, *smṛti*, *dhyāna*, *darśana*, and *sparśana*, these five things.

JOHN: *Stuti* means?

SWAMIJI: *Stuti* means, if you sing His glory. That is in the state of *jāgrat* [wakefulness]. If you remember Him, that is in the state of dreaming (in a dream, the mind). If you meditate on Him, that is the state of one-pointedness, that is *suṣupti* (deep sleep). *Jāgrat* is singing [His] glory. In *jāgrat,* you can sing His glory, [but] you can't see Him, you can't touch Him. In which state?

JOHN: In *jāgrat*.

SWAMIJI: In *jāgrat*. And, in *svapna* (the dreaming state), you can think of Him. In *suṣupti,* you can meditate on Him because, in *suṣupti*, you have no thoughts. That is a thoughtless state, so you can meditate on Him. *Darśane*, and in *turya*, you can see Him. And, in *turyātīta*, you can embrace Him.

And in all of these five states, He bestows you [with] joy. He is *ānanda vṛndāya*, He gives you a multitude of joy, a multitude of ecstasy, in all of these states. I bow to that Lord Śiva who is very dear to me (*daitāya* means, who is very dear to me).

Audio 3 (26:32)

किं स्मयेनेति मत्वापि मनसा परमेश्वर ।
स्मयेन त्वन्मयोऽस्मीति मामि नात्मनि कं मुदा ॥३७॥

kiṁ smayeneti matvāpi manasā parameśvara /
smayena tvanmayo'smīti māmi nātmani kiṁ mudā //37//

Sometimes I think, "Why should I get excited? I should not get excited." Whenever I see You, I get excitement. O Lord Śiva, whenever I see You, I get excitement. Sometimes I think, "I should not get excited because Lord Śiva is my own Self. Why should I get excited if I see Him, if I perceive Him?" And I tell my mind, I teach my mind, not to get excited. In my mind, Parameśvara, O Lord Śiva, after teaching it that, *smayena tvan-mayo'smīti*, but sometimes excitement comes again, and, by that excitement, I become one with You. It is such [a great] excitement that it rises to that extent that I become one with You and I cannot control my excitement afterwards. *Māmi nātmani kiṁ mudā*, is it my mistake, Lord Śiva? Would You teach me that I should not get excited? But I get excited and I can't control it afterwards. I get excitement.

Audio 3 (28:09)

चिन्तयित्वापि कर्तव्यकोटीश्चित्तस्य चापलात् ।
वोश्राम्यन्भव भावत्कचित्तानन्दे रमे भृशम् ॥ ३८॥

cintayitvāpi kartavyakoṭīścittasya cāpalāt /
viśrāmyanbhava bhāvatkacittānande rame bhṛśam //38//

O Lord Śiva, I have got one desire in my life. If You could fulfill it, that would be Your greatness. *Cintayitvāpi kartavya-koṭīḥ cittasya cāpalāt*, my mind is flickering always. It is true that my mind is always jumping here and there, not only to one point, [but] to numberless points: sometimes sex, some-times joy, sometimes cinema, sometimes money, sometimes house, sometimes . . . all of those things. My mind, because he is always jumping here and there, I am tired, I am exhausted now by this jumping. By jumping here and there, I am exhausted. Truly, I am exhausted. I want to take rest, and that lace I would like to have. That is *bhāvat-de, bas*, just I would [like to] reside in Your Self.

That would give me rest. I am restless, I have become restless, by going here and there in this world. This is my desire. If You could fulfill it for me, it would be Your greatness. I won't persist that You should do it. It would be Your greatness if You fulfill this desire in me.

Audio 3 (30:02)

सूक्ष्मोऽसि चेत्त्रिलोकीयं कलामात्रं कथं तव ।
स्थूलोऽथ किं सुदर्शो न ब्रह्मादिभिरपि प्रभो ॥ ३९ ॥

sūkṣmo'si cettrilokīyaṁ kalāmātraṁ kathaṁ tava /
sthūlo'tha kiṁ sudarśo na brahmādibhirapi prabho //39//

O my master, *sūkṣmo'si cet*, if You are subtle, if this is a fact that You are the subtlest element in this one hundred and eighteen worlds (in one hundred and eighteen worlds, the subtlest element is Lord Śiva), if You are the subtlest, wherefrom this gross cycle of the one hundred and eighteen worlds have come out? It is not due. This gross creation of the one hundred and eighteen worlds[73] must not come out from that subtlest point–if You are the subtlest. If You are the grossest (*sthūlo'tha*, if You are the grossest, if You are gross), then *sudarśo na brahmādibhir*, then why are You not seen by even the lords of these five great activities (*pañcakṛtya*)?[74] Why those five lords cannot see You, cannot perceive You, if You are gross? If You are the subtlest, then it is obvious that nobody will perceive You, because You are the subtlest. If You are the subtlest and nobody perceives You, wherefrom this universe has come out, this grossest universe? This is also a wonder. Now, if You are the grossest, then You must be known to everybody. [But] nobody knows [You]! Why these five lords, who are deputed on those five activities of the world (creation, protection, destruction, concealing, and revealing), why those

73 See fn 24 for and explanation of the 118 worlds.
74 Here, *brahmādi* refers to the five lords of the five great activities: Brahmā, Viṣṇu, Rudra, Īśvara, and Sadāśiva. See verses 33, 34.

lords cannot perceive You if You are gross? This is also another wonder to me.

Audio 3 (32:20)

वाच्य एषां त्वमेवेति नाभविष्यदिदं यदि ।
कः क्लेशं देव वाग्जाले ष्वकरिष्यत्सुधीस्तदा ॥४०॥

vācya eṣāṁ tvameveti nābhaviṣyadidaṁ yadi /
kaḥ kleśaṁ deva vāgjāle ṣvakariṣyatsudhīstadā //40//

Eṣāṁ, now go to those words of these *śāstra*s (these scriptures). These manuscripts, these *śāstra*s, *tantra*s, the Vedas, what is there in it? They are only words! Why do we exert ourselves to understand these words? What is there in understanding these words? But there is one point why we exert, there is the chief cause: the chief cause is that You are known from those words. If You were not known from these words of the *śāstra*s and the *tantra*s and the Vedas, who the devil would worry for understanding these *śāstra*s? Nobody would care to understand the *śāstra*s. Everybody cares to understand the *śāstra*s only [because] You are known from that. That is the point.[75]

Audio 3 (33:46)

क्रमेण कर्मणा केन कया वा प्रज्ञया प्रभो ।
ज्ञेयोऽसी त्युपदेशेन प्रसादः क्रियतां मम ॥४१॥

krameṇa karmaṇā kena kayā vā prajñayā prabho /
jñeyo'sī[76] *tyupadeśena prasādaḥ kriyatāṁ mama //41//*

---

75 "These Śaiva *śāstra*s don't explain anything new." *Stava Cintāmaṇi* (1990). "I indulge in Śaiva scriptures only because there is Your name, that is all! Without Your name, there is nothing, there is no exposition." *Stava Cintāmaṇi* (1991).

76. Swamiji said that *dṛśyo'si*, "by which knowledge You are seen," is a misprint and should be *jñeyo'si*, "by which knowledge You are felt." Ibid.

Prabho, 'O my Master', please do one favor to me. That is, successively teach me how I should meditate, how I should act, how I should concentrate, and how I should un-mind my mind. Please teach me. I cannot understand how to act, how to meditate, how to think of You, how to remember You–I cannot do that. Please teach me successively so that I can understand how we should meditate, how I should meditate. And by that meditation, You would be perceived by me. Teach me that. Please teach me. This is my . . .

DENISE: Request.

SWAMIJI: . . . request to You. Please do this favor to me, O my Master.

Audio 3 (35:00)

नमो निरुपकार्याय त्रैलोक्यैकोपकारिणे ।
सर्वस्य स्पृहणीयाय निःस्पृहाय कपर्दिने ॥४२॥

namo nirupakāryāya trailokyaikopakāriṇe /
sarvasya spṛhaṇīyāya niḥspṛhāya kapardine / /42/ /

I bow to that *kapardine*, that brown-haired Lord Śiva, who is *nirupakārya*, who does not want anybody's help (*nirupakārya*, who does not need anybody's help) and, on the contrary, *trailokyaiko*, who helps all of the three worlds. He doesn't need anybody's help but he helps all of the three worlds. I bow to that Lord Śiva who is brown-haired. *Sarvasya spṛhanīyāya*, and I bow to that Lord Śiva who is liked by everybody, who is embraced by everybody; who is liked by everybody and who is longed [for] by everybody.

Not "embraced."[77] You can't (laughter)[78] . . .

And *niḥspṛhāya kapardine*, and Himself, He is without any needs. He is desireless. He has no desire.

Bas, 42 ending.

Audio 3 (36:20)

77 *Spṛhaṇīyā*: to be wished or longed for, desirable, enviable.
78 Indicating that you can't embrace Lord Śiva.

अहो क्षेत्रज्ञता सेयं कार्याय महते सताम् ।
ययानन्तफलां भक्तिं वपन्ति त्वय्यमी प्रभो ॥ ४३ ॥

aho kṣetrajñatā seyaṁ kāryāya mahate satām /
yayānantaphalāṁ bhaktiṁ vapanti tvayyamī prabho //43//

O my Master, *satām—anugṛhītānām, aho—āścaryaṁ kṣetra -jñatā,*[79] there are some saints in this world who are blessed by You. Those saints who are blessed by You, their activity is wonderful! Their activity, whatever they act, it is all filled with wonder because:

Audio 3 (37:08)

सर्वक्लेशसंसरणत्राणहेतुभूतं त्वां क्षेत्रं प्रति ज्ञता-
बोद्धृता सा इयम् इति स्वात्मनि उपलब्धप्रभावा

sarvakleśasaṁsaraṇatrāṇahetubhūtaṁ tvāṁ kṣetraṁ prati jñatā–boddhṛtā sā iyam svātmani upalabdhaprabhāvā[80]

Because this activity sentences them, this activity of those saints sentences them, to get entry in God consciousness, in You, in Your body, just for becoming one with You (*tvat abhedāya*). And this *bhakti*, this devotion, which is shining in their minds, . . .

In whose minds?

DENISE: Those devotees.

SWAMIJI: . . . in the devotee's minds, *vyatirikta phala-vāñchātyāgena tvayi [kṣetre] vapanti,*[81] they put the seed of that devotion in Your body just for pleasing You, not for any other aim. They have no aim at all! This is the greatness in them, because they are blessed by You. Those devotees, they

79 Kṣemarāja's commentary: p52 of *Kashmir Series of Text and Studies (KSTS)*. vol. 10.
80 Ibid.
81 Ibid.

put *bhakti* (*bhakti* means, *seva*),[82] they serve You, they love You, they devote all of the time of their lives for You. For what purpose? For nothing!

DENISE: For no reason.

SWAMIJI: Just out of love. They don't want anything from You! They don't desire anything to gain from You–just for Your devotion. This is the greatness of their activity, because, by that activity, they sow the seed of their devotion in Your body to get the fruit without any fruit. To sprout it, it must . . . it will sprout out without any fruit. They don't want any fruit from it. They just sow the seed of devotion in Your body. This is the greatness in them.[83]

Audio 3 (39:26)

महतीयमहो माया तव मायिन्ययावृतः ।
त्वद्ध्याननिधिलाभेऽपि मुग्धो लोकः श्लथायते ॥४४॥

mahatīyamaho māyā tava māyinyayāvṛtaḥ /
tvaddhyānanidhilābhe'pi mugdho lokaḥ ślathāyate //44//

And there is one other problem in the cycle of this devotion. [In the cycle of the] devotion of Thee, there is another problem that has risen by the power of Your energy of illusion. You put the energy of illusion side-by-side with You, so You are a fraud. *Māyin* means, exactly You are a fraud, You are not simple, You are not straightforward. You have got some magic with You, and that illusive magic makes a devotee fall in the pit of magic. And what is that magic which You adjust in the cycle of the devotion of Thy devotees? When you devote time for God, just for His sake, for love, out of love, out of devotion, out of attachment, *tvad dhyāna nidhi* [*lābhe'pi*], and their mind is concentrated, their mind is centered, at that point of God consciousness, while their mind is centered in the point of God

82 Service.

83 "O Lord, I have found some secret in this. This secret is lying behind the sayings of yours: 'Actually, there is nothing to do, just wait with devotion." *Stava Cintāmaṇi* (1991).

consciousness, [then] it works, Your other cycle of illusive energy [also] works at that time. How [does] it work? *Mughdo lokaḥ ślathāyate*, they get bored in that meditation. They meditate and they find the joy in meditation, and just after five minutes, or six minutes, or ten minutes, twenty minutes, they get bored, they want to lie down.

DENISE: Bored of the joy?

SWAMIJI: Bored of doing this meditation.

ERNIE: No, "bold."

SWAMIJI: Bored.

ERNIE: "Bored?"

SWAMIJI: Bored doing this meditation.

JOHN: Bored, boredom.

ERNIE: They get bored?

SWAMIJI: Yes.

JOHN: This is God's, Lord Śiva's, illusive energy doing this.

SWAMIJI: They don't want to do meditation for Thy devotion. They want to lie down. This is the trick of Your *māyā*, O Magician! *Tvad dhyāna nidhilābhe'pi*, although they achieve the treasure of Your meditation, the treasure of Your contemplation, they throw it aside and they lie down. This is Your trick of this *māyā*.

ERNIE: (laughter)

Audio 3 (42:14)

आरम्भे भव सर्वत्र कर्म वा करणादि वा ।
विश्वमसतु स्वतन्त्रस्तु कर्ता तत्रैकको भवान् ॥४५॥

ārambhe bhava sarvatra karma vā karaṇādi vā /
viśvamstu svatantrastu kartā tatraikako bhavān //45//

Ārambhe bhava, O Lord Śiva, *ārambhe*, in all of the activities, in the beginning of all activities, everywhere, whatever action is done by Your devotees, or whatever means are produced, let them be there, let them remain there, but

[only] if You want to do it, it will be done. If You don't want to do it, you may put all of the means of your strength, [still] it won't be solved. If You want to have it solved, it will be solved, otherwise not, it will never be solved.

DENISE: What will never be solved?

SWAMIJI: Anything! If you want to prepare lunch, if you want to prepare a cake, if you want to do something, it will be done only when You wish it to be done. If You don't wish it, something will happen and it will be destroyed, it won't work. *Svatantrastu tatra eka ko bhavān*, You are the only independent cycle of doing all of the activities in completion. They will never be completed [without You].[84]

Audio 3 (43:45)

त्रिगुणत्रिपरिस्पन्द-द्वन्द्वग्रस्तं जगत्त्रयम् ।
उद्धर्तुं भवतोऽन्यस्य कस्य शक्तिः कृपाथ वा ॥४६॥

triguṇatriparispanda-dvandvagrastaṁ jagattrayam /
uddhartuṁ bhavato'nyasya kasya śaktiḥ kṛpātha vā / /46/ /

In this three-fold world (*jagat trayam*, in these three worlds: *bhūr*, *bhuvaḥ*, and *svaḥ*),[85] . . .

---

84 In this connection Swamiji quotes a verse by Vidyāpati, which is another name of the highly revered Śaiva saint, Bṛhaspāti: "As long as one is rising up, holding one state and residing in that state for one to two years, and he sees that it is not the right state, You coach him to another state and he goes on meditating on that state, and after twenty years, he again comes to the conclusion that this is not correct, and then You give him the third step, etc. If they are Your devotees, why do You make them go through steps and You finally push them to the 118th step and they become *jīvan mukta*?" *Stava Cintāmaṇi* (1990). See also: Swami Lakshmanjoo, *The Tantrāloka of Abhinavagupta*, translation and commentary (original audio recording, LJA archives, Los Angeles, 1972-1981), chapter 14.9b-10.

85 "There are three worlds: *bhūḥ*, *bhuvaḥ*, and *svaḥ* (*bhūrloka*, *bhuvarloka*, and *svarloka*). This is one world (*bhūrloka*, earth), where

Internally, these three worlds are said to be the three states of individuals. What are those? Wakefulness, the dreaming state, and the dreamless state (*jāgrat*, *svapna,* and *suṣupti*).[86]

. . . in these three worlds, you find *triguṇa tripari spanda dvandva*, there are three *guṇa*s, three *guṇa*s working in *jāgrat*, *svapna*, and *suṣuptī*, and *tripari spanda*, and three-fold waves are working. Sometimes there is the love of God that rises, sometimes the love for worldly pleasures rises, and sometimes the love for sluggishness rises in this three-fold world–*jāgrat*, *svapna*, and *suṣupti*. So, by this tripleness, *dvandva grastam*, the whole world is finished, the whole world is . . .

ERNIE: Consumed.

SWAMIJI: . . . consumed, yes. It is gobbled, swallowed. The whole world is swallowed in this *dvandva*[87] of the three *guṇa*s. Who else except You, who else has the strength, O Lord, to get these individuals out of this pit of the three *guṇa*s? Nobody [else] has got the power to get those [individuals] out from the pit of the three *guṇa*s. And *kṛpā*, and nobody has got that kind of *kṛpā*.

Kṛpā is . . . what is *kṛpā*?

ERNIE: Power.

SWAMIJI: No, *kṛpā* is . . .

ERNIE: Ability?

SWAMIJI: Not ability. *Kṛpā* is *anugraha*.

JOHN: Grace?

---

there are stars, moons, etc., that is another world (*bhuvarloka*), and above that, there is heaven–that is the third world (*svarloka*)." Swami Lakshmanjoo, *Festival of Devotion and Praise–Śivastotrāvali, Hymns to Shiva*, by Utpaladeva, ed. John Hughes, (Lakshmanjoo Academy, Los Angeles, 2014), 4.23.

86 Swamiji noted that creation, protection, and destruction are also included among these threefold cycles. *Stava Cintāmaṇi* (1990).

87 Opposites, duality or differentiatedness.

SWAMIJI: Grace, grace. Grace.[88] And only that Lord Siva has got that power and that grace to take out all of these individuals out of that pit. Who is that Lord Śiva?

Audio 3 (46:48)

"*Ācārya dehamāsthāya śivaḥ pāśānnikṛntati*,[89] where shall we find Lord Śiva? He is unknown to us. Lord Śiva, for us, is our Master." This is what [Kṣemarāja] says here. "He [Lord Śiva] has got the ability to take us out from that pit."[90]

DENISE: Having love for God, you know, being in that *sattvic guṇa*, . . .

SWAMIJI: Yes.

DENISE: . . . isn't it a sign of being close to God? Or no, it's a pit.

SWAMIJI: No, it is also a pit, because in *sattvaguṇa*, you find peace.

DENISE: Yes.

SWAMIJI: That peace should not be found.

DENISE: Why?

SWAMIJI: It must be your nature. If it is your nature, then you have crossed the cycle of *guṇa*.[91]

ERNIE: That's *mokṣa*.

SWAMIJI: That is *mokṣa*.

JOHN: So, in other words, in this case, *sattvaguṇa* is just another mood, and then *rajoguṇa* is another mood, and it

---

88 *Kṛpā* literally means, pity, tenderness, or compassion.
89 Kṣemarāja's commentary.
90 "In this world, there are so many Śaiva *gurus*. You should not treat them as human beings. You should treat them as Lord Śiva. A *guru* destroys all of the bondages of his devotees. Those *gurus* are hidden [amongst] human beings, walking around speaking with everyone. They know who they are." *Stava Cintāmaṇi* (1990).
91 Viz., *guṇātīta*.

changes and it will go . . .

SWAMIJI: Yes.

JOHN: Here today, gone tomorrow.

SWAMIJI: Yes.

JOHN: If it's real, it shouldn't go.

SWAMIJI: It shouldn't go. It will [not] go only when it becomes your nature. When you say, "Kashmir is a portion of India, Kashmir is a portion of India, Kashmir is a portion of India, part and parcel of India," it means it is not. They go on giving lectures like that–these leaders. It seems that it is not. If you are really Denise, why should you bother to tell everybody that, "I am Denise, I am Denise, I am Denise"? You are Denise by nature.

ERNIE: Yes, but don't you want to cultivate that nature, and so . . . ?

SWAMIJI: It must be your nature, it must not be your . . .

ERNIE: Yes, but don't you get closer to your nature when you do *sattvic* things?

SWAMIJI: When you stick to *sattvic* things, [but] *sattvaguṇa* does not stick to one point. It will change to *rajoguṇa*, then it will change to *tamoguṇa.*

ERNIE: But isn't the idea to lead a *sattvic* life?

SWAMIJI: Yes.

ERNIE: Not a *tamasic* life.

SWAMIJI: Yes, not *tāmasic*, not *rajasic*. Saints have got a *sattvic* life, they develop a *sattvic* life, but that life is also ignorance, that life is also residing in the pit.

ERNIE: A trap.

SWAMIJI: You are not liberated. You are liberated only when you become *guṇātīta*.

JOHN: Beyond these *guṇa*s.

SWAMIJI: Beyond these *guṇa*s.

BRUCE H: So what is the purpose of leading a *sāttvic* life?

SWAMIJI: *Sāttvic* life? To discard *rajoguṇa* and *tamoguṇa*. When this *rajoguṇa* and *tamoguṇa*, [appear] you don't allow your mood of *sattvic* activity to step in *rajoguṇa* or step in *tamoguṇa* at all. Then what happens? You'll rise above *sattvaguṇa guṇa*. You have to maintain that *sattvaguṇa* for the time being so that you cross that *sattvaguṇa*. The avenue for crossing the cycle of *guṇa* is through *sattvaguṇa*. It is not through *rajoguṇa*, it is not through *tamoguṇa*. This cycle, it has got three openings: one opening is *sattvaguṇa*, another is *rajoguṇa*, and another is *tamoguṇa*. By this opening [of *rajoguṇa*], you will fall in the pit. By this opening [of *tamoguṇa*], you will fall in the pit. By this opening [of *sattvaguṇa*], you will rise in the cycle of *guṇātīta*, above the *guṇa*s. So, masters have preferred to maintain *sattvaguṇa* all of the time.

JOHN: Can you answer me a question then? Why in Shaivism at some point–not now, but at some point–do they have all of these other practices, which, from the point of view of orthodoxy, are very much not *sattvaguṇa*? [For example], eating meat, drinking wine, etc. In a much later stage, this is still on practice and . . .

SWAMIJI: Yes. Then, once you have stepped/established your consciousness in the cycle of *guṇātīta*, then you can travel in all of the three *guṇa*s.

ERNIE: Yes, you can go out any of those openings.

SWAMIJI: Openings, and you'll be *guṇātīta*.

ERNIE: It's all the same then.

SWAMIJI: Yes, then it will all be the same.

JOHN: Then the point of these practices is it not, at some point, to also help establish that consciousness?

SWAMIJI: Establish, but after you cross the cycle [of the three *guṇa*s]. After you cross the cycle, then you can get entry again in the cycle in a divine way.

ERNIE: So you have to have that experience first . . .

SWAMIJI: First, yes.

ERNIE: . . . before you think that you can . . . ?

SWAMIJI: Yes, not till then. Till then, you have to maintain *sattvaguṇa*.

ERNIE: Otherwise you are a fraud.

JOHN: How can you say you are a fraud?

ERNIE: Well, if you don't have that experience, if you're not established in that consciousness . . .

SWAMIJI: That is right, that is right, yes (laughs).

ERNIE: . . . and you go to *rajoguṇa* and you say, "Oh, I am enlightened," you go out that exit, that's the pit.

SWAMIJI: No, that is not . . . that is only a pit.

JOHN: But *sattvaguṇa* is also a pit.

SWAMIJI: *Sattvaguṇa* is also a pit.

JOHN: Thinking that, "I'm oh so pure" and "I'm this and that," that's a . . .

SWAMIJI: Yes, when you think. It must be your nature.

DENISE: But aren't people with certain *prakṛti*s, they are just naturally *rajastically* inclined?

JOHN: That's really my question.

DENISE: And some are just naturally very *tamasic* and some are naturally *sattvic*–when they are born it seems! Doesn't it seem?

SWAMIJI: Yes.

DENISE: Then if they are that way, how can they change to *sāttvic*?

SWAMIJI: No, by *sādhana*s.

DENISE: *Acha*,[92] by meditation.

SWAMIJI: By meditation.

DENISE: That's the point of meditation.

SWAMIJI: Yes, meditation is meant for that purpose.

ERNIE: And grace.

---

92 Hindi for "okay".

SWAMIJI: Yes, the grace of Lord Siva or a master.

Audio 3 (52:36)

दोषोऽपि देव को दोषसत्वामाप्तुं यः समास्थितः ।
गुणोऽपि च गुणः को नु त्वां नाप्तुं यः समाथितः ॥४७॥

doṣo'pi deva ko doṣas-tvāmāptuṁ yaḥ samāsthitaḥ /
guṇo'pi ca guṇaḥ ko nu tvāṁ nāptuṁ yaḥ samāthitaḥ //47//

There is another point to be understood in this world, O Lord. If there is a defect, if one has a defect, *doṣo'pi deva ko doṣas tvāmāptuṁ yaḥ samāsthitaḥ*, if by Your grace, with that defect, having that defect, he will rise in God consciousness, [then] what kind of defect is it? It is not a defect at all.

ERNIE: (laughter)

SWAMIJI: If, by a defect also, by some defect also, you rise in God consciousness, is that a defect?

DENISE: No.

SWAMIJI: That is no defect. That is no defect at all! *Guṇo'pi*, if there is a qualification,[93] if there are qualifications in some, and by those qualifications they don't rise in God consciousness, what qualifications are they? They are not qualifications at all.

ERNIE: (laughter)

SWAMIJI: That is what he says here.

Audio 3 (53:40)

रागोऽप्यस्तु जगन्नाथ मम त्वय्येव यः स्थितः ।
लोभायापि नमस्तस्मै तवल्लाभालम्बनाय मे ॥४८॥

93 Such as being a Brahmin, etc.

rāgo'pyastu jagannātha mama tvayyeva yaḥ sthitaḥ /
lobhāyāpi namastasmai tvallābhālambanāya me //48//[94]

O Jagatnātha, O Master of the three worlds, let attachment govern in, shine in, my mind, in the cycle of my mind–attachment. *Mama tvayyeva yaḥ sthitaḥ*, that attachment which has appeared in me for You, let that attachment shine in me. I don't want to discard that attachment. People say there must be no attachment, but if I have got attachment for You, let that attachment shine in me. I don't want to discard that attachment. I want to be attached to You.[95] *Lobhāyāpi*, if there is greed for realizing Your nature, if I have got greed for realizing Your nature, I welcome that greed. People say that you should discard greed, but I don't say that. If there is greed in me for You, I bow to that greed. I bow to the cycle of that greed, *tvat lābhā lambanāya*, which greed carries me to God consciousness.

Audio 3 (55:08)

अहो महदिदं कर्म देव त्वद्भावनात्मकम् ।
आब्रह्माक्रिमि यस्मिन्नो मुक्तयेऽधिक्रियेत कः ॥४९॥

aho mahadidaṁ karma deva tvadbhāvanātmakam /
ābrahmākrimi yasminno muktaye'dhikriyeta kaḥ //49//

Now there is another wonderful point to be observed in the cycle of Your grace. If you shine with grace, *mahat idaṁ karma deva tvat bhāvanātmakam*, by that grace you become one-pointed, *ābrahma*, and that one-pointedness is meant not only for those who are well-qualified and Brahmaṇās [Brahmins]. Not outcasts, those who are outcasts, the Vedas say, outcasts are not supposed to be fit for meditation–outcasts.

---

94 Note: There was a misprint in the numbering of the original *Stava Cintāmaṇi*, *KSTS* (pages 56, 57), where verse 47 was numbered twice. From here the verse numbers have been corrected.
95 "If I have attachment for some person, that attachment is actually attachment for You." *Stava Cintāmaṇi* (1990).

DENISE: And not women either.

SWAMIJI: And not women either. But this grace of Your nature, when it works, it works without the restriction of caste, creed, and color. If it works there, it will work, no matter if you are an outcast or a Brahmin. If you are with a *tilak*[96] ten feet long, it doesn't matter.

DEVOTEES: (laughter)

SWAMIJI: If you have got a *tilak* ten feet long and you have no grace, you are degraded. If you have nothing, no qualifications, but [you have the] grace of Lord Śiva, you have everything!

That is what he says.

Audio 3 (57:06)

आरम्भः सर्वकार्याणां पर्यन्तः सर्वकर्मणाम् ।
तदन्तर्वृत्तयश्चित्रा-स्तवैवेश धियः पथि ॥५०॥

ārambhaḥ sarvakāryāṇāṁ paryantaḥ sarvakarmaṇām /
tadantarvṛttayaścitrā-stavaiveśa dhiyaḥ pathi //50//

O Lord Śiva, the beginning of all activities and the end of all activities only shines in the cycle of the body of Your God consciousness. So, whatever activity is done in this world, it is done in the kingdom of God consciousness. So, all activities and all perceptions, which we have, reside in That divine state, if there is Your grace.

End of Audio 3 (57:49)

Start of Audio 4 (00:00)

यावदुत्तरमास्वाद-सहस्रगुणविस्तरः ।
त्वद्भक्तिरसपीयूषान्नाथ नान्यत्र दृश्यते ॥५१॥

yāvaduttaramāsvāda-sahasraguṇavistaraḥ /
tvadbhaktirasapīyūṣān-nātha nānyatra dṛśyate //51//

96 A sacred mark worn by Hindus, especially the Brahmin caste, on the forehead.

In this universe, *uttaram āsvāda sahasara guṇa vistara*, whatever joy is found in its uppermost limit in this world, whatever joy you find–the utmost joy (keep that on one side, that utmost joy)–and *tvad bhakti rasapiyūṣāt*, and the joy which is perceived by Thy devotion, that joy, if you multiply that one thousand times (that joy, the previous joy), it will be more than that, the joy of Your devotion [will be more than that]. This is what I have understood in this world. There is no joy more than the joy of Your devotion, Your love, Your attachment.[97]

Audio 4 (01:25)

उपासंहृतकामाया कामायतिमतन्वते ।
अवतंसितसोमाय सोमाय स्वामिने नमः ॥५२॥

upāsaṁhṛtakāmāyā kāmāyatimatanvate /
avataṁsitasomāya somāya svāmine namaḥ //52//

I bow to my Master who is Lord Śiva, who has *upasaṁhṛta kāmāyā*, who has discarded all desires, who has no desires, and who is the producer of all desires. He produces all desires and He is beyond the cycle of desires. I bow to that Lord Śiva.[98] *Avatam sita somāya*, and that Lord Śiva who has decorated His forehead with the crescent moon (*somāya* is He who is embraced and married to Ūmā, Pārvatī), I bow to that Lord Śiva who is married to *soma* (*soma* means, Ūmā), with Ūmā, who is always with Ūmā (Ūmā is Pārvatī). And *āvataṁ sita somāya*, who has decorated His forehead with the crescent moon, and who is the producer of all desires, and who is beyond desires, I bow to that Lord Śiva.

Audio 4 (02:58)

किमशक्तः करोमीति सर्वत्रानध्यवस्यतः ।
सर्वानुग्राहिका शक्तिः शाङ्करी शरणं मम ॥५३॥

97 That is, devotion *for* You, love *for* You, and attachment *to* You.
98 "If You've destroyed all desires, where are they existing in Your Being so that You could bestow them on others?" *Stava Cintāmaṇi* (1990).

kimaśaktaḥ karomīti sarvatrānadhyavasyataḥ /
sarvānugrāhikā śaktiḥ śāṅkarī śaraṇaṁ mama //53//

In each and every avenue of this journey of life, in each and every turning point of this life, . . .

So when you begin one kind of life and you have to change it to another way, that is an avenue–that changing diversion.

. . . at that moment, at that place, at that point, I become helpless, I can't change. *Kim aśakta karomīti*, for instance, when a change comes, if my master dies–it is a change in your life–if my husband dies, my wife dies, my son dies–it is a change in [your] life–there, what to do, I don't know. I am *aśakta*, it is beyond my power to fix myself at that point. *Sarva-trānadhya vasyataḥ*, in the same way, in each and every avenue of this life, I am helpless, I become helpless. *Sarvatra anadhya vasyataḥ*, and I have no sources of being protected–on all sides. And there is only one hope for me, O Lord Śiva, that is, Your grace. If You grace me on these occasions, I will [continue] with [my] life, otherwise I am gone. So, the only hope for me for protection is just Your grace, Your helping hand. If You don't help me on these occasions, I am lost.

Audio 4 (05:12)

गुणातीतस्य निर्दिष्ट-निःशेषातिशयात्मनः ।
लभ्यते भव कुत्रांशे परः प्रतिनिधिस्तव ॥५४॥

guṇātītasya nirdiṣṭa-niḥśeṣātiśayātmanaḥ /
labhyate bhava kutrāṁśe paraḥ pratinidhistava //54//

You are *guṇātīta*, You are beyond the three *guṇa*s (*sattva-guṇa*, *rajoguṇa*, and *tamoguṇa*). *Niśeśatiṣātmana*, You are above all, You are the extreme of all.

You know "the extreme of all"?

DENISE: The highest of all?

SWAMIJI: Whatever highest you perceive in this world, it is more than that highest.

DENISE: Beyond the highest?

SWAMIJI: So, there is no comparison. Any element, which could compare with Your beauty, with Your glamour, it is not found in this world. There is no *pratinidhi* (*pratinidhi* is "opposite").[99] Lord Śiva is beautiful. There is no other beautiful [thing]. . .

JOHN: To compare Him with.

SWAMIJI: . . . to compare with.[100]

Audio 4 (06:26)

निरद्वन्द्वे निरुपाधौ च त्वय्यात्मनि सति प्रभो ।
वयं वञ्च्यामहेऽद्यापि माययामेयया तव ॥५५॥

nirdvandve nirupādhau ca tvayyātmani sati prabho /
vayaṁ vañcyāmahe'dyāpi māyayāmeyayā tava //55//

O my Master, You are existing before me to help me. *Nirdvandve*, You are without *dvandva* [duality]. Without *dvandva* [means], You don't love those who love You, You don't hate those who hate You. You are the same to those who love You and for those who hate You. You are the same to both sections. Anybody who hates You, kicks You, ignores You, You don't ignore him. Anybody who loves You, You don't love him, because You are *nirdvandva*, You have no *dvandva* (*dvandva* means, opposites), You don't find any opposites.

Because what can he do? [He] who hates Lord Śiva, what

---

99 Lit., substitution, likeness.

100 "The *śāstras* have defined that the topmost seat is possessed by You, but it seems You have another topmost seat for Parabhairavī who sits face-to-face with You. She is just like You. If You are the Topmost Being, how does another great Being exist on the same level as You?" *Stava Cintāmaṇi* (1990).

can he do to Lord Siva?

DENISE: Nothing.

SWAMIJI: If you love Lord Śiva, what benefit can you give to Lord Śiva by loving Him? It is for you to get satisfaction. For your satisfaction you love Him, not for His upliftment.

DENISE: He is already uplifted.

SWAMIJI: He is already above that cycle.

And *nirupādhau*, there is no *upādhi*[101] for Lord Śiva. And You are existing in front of me; this way, You are existing in front of me. Still, this is a great pitiable condition for You. This is the greatest pitiable condition for You that we are begging, still we are begging in this world, having such a Lord in front of us. Is it fair for You? Why don't You make it work like that so we won't [have to] beg. We beg from everywhere. For *śabda* we beg, for *sparśa*, *rūpa*, *rasa*, *gandha*,[102] all of the senses, we are hankering after these senses in each and every way of our life. Is it good for You that You tolerate this pitiable condition of ours?

This is the meaning of this *śloka*.[103]

Audio 4 (09:36)

अणिमादिगुणावाप्तिः सदैश्वर्यं भवक्षयः ।
अमी भव भवद्भक्ति-कल्पपादपपल्लवाः ॥५६॥

aṇimādiguṇāvāptiḥ sadaiśvaryaṁ bhavakṣayaḥ /
amī bhava bhavadbhakti-kalpapādapapallavāḥ //56//

O Lord Śiva, You are just like a *Kalpa Tree*.

You know the *Kalpa Tree*?

DENISE: Wish-fulfilling tree.

101 Without foreign attribute, adjustment or limitation.
102 Sound, touch, form, taste, and smell, respectively.
103 "You are the possessor of *māyā*, but *māyā* does not affect You. If, by Your grace, we have come out of *māyā*, why does *māyā* continue to affect us and not You? This is Your situation. Isn't it shameful that we people are mislead by Your *māyā* altogether?" *Stava Cintāmaṇi* (1990).

STEPHANIE: Boon-giving tree.

SWAMIJI: Boon-giving tree.

You are Yourself a boon-giving tree, and there is another boon-giving tree just opposite You. That is Your devotion. Anybody who devotes his life for Your sake, that devotion has become another boon-giving tree. And these two boon-giving trees (Yourself and Your devotion), they have produced sprouts, they have produced branches, they have produced fruits. What are those fruits? *Aṇimādi guṇā vāpti*, the great *yogic* powers. The eight great *yogic* powers come out . . . these are the eight fruits of those trees.[104] Which trees?

JOHN: The boon-giving trees.

SWAMIJI: Lord Śiva and Lord Śiva's devotion. And *sad aiśvaryaṁ*, you are always glorified if you have got these two trees at your disposal. *Bhava kṣaya*, and the destruction of pain, sadness, etc., these are also sprouts of This tree. No sadness remains, all sadness vanishes, all glory comes forth, and all great *yogic* powers are there as the fruit. This is what comes out from Your *Kalpa Tree* and Your devotion.

You know "devotion"? *Bhakti.*[105]

---

104 The eight worldly powers are: *aṇimā* (the power to make one's body extremely small), *mahimā* (the power to make one's body infinitely large), *garimā* (the power to become infinitely heavy), *laghimā* (the power to become weightless), *prāpti* (the power to be anywhere), *prākāmya* (the power to achieve any desire), *īśitva* (the power to possess absolute sovereignty), and *vaśitva* (the power to subjugate).

105 "O Lord, O universal Master, there are those three great gods, Brahmā, Viṣṇu, and Rudra, who have possessed the eight *yogic* powers as mentioned in Yoga Darśana. And, at the time of *samādhi*, some *yogi*s attain the states of Sadāśiva, Īśvara, and Śiva, so they have achieved greater power than those gods. And there are some great souls greater than Sadāśiva, etc., who have unminded their minds. For them, repeated births and deaths have been put to an end and they are mixed with the Parabhairava state. But I (Bhaṭṭa Nārāyaṇa) achieved those great powers when I maintained Your devotion, Your *bhakti*, so I am united in such a way in Your Being

Audio 4 (12:15)

या या दिक्तत्र न क्वासि सर्वः कालो भवन्मयः ।
इति लब्धोऽपि कर्हि त्वं लप्स्यसे नाथ कथ्यताम् ॥५७॥

yā yā diktatra na kvāsi sarvaḥ kālo bhavanmayaḥ /
iti labdho'pi karhi tvaṁ lapsyase nātha kathyatām //57//

O Lord Śiva, please tell me, please make me understand, because I know this from the Śaiva point of view that, *yā yā dīk*, whatever space there is, whatever space you find in this universe, whatever time you find in this universe, all of this time and all of this space is one with You, it is not separated from You. All space is Your Self and all time is Your Self. So, by this understanding, I think I have achieved You (*iti labdho'pi*), but there is not such confirmation in my mind that I have achieved You. Please tell me when You will confirm this, this perception that I have achieved You. I have already achieved You because whatever space you find in this world is one with You, whatever time you find in this world is one with You. So, I have achieved You in one sense, but there is not such satisfaction in my mind that I have achieved You because I [can't] confirm it. Please tell me when You'll confirm this understanding in me.

Audio 4 (14:04)

नमः प्रसन्नसद्वृत्त-मानसैकनिवासिने ।
भूरिभूतिसिताङ्गाय महाहंसाय शंभवे ॥५८॥

namaḥ prasannasadvṛtta-mānasaikanivāsine /
bhūribhūtisitāṅgāya mahāhaṁsāya śaṁbhave //58//

I bow to Lord Śiva, who is just like *haṁsaḥ* (*haṁsaḥ* means, a duck).

---

that these great gods and the power they have attained are like leaves of that *Kalpa Tree*. I have been blessed with Your *bhakti* (devotion) and that is the greatest achievement of all." *Stava Cintāmaṇi* (1990).

DEVOTEE: Swan?

SWAMIJI: Swan, swan, swan. Not a duck.

The great swan is Lord Śiva. I bow to Lord Śiva. These swans are generally *prasanna sat vṛtta mānasaika nivāsine*, they generally live in *sarovar*, in a lake, in the Mānasarovara Lake.[106] The Mānasarovara Lake is *prasanna sat vṛtta*, it is pure water there in that lake, and it is quite clean and shining water. In that lake, these swans are found, but You are also a swan and You are found in such a lake. And what is that lake? That is *prasanna sat vṛtta mānasaika nivāsine*, the mind of the individual, the mind of that individual who is purified, who is all-around purified, who has discarded all desires for worldly objects, and who has devoted, focused, all of his energy towards attaining Your Self–that mind! That mind is [the Mānasarovara] Lake. In that lake, You shine. And *bhūribhūti sitāṇgāya*, and You have a white body. These swans also have white bodies. You also have a white body, and that white body is just beyond the mind, [where] there is no hypocrisy, there is no crookedness, there is no lack of truth. It is all divine, divine with glory. So, You have got those glorified limbs. You, Swan, have those glorified limbs. I bow to that Swan who is Lord Śiva.[107]

Audio 4 (16:34)

हृतोद्धततमस्तान्तिः प्लुष्टाशेषभवेन्धना ।
त्वद्बोधदीपिका मेऽस्तु नाथ त्वद्भक्तिदीपिका ॥५९॥

106 According to ancient mythology, the Mānasarovara Lake was first created in the mind of Brahmā after which it was manifested on Earth. Hence it is called *manasa* (mind) *sarovara* (lake), which is said to be the abode of the *haṁsa*. This is also the name of the great lake near Mount Kailash in modern day Tibet.

107 "I bow to Thee, O Lord Śiva. Do you know where You are residing? You are residing in the mind of great souls. In which manner? You are glorified with the *basam* (holy ash) of destroying this whole universe, and You are just like *haṁ-saḥ* ('I am He'). I bow to Thee there." *Stava Cintāmaṇi* (1990).

hṛtoddhatatamastāntiḥ pluṣṭāśeṣabhavendhanā /
tvadbodhadīpikā me'stu nātha tvadbhaktidīpikā //59//

There are two kinds of candles in this world [that are] found in the cycle of Your kingdom. One is *bodha dīpikā* (*bodha dīpikā* is, just experiencing Your nature). This is one candle. It is shining always–*bodha dīpikā*. When you have got absolute knowledge of God consciousness, that is one candle which shines always in the minds of devotees. And another candle is *tvad bhakti dīpikā*, just Your love, just Your attachment. That is also another candle. These two candles are shining in this world. I know these two candles are shining. One is from *bhakti* and one is from knowledge. In these two candles, I would prefer to have, to own, one candle of devotion. I don't want knowledge. Because [the candle of devotion] is *hṛtoddhata tamastāntiḥ*, all darkness has vanished there. There is some darkness possible in the light of the candle of knowledge, but in the light of the candle of *bhakti*, there is no such possibility of any darkness. Because when there is knowledge, there is something, something more to be known. When there is love, what else do you need?

DENISE: Nothing.

SWAMIJI: [If] you have love, that is all [you need]. It does not rise, it does not become less, when there is devotion, when there is love, when there is attachment, that is all. When there is knowledge, you [still] have more to understand by-and-by, step-by-step, so there is the possibility of darkness. Some shades of darkness are sure to appear. But here, in the candle of Thy devotion, there is not that possibility. Between these two candles, I would like to have that candle of Thy devotion, O Lord. Please accept this request from me.[108]

Audio 4 (19:37)

विसृष्टानेकसद्बीज-गर्भं त्रैलोक्यनाटकम् ।
प्रस्ताव्यं हर संहर्तुं त्वत्तः कोऽन्यः कविः क्षमः ॥६०॥

108 "Only *bhakti* (devotion), only attachment, that intensity of love, is the nearest way to reach at Your feet." *Stava Cintāmaṇi* (1991).

visṛṣṭānekasadbīja-garbhaṁ trailokyanāṭakam /
prastāvyaṁ hara saṁhartuṁ tvattaḥ ko'nyaḥ kaviḥ kṣamaḥ / /60

This *trailokya nāṭakam*, this drama of the three worlds, this drama which appears in these three worlds, . . .

> This is the drama of the three worlds. In the outside cycle, you'll find three worlds: *bhūr*, *bhuvaḥ*, and *svaḥ* (this world, the *antarikṣa* world,[109] and heaven). In the individual cycle, you'll find three worlds.
>
> **DENISE:** Waking, dreaming, and deep sleep.
>
> **SWAMIJI:** Yes, waking, dreaming, and deep sleep.

. . . and this is the drama which You have put in front of us, the drama of the three worlds, the drama of the three states (wakefulness, dreaming, and dreamless). You created this. *Visṛṣṭa aneka sat bīja garbhaṁ*, and in this cycle of this drama of the three worlds, You have put the seed of *bhakti*, You have put the seed of devotion. But devotion does not appear! Because, as long as we are living in this world, do you find any devotion here? We don't! We feel like going to the cinema, to these pleasures, and movies, and motorcars, and all of these things–enjoyments. We don't go to the depth of the seed which is existing in this drama. What is that seed? Thy devotion. Who can produce that seed? Who can give sprout to that seed? Who can withdraw that sprout? It is only You who can give life to that sprout or withdraw that sprout of *bhakti*. Please do that for me. Please give sprout to this *bhakti* in this drama of the three worlds.

He means that, "In wakefulness, I must not ignore You; in the dreaming state, I must not ignore You; and in the dreamless state, I must not be away from You. I want to be one with You, wholeheartedly devoted to You, because there is no other power which can produce it or withdraw it (withdraw this seed out of this drama). Please do this for me."

---

109 *Bhuvaḥ*, lit., atmosphere, viz., the planets which fill the space between heaven and earth. See verse 46, fn 85.

Audio 4 (22:53)

नमः सदसतां कर्तुमसत्त्वं सत्त्वमेव वा ।
स्वतन्त्रायास्वतन्त्राय व्ययैश्वर्यैकशालिने ॥ ६१ ॥

namaḥ sadasatāṁ kartumasattvaṁ sattvameva vā /
svatantrāyāsvatantrāya vyayaiśvaryaikaśāline //61//

I bow to that Lord Śiva who is *svatantra*, who is always independent for those who have ignored Him, and who is always dependent to those who remember Him. Those who remember Him, He is dependent to them. Those who do not remember Him, He is independent to them, He does not care for them. He is a slave of His devotees. Who?

DENISE: Lord Śiva.

SWAMIJI: Lord Śiva is a slave of His devotees. So, He is *svatantra* and *asvatantra*, both. *Svatantra* for those who ignore Him, *asvatantra* (dependent) for those who love Him. So, I bow to that Lord Śiva who is *svatantra* and *asvatantra* (*paratantra*), who is dependent and independent. Because He is *sat asatāṁ kartum*, He can change an existing [element] into a non-existing element, and He can change a non-existing [element] into an existing element.

For instance, I love Lord Śiva, but the nearness of Lord Śiva does not appear to me, the nearness of Lord Śiva is non-existent to me, but He can make it existent for me. And He can, if that seed[110] is existing in those who ignore Lord Śiva, He can make it non-existent for them.

I bow to that Lord Śiva.

Audio 4 (25:00)

त्रैलोक्येऽप्यत्र यो यावानानन्दः कश्चिदीक्ष्यते ।
स बिन्दुर्यस्य तं वन्दे देवमानन्दसागरम् ॥ ६२ ॥

trailokye'pyatra yo yāvān-ānandaḥ kaścidīkṣyate /
sa binduryasya taṁ vande devamānandasāgaram //62//

110 The seed of the love for, and the nearness of, Lord Śiva.

I bow to that God, Lord Siva, who is just an ocean of ecstasy, an ocean filled with bliss and joy. I bow to that Lord Śiva, that ocean of joy. Which ocean of joy? *Trailokye'pyatra yo yāvān ānandaḥ kaścidīkṣyate*, just go on finding out, investigating, where is the highest joy in this universe.

> [To Denise]: Go on investigating the highest joy in the nearness of Viresh. The highest joy is something more than that, the highest joy is something more than that, something more than that.

And in all of these three worlds, after going on investigating for the appearance of joy, you'll come to this conclusion that, when there is the highest joy, that is in heaven, where there is no fear, there is no nothing, no pain, no headache, no migraine, no heartache; *sa bindur*, and you'll find, in the end you will find, that that joy which you find in that heavenly abode, that highest joy, you will find that it is just like one drop of the ocean, the ocean of that joy of Lord Śiva. I bow to That ocean.

Audio 4 (26:46)

अहि ब्रह्मादयो धन्या ये विमुक्तान्यसंकथम् ।
नमो नमः शिवायेति जपन्त्याह्लादविह्वलाः ॥ ६३ ॥

aho brahmādayo dhanyā ye vimuktānyasaṁkatham /
namo namaḥ śivāyeti japantyāhlādavihvalāḥ / /63/ /

It is a great wonder to tell you, this is the greatest wonder to tell you, that *brahmādayo dhanyā*, those [gods], Brahmā, Viṣṇu, and Rudra, are the most fortunate people. Brahmā, the creator of this universe, and [Viṣṇu] the protector of this universe, and [Rudra] the destroyer of this universe, these three gods are most fortunate because *ye vimuktānya saṁkatham*, they discard all other topics of life and they, after discarding all other topics of life, [only recite], "*Namo namaḥ śivāya.*" They [come] to this conclusion: "*Namo namaḥ śivāya, śivāya namaḥ, śivāya namaḥ*, we bow to Lord Śiva, we bow to

Lord Siva." *Japantī*, and they recite this *mantra*, "*Namaḥ śivāya*," this *mantra*, *āhlāda-vihvalāḥ*,[111] after getting soaked in the ocean of nectar. They are most fortunate in this world–those three gods.[112]

Audio 4 (28:08)

निष्कामायापि कामानामनन्तानां विधायिने ।
अनादित्वेऽपि विश्वस्य भोक्त्रे भव नमोऽस्तु ते ॥ ६४ ॥

niṣkāmāyāpi kāmānām-anantānāṁ vidhāyine /
anāditve'pi viśvasya bhoktre bhava namo'stu te //64//

O Lord Śiva, I bow to Thee. *Niṣkāmāyāpi*, You have no desire. [Although] You have no desire Yourself, *kāmānām anantānām vidhāyine*, but You produce all desires, You fulfill all desires, of Your devotees. *Anāditve'pi*, You have no beginning, You are beginningless, *viśvasya bhoktre bhava namo*, but although You are beginningless, You enjoy the nectar of this whole universe.[113] Because, whoever enjoys, [their enjoyment] will have its end, but [His enjoyment] is not that kind of joy–He enjoys this universe endlessly! We enjoy this universe with an end, with its end. I have enjoyed so much and now I am in its ripening, falling position. There is an end; in each and every joy, there is an end, but in Your enjoyment, there is no end because You are above desires. When there are no desires, there is no end of joy.

Bas, 64 ending.

Audio 4 (29:58)

स्तुमस्त्रिभुवनारम्भमूलप्रकृतिमीश्वरम् ।
लिप्सेरन्नोपकारं के यतः संपूर्णधर्मणः ॥ ६५ ॥

111 Lit., agitated (*vihvala*) with joy, delight (*āhlāda*).

112 "They don't find any joy other than to recite the name of Lord Śiva." *Stava Cintāmaṇi* (1990).

113 "You Yourself don't eat anything, but in another sense, You eat all of the production grown in the world, both here and hereafter." Ibid.

stumastribhuvanārambha-mūlaprakṛtimīśvaram /
lipserannopakāraṁ ke yataḥ saṁpūrṇadharmaṇaḥ //65//

We sing the glory of Lord Śiva (*stuma*), *tribuvanāram mula prakṛtim*, who is the only cause of the creation of the three worlds (*mūla prakṛtim*, who is the cause of creating the whole universe, the threefold universe). We sing the glory of that Lord, *lipserannopakāraṁ ke yataḥ saṁpūrṇa dharmaṇaḥ*, because He is *saṁpūrṇa dharmaṇaḥ*, He is the embodiment of all aspects, which are found in this world. All of those aspects are found in His Self, in His Nature. And from that Lord, *ke upakāram na lipseran*, other lords who are Brahmā, Viṣṇu, Rudra, Īśvara, and Sadāśiva,[114] all of those lords, they always long to get protection from Him.[115] I bow to and sing the glory of that Lord.

Audio 4 (31:34)

महत्स्वप्यर्थकृच्छ्रेषु मोहौघमलिनीकृताः ।
स्मृते यस्मिन् प्रसीदन्ति मतयस्तं शिवं स्तुमः ॥६६॥

mahatsvapyarthakṛcchreṣu mohaughamalinīkṛtāḥ /
smṛte yasmin prasīdanti matayastaṁ śivaṁ stumaḥ //66//

Mahatsu api artha kṛt śreṣu, in [solving] the great problems, for putting a solution for those problems, how these problems would be solved, and by this [*moha*],[116] all understandings of various schools of thought have become *malinī kṛta*, have become confused. By becoming "dirty," they cannot find the problem, they can't find the solution of getting rid of those problems. But, at the very moment when they remember Lord Śiva, all problems are solved for them.[117]

---

114 See verses 33, 34 for an explanation of the five lords.

115 "You are the possessor of complete *dharma*, the energy of *svātantrya śakti*, and, being the possessor of *svātantrya śakti*, these great lords want to be blessed by You." Ibid.

116 Darkness or delusion of mind, viz., *māyā*.

117 *Yasmin smṛte prasīdanti.*

JOHN: So we bow to that Lord Siva by whose very remembrance all of the great problems of the world, . . .

SWAMIJI: Are solved at once!

JOHN: . . . which these fools have become confused by in trying to solve, are solved immediately.

SWAMIJI: Yes.[118]

Audio 4 (32:42)

प्रभो भवत एवेह प्रभुशक्तिरभङ्गुरा ।
यदिच्छया प्रतायेते त्रैलोक्यस्य लयोदयौ ॥ ६७ ॥

prabho bhavata eveha prabhuśaktirabhaṅgurā /
yadicchayā pratāyete trailokyasya layodayau //67//

Prabho, O Lord, *bhavata eveha prabhuśaktir*, You only possess that strength of Your masterly strength, only You possess that masterly strength, which is indestructible, which is not destroyed in any case.[119]

JOACHIM: *Abhaṅgurā.*

SWAMIJI: *Abhaṅgurā.* And by whose mere will, *trailokyasya layodayau pratāyete* (*trailokyasya layodayau*; *layodayau* means, destruction and creation), the destruction and creation of the three worlds takes place, and the whole universe, which is the threefold universe (*bhūḥ*, *bhuvaḥ*, and *svaḥ*),[120] the destruction and creation of these three worlds takes place–by whose mere will.[121]

---

118 "I bow to that Lord Śiva by whose remembrance all confusion of the gods of the five great acts is cleared." *Stava Cintāmaṇi* (1990).

119 "*Prabhu śakti* is possessed of wisdom without any side effects." Ibid.

120 *Bhu* (earth), *bhuvaḥ* (sky), and *svaḥ* (heaven). See verse 46, fn 85.

121 "By Your mere will, the whole world is created, protected, destroyed, concealed, and revealed." Ibid.

Audio 4 (33:57)

कुकर्मापि यमुद्दिश्य देवं स्यात्सुकृतं परम् ।
सिकृतस्यापि सौकृत्यं यतोऽन्यत्र न सोऽसो भोः ॥६८॥

kukarmāpi yamuddiśya devaṁ syātsukṛtaṁ param /
sukṛtasyāpi saukṛtyaṁ yato'nyatra na so'si bhoḥ //68//

O Lord Śiva, *yamuddiśya*, when Lord Śiva is realized, once Lord Śiva is realized, *kukarmāpi param sukṛtaṁ syāt*, all bad actions turn into good actions, they appear as good actions. All bad actions which you do in this world, they become good actions. They become really good when the Lord is realized–then, only then. And *sukṛtasyāpi saukṛtyaṁ*, when the Lord is realized . . . *sukṛta* means, the good actions of individuals become divine (*saukṛta* means, divine, too good).[122] And this kind of action is not found anywhere except in You; *yato anyatra nā*, this kind of position is not found in any other being except You. *So'si bhoḥ*, You are that Lord.

Audio 4 (35:24)

एष मुष्ट्या गृहीतोऽसो दृष्ट एष क्व यासि नः ।
इति भक्तिरसाध्माता धन्या धावन्ति धूर्जटिम् ॥६९॥

eṣa muṣṭyā gṛhīto'si dṛṣṭa eṣa kva yāsi naḥ /
iti bhaktirasādhmātā dhanyā dhāvanti dhūrjaṭim //69//

Those who are divinely shining by the intensity of devotion towards Thee (*bhakti rasa ādhmātā*; *ādhmātā*, who are shining with the *rasa*[123] of devotion)–how can we know that they are shining with the *bhakti rasa*?–they always say, "*Eṣa muṣṭyā gṛhīto*, O Lord, I have found You and have kept You in my clutches. *Dṛṣṭa eṣa*, I have found You, I have seen You. *Kva*

122 "When somebody does the purest deed, I'll be excited because You are in charge of all deeds. O Lord Śiva, this is a fact." Ibid.
123 "*Rasa* means the nectar of Thy devotion." *Śivastotrāvali*, 5.22.

yāsi naḥ, You can't go anywhere [away] from me now. You are trapped in my mind." This is the divine shining in the heart of devotees. And by this divinity, those glorified *sādhakas*, *dhanyā dhāvanti dhūrjaṭim*, they are sentenced to the state of the feet of Lord Śiva, they always remain at the feet of Lord Śiva.

Audio 4 (36:54)

स्तुमस्त्वामृग्यजुः साम्नां शुक्रतः परतः परम् ।
यस्य वेदात्मिकाज्ञेयमहो गम्भीरसुन्दरी ॥७०॥

stumastvāmṛgyajuḥ sāmnāṁ śukrataḥ parataḥ param /
yasya vedātmikājñeyam-aho gambhīrasundarī //70//

We sing the glory of Thee (*stumastvām*). *Ṛk yajuḥ sāmnāṁ śukrataḥ parataḥ param*, *yasya vedātmikā jñeyam aho gambhīra sundarī*, the *Ṛk Veda*,[124] *Yajur Veda*, and *Sāma Veda*, these three Vedas, you find in these three Vedas (*Ṛk Veda*, *Yajur Veda*, *Sāma Veda*) *śukrata* (*śukrata* means, *tejā*, light). I bow to Thee, who is the Light of that Light, the Light of all Lights of the three Vedas. *Śukrata parataḥ param*, the supreme Light, the supreme Light of the Light of all of the three Vedas, I bow to Thee, *yasya*, whose, *vedātmika ājña* (*ājña* means, the order),[125] the order of the Vedas, the order of the *Ṛg Veda*, *Yajur Veda*, and *Sāma Veda*, becomes His divine mistress (*gambhīra sundarī*).

Gambhīra sundarī means, the divine mistress is . . . His divine mistress is who?

ERNIE: The light.

SWAMIJI: The Light of all of the three Vedas.

ERNIE: I thought there was four Vedas.

SWAMIJI: No, because the *Ārtharva Veda* has been

124 Also known as the *Ṛig Veda*.
125 Or "command," "authority," "unlimited power."

written afterwards. Out of the manifestation of the three Vedas, the *Ārtharva Veda* is an added Veda for engineering; engineering courses and making planes and airplanes and ships and . . .

GANJOO: Music and everything.

SWAMIJI: Music? No music. Music is ancient. That is the *Sāma Veda*. The *Ṛg Veda*, *Yajur Veda*, and *Sāma Veda* are the ancient three Vedas, and the *Ārtharva Veda* is added afterwards because there was the need of construction, there was the need of airships, there was the need of sea ships.

JOACHIM: You see these medicines and things in the *Ārtharva Veda* also.

SWAMIJI: Medicines also, yes. All manufacturing systems are found in the *Ārtharva Veda*.

ERNIE: No light there.

SWAMIJI: There is light also, but the *Ṛg Veda*, *Yajur Veda*, and *Sāma Veda* are the ancient three Vedas. So he has mentioned only these three Vedas.

The Light of the three Vedas is Lord Śiva. I bow to Him, whose order of the three Vedas has become His divine mistress.

Audio 4 (40:04)

विधिरादिस्तथान्तोऽसि विश्वस्य परमेश्वर ।
धर्मग्रामः प्रवृत्तो यस्त्वत्तो न स कुतो भवेत् ॥७१॥

vidhirādistathānto'si viśvasya parameśvara /
dharmagrāmaḥ pravṛtto yas-tvatto na sa kuto bhavet //71//

Vidhir, there are orders of discipline which are found in the Vedas, e.g., you should do this, you should do a *havan*,[126] you should do *sādhana*,[127] you should maintain discipline. All of

126 A fire ceremony.
127 Contemplative practice.

those ways and regulations of how a human being should act in this world, these are called "*vidhi*". O Lord Śiva, *ādiḥ tathānto'si viśvasya parameśvara*, You are the source of all of these rules and regulations, and You are the ending place of the rest of all of these regulations. You rest there and all of the rules and regulations come out from You and all of these regulations rest in Thy nature. You are the *ādi* and *anta* of all of these *vidhi*s, all of these . . .

JOHN: Beginning and end.

SWAMIJI: The beginning [*ādi*] and the end [*anta*]. Because *dharma grāmaḥ pravṛtto yaḥ*, all these aspects which have come out from these rules and regulations, *tattvo*, they have come out from You, You alone. *Na sa kuto bhavet*, there is no possibility of this flowing out from another source. All of these rules and regulations have come out from Your nature.[128]

[Kṣemarāja] puts this verse:

> *'tameva bhantāmanu bhāti sarvaṁ tasya bhāsā sarvamidaṁ bibhāti'*[129]

Tameva bhantām, when You are shining, all of these rules and regulations shine, *tasya bhāsā*, and by Your shining, *sarvam-idaṁ*, everything begins to shine.

Audio 4 (42:10)

नमस्ते भवसंभ्रान्त-भ्रान्तिमुद्भाव्य भिन्दते ।
ज्ञानानन्दं च निर्द्वन्द्वं देव वृत्त्वा विवृण्वते ॥७२॥

namaste bhavasaṁbhrānta-bhrāntimudbhāvya bhindate /
jñānānandaṁ ca nirdvandvaṁ deva vṛttvā vivṛṇvate //72//

I bow to Thee, O Lord Śiva, who is the creator of *bhava saṁbhrānta bhrāntim*, the creator of the rise of wrong notions

128 "The first rule says that you should not kill or give trouble to any living being. This is the general order of behavior as given in the Laws of Manu (*Manusmṛti*)." *Stava Cintāmaṇi* (1990).

129 From the *Kaṭha Upaniṣad*, 2.2.15.

in ignorant people. *Bhava saṁbhrānta*, those who have become ignorant in the field of this universe, they possess wrong notions, always wrong notions. The creator of wrong notions is You. I bow to You who is the creator of wrong notions in ignorant persons, and *bhindate*, who is the destroyer of wrong notions in the cycle of elevated souls.

"*Bhindate*" is, he who cuts it into pieces. What? A wrong notion [*bhrānti*]. A wrong notion is cut by Lord Śiva for whom? For those who are elevated. And a wrong notion is maintained for those who are ignorant. By whom? Lord Śiva. Lord Śiva creates this wrong notion and Lord Śiva destroys this wrong notion for those who are likely to be elevated.

Jñānānandaṁ ca nirdvandvaṁ, and the bliss of the knowledge of oneness (*nirdvandvaṁ*), the bliss of the knowledge of oneness, O Lord Śiva, the bliss of the knowledge of oneness, You *vṛttvā*, You conceal that for those who are [not] worthy of that, and You *vivṛṇvate*, You reveal that supreme peace (*ānanda*) of knowledge to those who are [worthy of] that. So, You do it in both ways, You act in both ways. You create this misunderstanding and You destroy this misunderstanding. You create this misunderstanding for those who are likely to remain in the ignorant field of understanding. [For those] whom You want that they should come out from this ignorance, You destroy wrong notions in them. And You conceal the joy of knowledge of oneness; the joy of knowledge of oneness, You conceal this for those who are ignorant, and You reveal that joy of knowledge and oneness to those who are . . .

ERNIE: Deserving.

SWAMIJI: . . . who deserve that.[130]

---

130 "O Lord Śiva, I bow to You. Among all philosophers, that misunderstanding (*bhrānti*) has spread all over the world from [the element of] earth to [the element of] Sadāśiva. In the Pratyabhijñā *Śāstra*s, Utpaladeva and Abhinavagupta have said, 'O Lord Śiva, You create the various misconceptions of scholars of other systems, and by the wisdom of Your real philosophy, You destroy those misunderstandings one-by-one. And this wisdom You infuse only in Your greatest devotees.' So, You hide it from some people, and for those

Audio 4 (45:26)

यस्याः प्राप्येत पर्यन्त-विशेषः कैर्मनोरथैः ।
मायामेकनिमेषेण मुष्णंस्तां पातु नः शिवः ॥ ७३ ॥

yasyāḥ prāpyeta paryanta-viśeṣaḥ kairmanorathaiḥ /
māyāmekanimeṣeṇa muṣṇaṁstāṁ pātu naḥ śivaḥ //73//

Let that Lord Śiva protect us (*pātu naḥ śiva*; *naḥ* means, us), let that Lord Śiva protect us from all sides, whose *māyā*, whose illusive energy of *māyā*, *paryanta viśeṣaḥ kairmanorathaiḥ prāpyeta*, . . .*

Paryanta viśeṣaḥ: *Paryanta viśeṣaḥ* means, the last understanding of what *māyā* really is. *Māyā* is just the concealing nature of Lord Śiva. The concealing energy of Lord Śiva is *māyā*. But, in fact, this concealing energy of *māyā* is just the *svātantrya śakti* of Lord Śiva.

ERNIE: His freedom.

SWAMIJI: It is only freedom! It is only [because of] freedom that He conceals His nature–out of His freedom, free will.[131]

JOHN: He's not forced by any *karma* or anything else to do that.

SWAMIJI: No, He conceals according to His play. That is *paryanta viśeṣaḥ*. That is the ending quality of *māyā*. The last ending quality of *māyā* . . . what is that last ending?

JOHN: *Svātantrya śakti*.

SWAMIJI: *Svātantrya śakti*, entry in *svātantrya śakti*. And that entry in *svātantrya śakti* of *māyā*, that is *paryanta viśeṣaḥ*; *paryanta viśeṣaḥ*, the last understanding of *māyā*, what *māyā* actually is. It is said in the Pratyabhijñā *Darśana*:[132] *Māyā* is actually the energy of *svātantrya*

---

who deserve it, You expose it to them." *Stava Cintāmaṇi* (1990).

131 See Appendix 5 for an explanation of *svātantrya śakti*.

132 The Doctrine of Recognition (*pratyabhijñā*). "The Trika System is comprised of four sub-systems: the Pratyabhijñā System, the Kula

śakti of Lord Siva. *Māyā* is not ignorance. Actually, *māyā* is not ignorance, *māyā* is just the freedom of Lord Śiva. By His free will He conceals His nature, [but it is] not that He has concealed His nature and now He has not revealed His nature. Although It is revealed to [a person], at the same time, He makes ignorant persons feel that It is concealed. Actually, It is not concealed. This is the position of *māyā*. *Māyā* is nothing, *māyā* is divine.

ERNIE: Swamiji, in other schools, *māyā* is . . .

SWAMIJI: *Māyā* is very bad. In our school, *māyā* is divine.

ERNIE: Is divine. And they hold that that is . . . what is it?

SWAMIJI: What is it? For instance, [they say], don't go to sex, don't go . . . [but we say], see the beauty of Ellen[133] and divert your attention towards God consciousness, *bas*.

JOHN: This is ours, not theirs.

SWAMIJI: That is ours.

JOHN: Theirs is?

SWAMIJI: (question ignored) This *māyā* becomes *svātantrya śakti* then.[134]

JOHN: And they would [say] to just reject everything?

SWAMIJI: If you find attachment, individual attachment, that is *māyā*. That you should leave. You should feel everything [as] divine, then there is no *māyā*, there is *svātantrya śakti*.[135]

System, the Krama System, and the Spanda System. These four Systems, which form the one thought of the Trika System, all accept, and are based on, the same scriptures." *Kashmir Shaivism–The Secret Supreme*, 19.129.

133 Ernie Montano's girlfriend at that time.

134 This is the Śaivite understanding of *māyā*.

135 "*Svātantrya śakti* and *māyā* are one. *Svātantrya śakti* is that state of energy which can produce the power of going down and coming up again. And *māyā* is not like that. *Māyā* will give you the strength of coming down and then no ability of going up. *Māyā śakti*

ERNIE: No but, in the Buddhist School, they feel that it's the absence of knowledge?

SWAMIJI: They feel [that], yes.

JOACHIM: It is unreal, it is not reality.

SWAMIJI: It is not real.

ERNIE: It's not real. In Vedānta, they hold that *māyā* is . . . ?

SWAMIJI: Ignorance.

JOHN: Yes, but in this particular illustration . . .

SWAMIJI: Not only in Ellen, I mean, anybody.

DEVOTEES: (laughter)

JOHN: But in this particular one, for a Vedāntin to look at Ellen and see anything, that would just all be false.

SWAMIJI: Vedānta directs us [that] you should not see –"*citra nikatam api naram na paśyati*"–you must not see a woman, [even] a photograph of a woman. What to say of seeing a woman and talking to her? It is a blunder [according to Vedānta].

ERNIE: This is a very important difference in Śaivism, . . .

SWAMIJI: Yes.

ERNIE: . . . this concept of *māyā*.

SWAMIJI: Everything is divine, if you feel like that. So, that is *paryanta viśeṣaḥ*.

*. . . and *kairmanorathaiḥ prāpyeta*, and Brahmā, Viṣṇu, Rudra, all of these gods and sages and *ṛṣi*s and *yogi*s are craving for that last point of *māyā*'s understanding, what *māyā* is, and that *māyā*, that ignorance, *eka nimeṣeṇa muṣṇaṁ*, You destroy it; instantaneously You destroy that misunderstanding

---

is that energy, universal energy, which is owned by the individual being, the individual soul. The same energy, when it is owned by the Universal Being, is called *svātantrya śakti*." *Kashmir Shaivism–The Secret Supreme*, 7.47.

of *māyā*. Let that Lord Siva protect us in this way.[136]

Have you understood it?

JOACHIM: Yes.

SWAMIJI:

Audio 4 (50:50)

वैराग्यस्य गतिं गुर्वीं ज्ञानस्य परमां श्रियम् ।
नैःस्पृह्यस्य परां कोटिं बिभ्रतां त्वं प्रभो प्रभुः ॥ ७४ ॥

vairāgyasya gatiṁ gurvīṁ jñānasya paramāṁ śriyam /
naiḥspṛhyasya parāṁ koṭiṁ bibhratāṁ tvaṁ prabho prabhuḥ 74

Prabho ("*prabho*" is *āmantraṇa*),[137] O Lord Śiva, those persons who *bibhratāṁ*, who possess . . . *bibhratāṁ*, who possess–what?–the deep state of detachment (*gurvī* means, deep; *gati* means, state), those persons who possess the deep state of detachment, and who possess the supreme glory of knowledge, and those who possess the supreme *koṭi*, the supreme state of *naiḥspṛhyasya*, . . .*

Naiḥspṛhyasya is . . .

JOACHIM: Detachment.

SWAMIJI: It is not actually "detachment", it is more than detachment–*naiḥspṛhyasya*.[138] You don't like anything in this world, that is *naiḥspṛhyasya*. *Naiḥspṛhya* is when you don't like to live also, you don't like to breathe, you don't like anything in this world. When you are fed up with this universe, you don't like to do anything, you don't like to breathe, you don't like to have a body, that is *naiḥspṛhyasya*.

ERNIE: It is disgusting, all of this.

136 "Bhaṭṭa Nārāyaṇa does not [only] say "me", as he includes all of his brothers and sisters who are with him, [that they] should be protected." *Stava Cintāmaṇi* (1990).
137 Vocative case, i.e., a calling or an addressing. *Prabho*, lit, calling to one's Master or Lord.
138 Lit., the absence of longing for anything.

SWAMIJI: You feel that all-around it is filled with disgusting [things].

GANJOO: Absolution of attachment.

SWAMIJI: That is "*vairāgya*". [*Naiḥspṛhyasya*] is something more than *vairāgya*. *Vairāgya* is, you possess a body, you feel that you are living in a body, and you go in the forest, seclusion, and perform *tapāsya*, perform penance, and *sādhana* (and meditation), and get elevated. That is *vairāgya*. But *naiḥspṛhya* is, you don't want to live, you don't want to breathe!

JOACHIM: Its the same like "*glāni*", depression or . . . ?

SWAMIJI: What is *glāni*? *Glāni*, it is just like *glāni*, yes.[139]

ERNIE: You don't want to breathe because? Is there a reason?

SWAMIJI: The reason is, you don't enjoy anything, you don't enjoy anything in this world. This stage also comes to some aspirants. This stage also [occurs] in this universe. They don't want anything. This stage had come to one person in my period. He wanted to die, he didn't want to live. He was quite healthy, a young man, and he poisoned [himself]. He wanted to see what is behind this life.

ERNIE: But isn't that suicide?

SWAMIJI: That is suicide but he couldn't . . .

JOACHIM: Couldn't help.

SWAMIJI: . . . he couldn't help.

ERNIE: But isn't that a bad thing?

SWAMIJI: From our viewpoint, it is a bad thing, but from his viewpoint, it was good. He did it!

GANJOO: It was his only solution to it.

SWAMIJI: This is the state of *naiḥspṛhyasya*.

ERNIE: But that's not an elevated state.

---

139. Lit., exhausted or debilitated. In other texts, Swamiji translates *glāni* as "shrunken" or "squeezed."

SWAMIJI: This is not an elevated state. This comes first. This state . . .

JOHN: But this state is only for spiritual devotees. This isn't simply depression with the world. This is depression where you want to get to that other spiritual state, not just to get rid of your . . .

SWAMIJI: Yes, you want to find out something else. [It is] not this [ordinary depression].[140]

*. . . and those persons who possess this kind of position of mind, those persons who possess detachment, deep detachment, and those who possess supreme knowledge, and those persons who possess this *naiḥspṛhyasya*, *bibhratāṁ tvaṁ prabho prabhuḥ* (*bibharatām* means, those who possess), *tvaṁ prabho prabhuḥ*, You are their protector, You are the only means to get them out from this crisis. This is the threefold crisis.

ERNIE: Supreme knowledge? What was the knowledge?

SWAMIJI: Supreme knowledge is also a crisis. "I want that supreme knowledge, to find out supreme knowledge. I want to have that supreme knowledge," this craving, it is a crisis. Is it not a crisis?

JOHN: These are all spiritual cravings then.

SWAMIJI: Yes, spiritual cravings. You are the protector for all of these three kinds of people.

Audio 4 (55:48)

ब्रह्माणोऽपि भवान्ब्रह्म कस्य नेशस्त्वमीशितुः ।
जगत्कल्याणकल्याणं कियत्त्वमिति वेत्ति कः ॥७५॥

140 "Lord Buddha was married and slept with his wife, but he had lost all interest in sex. He had reached the topmost stage of detachment. He had the supreme wealth of Parabhairava and that knowledge was his. He ate food with tears in his eyes. He had no interest in anything although he did everything." *Stava Cintāmaṇi* (1990).

brahmāṇo'pi bhavānbrahma kasya neśastvamīśituḥ /
jagatkalyāṇakalyāṇaṁ kiyattvamiti vetti kaḥ //75//

You are the *brahma* of Brahmā, You are the creator of Brahmā, You are the Creator of the creator He who creates this universe is called Brahmā. You are his creator. *Kasya neśastvam īśituḥ* (*kasya īśituḥ tvam na īśa*), any person who governs in this universe, whom don't You govern? [Which] governing personality don't You govern?

The governing personalities, there are five governing personalities. The creator is one personality, the protector is one personality of this universe, the destroyer is another personality, the concealing embodiment is another personality, and revealing is another personality.[141] These three governing . . .

ERNIE: Five.

SWAMIJI: . . . these five governing beings are governed by You! *Kasya īśituḥ* (*īśitu* means, who are governing), . . .

ERNIE: The governors.

SWAMIJI: Governors.

. . . You are their governor. *Kasya na īśa*, whom don't You govern? *Jagat kalyāṇa kalyāṇam*, You are the *kalyāṇa* of all *kalyāṇas* of the world.

Kalyāṇa means . . .

JOACHIM: Beautiful or . . .

SWAMIJI: *Kalyāṇa* is "the graceful state," the graceful position of the [whole] all-graceful world. *Jagat kalyāṇa*, the grace of the universe, You are the Grace of the grace of the universe.[142]

JOHN: Grace means "harmony" here, not grace like *anugraha*. Grace means . . .

---

141. Brahmā, Viṣṇu, Rudra, Īśvara, and Sadāśiva, respectively. See verses 33, 34 for an explanation of these five lords.

142 "*Jagat kalyāṇa* are those who attain the power to be united with Lord Śiva, i.e., Īśvara, Sadāśiva, and Śiva. How can I describe [them], O Lord, those who produce bliss to everyone? That force they have achieved from one drop of Your Being." *Stava Cintāmaṇi* (1990).

SWAMIJI: No, [here it means] "harmony."

Kiyattvam, how very [great] are You, it is beyond our imagination. Who can know this (*iti vetti kaḥ*, who can know You)? You are the unknown beauty of this whole universe.[143]

Audio 4 (58:20)

किमन्यैरबन्धुभिः किं च सुहृद्भिः स्वामिभिस्तथा ।
सर्वस्थाने ममेश त्वं य उद्धर्ता भवार्णवात् ॥ ७६ ॥

kimanyairbandhubhiḥ kiṁ ca suhṛdbhiḥ svāmibhistathā /
sarvasthāne mameśa tvaṁ ya uddhartā bhavārṇavāt //76//

What have I to do with my relatives, with other relatives (*kim anyair bandhubhiḥ*)? I have nothing to do with other relatives of mine. *Kiṁ ca suhṛdbhiḥ*, I have nothing to do with other *suhṛdbhiḥ*, kith and kin; *suhṛdbhiḥ*, who are friends, fast friends of mine, I have nothing to do with them. *Svāmibhiḥ*, I have nothing to do with other masters in this world. *Sarva sthāne*, in all of these states, You are my Lord, You are my Lord as my relative, You are my friend, and You are my master. You are my master, I have no other master. You are my friend, I have no other friend in this world. And You are my relative, I have no other relative in this world. Because *sarva sthāne mameśa tvaṁ*, You are existing in all of these . . .

GANJOO: Places.

ERNIE: Roles.

SWAMIJI: . . . places for me, who is likely to *uddhartā*, who is likely to [uplift me from the] furious ocean of the universe of repeated births and deaths.

---

143 In his commentary, Kṣemarāja gives the reference of *Bhagavad Gītā* 14.3: "O Lord (this Para Brahman), Īśvara, Sadāśiva, and Śiva are eunuchs and have no strength. They will not produce fruit [because] they have no sperm (barren women are in this same class). They will produce only a fruitless egg. They will try to elevate the universe but it will have no effect. The real elevator is You, Lord Śiva, and I don't think anybody else knows." Ibid.

End of Audio 4 (59:48)
Start of Audio 5 (00:00)

जयन्ति मोहमायादि-मलसंक्षालनक्षमाः ।
शैवयोगबलाकृष्टाः दिव्यपीयूषविप्रुषः ॥७७॥

jayanti mohamāyādi-malasaṁkṣālanakṣamāḥ /
śaivayogabalākṛṣṭāḥ divyapīyūṣavipruṣaḥ //77//

Glory be (*jayanti*, glory be) to those *divyapīyūṣa*, those divine drops of knowledge. Glory be to those divine drops of knowledge, which are existing in the cycle of Śaiva Yoga, the *yoga* of Śaivism. Glory be to those drops, those divine drops of Śaiva Yoga, which are *mohamāyādi malasaṁkṣālana kṣamāḥ*, [which] have the ability of destroying or washing off all of the three *mala*s (all of the three *malas*: *āṇavamala*, *māyīyamala*, and *kārmamala*).[144]

ERNIE: What has that ability?

SWAMIJI: Who have that ability of washing that *mala*.

ERNIE: Who?

BRUCE H: The drops of knowledge.

SWAMIJI: The drops of knowledge.

ERNIE: Of Śaivism.

SWAMIJI: Śaiva Yoga.

Audio 5 (01:20)

गायत्र्या गीयते यस्य धियां तेजः प्रचोदकम् ।
चोदयेदपि कच्चिन्नः स धियः सत्पथे प्रभुः ॥७८॥

gāyatryā gīyate yasya dhiyāṁ tejaḥ pracodakam /
codayedapi kaccinnaḥ sa dhiyaḥ satpathe prabhuḥ //78//

---

144 "By these three coverings, Śiva, in the formation of being an individual, is enwrapped." *Paramārthasāra–Essence of the Supreme Reality*, verse 24.
See Appendix 8 for an explanation of the *malas*.

There is the *mantra* of the Gāyatrī *mantra*.[145]

The Gāyatrī *mantra* is: *"Oṁ bhūr bhuvaḥ svaḥ, tat savitur vareṇyaṁ, bhargo devasya dhīmahi, dhiyo yo na, pracodayāt."* *Oṁ*, I accept,[146] *bhūr bhuvaḥ svaḥ*, there are three worlds (*bhūḥ*, *bhuvaḥ*, and *svaḥ*). There is this universe, there is the universe of planets, and there is the universe of . . .[147]

ERNIE: Heavens.

SWAMIJI: *Tat savitur*, the sun of all of these three worlds, the shining embodiment of . . .

ERNIE: Light.

SWAMIJI: . . . He puts, He induces, the light on these three worlds, which are existing, which I confess they are existing (*bhūḥ*, *bhuvaḥ*, and *svaḥ*); *tat savitur*, He who is the light giver of these three worlds, and His effulgent light is *vareṇyam* (*vareṇyam* is "worth having, worth possessing"). *Tat savitur vareṇyam bharga* (*bharga* means, light), His effulgent light is worth having, worth possessing. I meditate on That light.

ERNIE: That's the *mantra*.

SWAMIJI: This is the meaning of this Gāyatrī *mantra*. *Vareṇyam teja*, *vareṇyam bharga*, *bhargo devasya dhīmahi*, I meditate on It, I contemplate on That light of the Lord, *dhiyo yo naḥ*, who will elevate our shrunken . . . "Shrunken"?

JOACHIM: Yes.

---

145 "The Gāyatrī *mantra* is traditionally recited during the sacred thread ceremony, but in this verse Bhaṭṭa Nārāyaṇa indicates something else." *Stava Cintāmaṇi* (1990).

146 "The recitation of *"oṁ"* means, [the acceptance of] That state which is condensed with consciousness and bliss, and in which all of these thirty-six elements are merged, are digested." Swami Lakshmanjoo, *Bhagavad Gitartha Saṁgraha of Abhinavagupta*, translation and commentary (original audio recording, LJA archives, Los Angeles, 1978), 8.14.

147 See verse 46, fn 85.

SWAMIJI: . . . shrunken intellectual position, who will elevate our shrunken intellectual position and insert it in that effulgent light of the universal sun–Gāyatrī. This is the *mantra* of Gāyatrī. He says . . . now he refers to that *mantra*.

JOHN: Gāyatrī means, the universal light, or . . . the word "*gāyatrī*"?

SWAMIJI: The meaning of *gāyatrī*? *Gāyatrī* means, he who sings His glory, he is protected by That–the singer is protected.

ERNIE: And the singer sings this *mantra*?

SWAMIJI: Yes.

Gāyatryā gīyate yasya dhiyāṁ tejaḥ pracodakam; *yasya tejaḥ*, *yasya gāyatryā tejaḥ*, *gāyatryā gīyate*, by this *mantra* of Gāyatrī, [the purpose for which] it is sung, "Whose effulgent light," is *dhiyām pracodakam*, is inducing the power of your individual understanding to insert it in the universal understanding.[148] It is *pracodakam*.[149] [Bhaṭṭa Nārāyaṇa says]: I don't want that! I don't want that thing to be done in my intellectual cycle. *Codayet api kaccit naḥ sa dhiya*, let that power of that effulgent light insert me, or direct me, *codayet api*, on the path of Śaivism. That is my *pracodaka*. I don't want to elevate my intellectual cycle. I want to get myself on the path of Śaivism. That is what I . . . I long for this favor from Gāyatrī.

ERNIE: Why? Because that . . .

SWAMIJI: I want Śaivism, *bas*, that is all.

ERNIE: That is more.

SWAMIJI: That is more than That. I don't want to get my intellectual cycle elevated only. I don't want that elevation. I want myself to be steeped in the path of Śaivism.

148 "The greatest energy of all *śāstras* has sunk in that light of Gāyatrī, which is produced by the sun (*savitur*): *oṁ*, *bhuḥ*, *bhuvaḥ*, *svaḥ*." *Stava Cintāmaṇi* (1990).
149 Lit., instigating, to impel.

ERNIE: As with before about supreme knowledge and having that desire.

Audio 5 (06:06)

[The following verse is not included in this audio.][150]

अष्टमूर्ते किमेकस्यामपि मूर्तौ न नः स्थितिम् ।
शाश्वतीं कुरुशे यद्वा तुष्टः सर्वं करिष्यसि ॥७९॥

aṣṭamūrte kimekasyām-api mūrtau na naḥ sthitim /
śāśvatīṁ kuruśe yadvā tuṣṭaḥ sarvaṁ kariṣyasi //79//

You have got eight formations, O Lord Śiva: *pṛthvī* (earth), *jala* (water), *agni* (fire), *vayu* (wind), *akāśa* (ether), *sūrya* (sun), *soma* (moon), *yajamāna* (individuals).[151]

From earth to *śāntātīta kalā*,[152] you can't count [the number of] individuals [because] all of these eight formations are so vast [that] they can't be measured.

Is it possible, O Lord Śiva, that You would make us worthy to dwell and be seated in these eight formations of Yours? And is it possible that we will dwell in those eight formations forever?

> According to the statement of Pāṇini's grammar, "*sthita iti*" means, the future tense of "Will you do it?" Sometimes the future tense is *kṣipravacane*, which means, the very near future which will come soon.[153]

---

150 This verse, along with its translation, was missing from the original recording. The translation used here is taken from Denise Hughes' handwritten notes from *Stava Cintāmaṇi* (1990).
151 Lit., one who performs a sacrifice or worship.
152 *Śāntātīta kalā* is the highest of the five circles (*kalā*s) which enclose the 118 worlds from earth to Śiva. See *Kashmir Shaivism–The Secret Supreme*, chapter 2, *Ṣaḍadhvan*, "The Sixfold Path of the Universe."
153 Kṣemarāja's commentary.

Let this near future come by tomorrow because we are dying for that. If You are pleased with us, I think You will do it.

[Swamiji's original audio resumes from here.]

Audio 5 (06:06)

वास्तुतत्त्वं पदार्थानां प्रायेणार्थक्रियाकारम् ।
भवतस्त्वीश नामापि मोक्षपर्यन्तसिद्धिदम् ॥८०॥

vastutattvaṁ padārthānāṁ prāyeṇārthakriyākāram /
bhavatastvīśa nāmāpi mokṣaparyantasiddhidam //80//

Just to complete some objective, solid work (*padārthānām vastu tattvam*, just to complete some solid work), *prāyeṇārtha kriyākāram*, it is not [for] sure that you will finish it to your [entire] satisfaction. For instance, if you want to do something. It may be completed according to your satisfaction or it may not be completed at all, whatever you have to do in this world. But, only reciting Your name, O Lord, just by the recitation of Your name, only by thinking of Your name, that will end in its complete satisfactory results! There is cent-per-cent[154] assurance there, cent-per-cent guarantee, that when you recite and take, remember, the Lord's name, that will make you finish/complete that whole work completely according to your satisfaction. This is the greatness of Your name.

Audio 5 (07:46)

मुहुर्मुहुर्जगच्चित्र-स्यान्यान्यां स्थितिमूहितुम् ।
शक्तिर्या ते तया नाथ को मनस्वी न विस्मितः ॥८१॥

muhurmuhurjagaccitra-syānyānyāṁ sthitimūhitum /
śaktiryā te tayā nātha ko manasvī na vismitaḥ //81//

Jagat citrasya anyānyām sthitim, *jagat citrasya*, the

154 One hundred percent.

varieties of this creation of the universe, the various creations of this universe, how is it done, which way is it done, how is it adopted, how is it adjusted (this whole creation of one hundred and eighteen worlds),[155] and which energy does this, which energy is put by Lord Śiva to complete this whole creation of nature, while thinking of That energy (what energy is that existing here that works in each and every blade of grass, in trees, in plants, in human beings, in mountains, everywhere, in streams), with this verification, just to investigate, when you investigate this strength and the way which it is being adjusted to create this whole universe, the varieties of the universe, *ko manasvī na vismitaḥ* (*manasvī* means, all of those informed souls), those who are intellectually advanced souls, they have failed to understand, they have failed to understand how it is done, how it is adjusted. You can't imagine this adjustment, how it is done, how it is . . .

DEVOTEE: How it takes place.

SWAMIJI: For instance, you are conceived. How is it done, how is it adjusted, how is it handled, you can't understand, you become just confused. Not only this, everywhere you will find the same greatness of That power that works secretly everywhere.

JOHN: This power is *prāṇana*?

SWAMIJI: *Prāṇana*,[156] but derived from Lord Śiva Himself.[157]

Audio 5 (10:26)

दुष्करं सुकरीकर्तुं दुःखं सुखयितुं तथा ।
एकवीरा स्मृतिर्यस्य तं स्मरामः स्मरद्विषम् ॥८२॥

155 See fn 24 for an explanation of the 118 worlds.

156 Lit., life. The source of the five *prāṇa*s (breaths).

157 "O my Lord, Your *śakti* has so much strength and energy that It creates the universe in varieties, all different from each other. You can't imagine how great this creation is. Some *yogi*s who observe this strength of Yours, they become wonderstruck and cannot imagine how much strength You have." *Stava Cintāmaṇi* (1990).

duṣkaraṁ sukarīkartuṁ duḥkhaṁ sukhayituṁ tathā /
ekavīrā smṛtiryasya taṁ smarāmaḥ smaradviṣam //82//[158]

Whose remembrance, only one remembrance (*ekavīrā* means, remembering the Lord only once), if you remember Lord Śiva only once, one time, one time only–what result [will] you get from this by remembering the Lord only once?–*duṣkaraṁ sukarī kartuṁ*, that thing which is difficult to be done becomes very easy to be done, very easily it is done, and *duḥkham*, when there is grief, it turns into pleasure, it turns into joy–by only remembering Lord Śiva only once! This is the greatness of His remembrance. And how fortunate we are that we remember Him always; *taṁ smarāmaḥ smaradviṣam*, we remember Him always, how fortunate we are. Whom [do we remember]? *Smaradviṣam*, [He] who hates the god of love (*smaradviṣam*,[159] who is the enemy of the god of love).

JOACHIM: Kāmadahanam.[160]

SWAMIJI: Yes.

JOHN: What does that mean?

DENISE: Who is the enemy of the god of love?

SWAMIJI: Lord Śiva. Lord Śiva is the enemy of the god of love. He doesn't want sex. He has no interest in sex.

ERNIE: But why is it fortunate to remember?

SWAMIJI: Because only remembering Lord Śiva one time will do such and such things, [have] such and such tremendous effects. And we remember Him always! How fortunate we are!

ERNIE: Then we are not bothered with love, hate, this, that.

SWAMIJI: You have nothing!

---

158 See also: *Special Verses on Practice*, verse 40.
159 Lit., the enemy (*dviṣa*) of the one who induces lust (*smara*), i.e., Kāmadeva.
160 The burning, scorching, or destroying (*dahanam*) of the god of desire (Kāma).

JOHN: So they are only calling Him this . . . this is one of His names.

SWAMIJI: *Smaradviṣam*, yes, the enemy of the god of love.

JOHN: But why is He the enemy of the god of love when He is the greatest lover in the universe? He is the . . .

SWAMIJI: He doesn't want to love Pārvatī because of the thrust of the god of love! He wants to love Pārvatī according to His own sweet will, not that [the god of love] will put force that [He] should love her. Once [Kāmadeva] did [try] and he was put to ashes by Him.

ERNIE: (laughter)

SWAMIJI: He tried to do that, to overpower Lord Śiva.

JOACHIM: Kālidāsa . . .[161]

JOHN: So what is the teaching here then about the god of love? It's not that sex is bad, it's that you shouldn't . . .

SWAMIJI: You want to have sex?

DEVOTEES: (laughter)

JOHN: No, I'm trying to understand because Śaivism doesn't teach that sex is bad. Śaivism teaches that the loss of awareness is . . .

SWAMIJI: *Smaradviṣam* means, sex is bad when you are overpowered by sex.

ERNIE: Overshadowed.

SWAMIJI: Overpowered by sex. When you do it according to your own free will, then it is good, then it is divine–not by anybody's force [making] you have to do it. Forcibly, it is not [to be] done like that.

JOHN: "Forcibly" means what? Internal urge?

SWAMIJI: There must be *svātantrya* [freedom] in sex, then it is divine. If there is not *svātantrya*, then you are

---

161 Though Kāmadeva is mentioned in the Vedas, the story regarding his incineration by Lord Śiva (*madana bhasma* or Kāma *dahana*) appeared first in the Matsya Purāṇa, and afterwards with variations in the Shiva and other Purāṇas (Hindu mythologies).

overpowered. She[162] will rule on you!

DEVOTEES: (laughter)

SWAMIJI: Don't let her rule on you. Just do whenever you like, *bas*!

ERNIE: With love.

SWAMIJI: With love, yes.

ERNIE: True love.

SWAMIJI: True love–free!

JOHN: So this urge, this overpowering urge, means, her or some person pressurizing you to do something, or it means by your own internal urges?

SWAMIJI: Not by pressure.

JOHN: Your own internal urges can also be a pressure.

SWAMIJI: Not urge, there must not be an urge, there must be [the freedom of] will. There is a big difference between urge and will. Urge is when you are overpowered by your desire. Will is when you just like to do it, *bas*, according to your choice. That is something else.

ERNIE: There is freedom there.

SWAMIJI: Yes. There must be *svātantrya*. It is not taught in Śaivism that you must be a slave of sex. You must govern on sex.

ERNIE: So He is the enemy of love because love is [means] urges.

SWAMIJI: Urges. There must not be an urge.

ERNIE: This is the enemy of love.

SWAMIJI: Yes.

JOHN: *Kāma* means "desire," right?

SWAMIJI: Because this idea came in Lord Śiva's mind when [Kāmadeva] thrusted that arrow of five flowers [in Him]. [When it was shot in] Him, He [suddenly] started thinking that, "Pārvatī is so beautiful to have, We must

---

162 Your partner.

possess Pārvatī." *Bas*, then He came to His senses and burnt him to ashes. Otherwise, He didn't hate Pārvatī.

DEVOTEES: (laughter)

JOHN: So, *kāma* doesn't mean "love" in our western sense. *Kāma* means "desire".

SWAMIJI: Yes, desire.

JOHN: Not "love". Love is carnal love.

SWAMIJI:

Audio 5 (15:54)

जयन्ति गीतयो यासां स गेयः परमेश्वरः ।
यन्नाम्नापि महात्मानः कीर्यन्ते पुलकाङ्कुरैः ॥८३॥

jayanti gītayo yāsāṁ sa geyaḥ parameśvaraḥ /
yannāmnāpi mahātmānaḥ kīryante pulakāṅkuraiḥ //83//

Gīta yāsāṁ sa geyaḥ parameśvaraḥ, these songs which are sung in the name of Lord Śiva, these songs, glory be to those songs which are sung in the name of Lord Śiva, *yat nam napi*, by whose thinking, by whose nomination, when you nominate this is the song sung by such and such great soul on Lord Śiva's . . .

GANJOO: Praise of Lord Śiva.

SWAMIJI: . . . in the name of Lord Śiva, and by that, *mahātmānaḥ* (great souls)[163] start feeling the *pulaka aṅkuraiḥ.*[164] When [they] just think of those songs, which are sung in the name of Lord Śiva, in the body of those great souls this appearance takes place, this appearance of these [goose-bumps].

---

163 "*Mahātmā* means, *mahā-ātma*, two words. *Mahā* means, brilliant by Your *tīvra tīvra śaktipāta*, *ātma* means, his mind. Those *mahātmās* sing Your glory in each and every respect." *Stava Cintāmaṇi* (1990).

164 *Harśa romahcha*: erection or bristling of bodily hair, i.e., goose-bumps.

GANJOO: We have seen it very often when Swamiji teaches the *Śivastotrāvali.*[165]

SWAMIJI:

Audio 5 (17:19)

भवानिव भवानेव भवेद्यदि परं भव ।
स्वशक्तिव्यूहसंव्यूढ-त्रैलोक्यारम्भसंहृतिः ॥८४॥

bhavāniva bhavāneva bhavedyadi paraṁ bhava /
svaśaktivyūhasaṁvyūḍha-trailokyārambhasaṁhṛtiḥ //84//

O Lord (*bhava*, O Lord), O Lord Śiva, *svaśakti-vyūḍha-saṁvyūḍha trailokyārambha saṁhṛtiḥ*, when You create the three worlds and destroy these three worlds (*ārambha saṁhṛti*; *ārambha* means, at the time of creating these three worlds and [*saṁhṛti* means], at the time of destroying these three worlds), who is the hero in that? Who does that? Who creates this whole universe and who destroys this whole universe? Only You do it, You can do it, and only that person can do it who has become one with You (*bhavāniva bhavāneva*; *bhavāneva*, just like You). He who has become just like You, he can do it, or You can do it. Only these two beings can handle this kind of creation and destruction of this three-fold universe. Who? Either You can do it or the person who has become just like You, he can do it (that is, Your devotee).[166]

Audio 5 (18:52)

मन्त्रोऽसि मन्त्रणीयोऽसि मन्त्री त्वत्तः कुतोऽपरः ।
स मह्यं देहि तं मन्त्रं त्वन्मन्त्रः स्यां यथा प्रभो ॥८५॥

---

165 A devotional treatise by Utpaladeva.

166 "By Your energies of *cit*, *ānanda*, *icchā*, *jñāna*, and *kriyā*, You conduct the creation and the destruction of the universe. You don't need any other element to destroy or create. You create and destroy with Your own energies." *Stava Cintāmaṇi* (1990).

mantro'si mantraṇīyo'si mantrī tvattaḥ kuto'paraḥ /
sa mahyaṁ dehi taṁ mantraṁ
tvanmantraḥ syāṁ yathā prabho //85//

Prabho, O Master, *mantro'si*, You are *mantra*, You are the *mantra* which is recited. *Mantraṇīyo'si*, You are that person for whom the *mantra* is recited–God. You are the God for whom this *mantra* is recited, You are the *mantra* which is being recited, [and the] *mantrī* (who recites), You are that *sādhaka* who recites the *mantra*. *Tvattaḥ kuto paraḥ*, who can be other than You? *Artha arthāt*, the person who recites the *mantra* is You, and the *mantra* itself is one with You, and for whom this *mantra* is recited is one with You. So, You are *mantra*, You are *mantrī*, and You are *mantraṇīya*.

Mantraṇīya is God (for whom this *mantra* is recited), *mantra* is the *mantra* (these sacred words which are recited), and *mantrī* is the one who recites (the *sādhaka*). All of the three are You. *Tvattaḥ kuto paraḥ*, who can be other than That? You are *mantra*, You are *mantrī*, and You are *mantraṇīya*.

May I venture to ask you, O Lord, to give me that kind of *mantra* by which *tvanmantraḥ syāṁ yathā prabho*, I'll become one with You? Because, whenever I recite, I [want to] become one with You [during the] recitation. *Arthāt mantrī* (*mantrī* means, he who recites, the reciter), the one who recites a *mantra* becomes Lord Śiva, the *mantra* becomes Lord Śiva, and for whom this *mantra* is recited, he is one with Lord Śiva. Make me fit to have this kind of state.[167]

Audio 5 (21:00)

भारूपः सत्यसंकल्पस्त्वमात्मा यस्य सोऽप्यहम् ।
संसारीति किमीशैष स्वप्नः सोऽपि कुतस्त्वयि ॥८६॥

167 Kṣemarāja gives a reference from the *Śrīkaṇṭha Saṁhitā* of Śrī Kaṇṭhanātha addressing His Śakti: "If you recite that *mantra* with devotion and keep the *mantrī* separate, then you will never achieve the final achievement. If you think the *mantra* pervades all three, then you will achieve the final achievement." *Stava Cintāmaṇi* (1990).

bhārūpaḥ satyasaṁkalpas-tvamātmā yasya so'pyaham /
saṁsārīti kimīśaiṣa svapnaḥ so'pi kutastvayi //86//

O Lord Śiva, You are my soul, You are my . . . you are my marrow, You are my flesh, You are my bones, You are my everything (*tvam ātmā yasya*). What is the qualification of Yours? What is Your qualification? You are *bhārūpaḥ*, always shining. *Satya saṁkalpa*, Your *saṁkalpa*[168] is always true.

> What is *satya saṁkalpa*? *Satya saṁkalpa* is [to say], "It will be done," and it is done, [or] "It will take place," and it takes place. Not [that] "I will cure you" and you are not cured–not like this. This is not *satya saṁkalpa*. This is *asatya saṁkalpa*. [When] you wish that it should be done and it does not come true, that is *asatya saṁkalpa*. But Lord Śiva has *saṁkalpa* that is *satya saṁkalpa*. Whatever He thinks, it becomes true.

And You are like that, You are *satya saṁkalpa*, You are *prakāśa rūpa*,[169] and You are one with me (*tvam ātma yasya*, You are one with me, You have become one with me). But, the tragedy is, *so'pi haṁ saṁsārī*, I am roaming here and there and I am tossed down just like an ordinary person in this field of the universe–mortality. In this mortal field, I am just begging from door-to-door. This is my position. If You say, "*Kimīśaiṣa svapna*," if you say, "You are dreaming like that, actually you are not like that, you are not a beggar because you are one with Me, you are not a beggar, you are dreaming like that, dreaming that you are a beggar in this world," [then my reply is], "*So'pi kutastvayi*, how can that dream also exist in Your nature? That dream also should not take place in Your universal body."

Do you understand what he means?

ERNIE: The dream of separation?

SWAMIJI: No, the dream that, I am ignorant, I am ignor-

168 Lit., Conception, idea or notion formed in the mind or heart.
169 The embodiment (*rūpa*) of light (*prakāśa*), viz., *bhārūpaḥ*.

ant, I have become ignorant. You are my soul, You are one with me, and You are *prakāśa* (You are all light), and You are *satya saṁkalpa*, and I am one with You–it is a fact–but still I am just like an ordinary person roaming from door-to-door just like a beggar, just like a trodden down person, an ignorant person (*ajñāni*). If You say, "No, this is a dream, you dream like that, actually you are not like that, you are not just an ignorant person, you dream like that," [then my reply is], "But how can that dream also exist in Your nature?" That is to be discussed.

This is what he says in this *śloka*.

Audio 5 (24:04)

तद्भङ्गि तदग्राम्यं तदेकमुपपत्तिमत् ।
त्वयि कर्मफलन्यास-कृतामैश्वर्यमीश यत् ॥८७॥

tadabhaṅgi tadagrāmyaṁ tadekamupapattimat /
tvayi karmaphalanyāsa-kṛtāmaiśvaryamīśa yat //87//

O Lord (Īśa, O Lord), that [*grāma*] is not destroyable. *Tat agrāmyaṁ*, that is not *grāmya*.

> There are two aspects, positions, of this organic action–two aspects. One is *grāma* and one is *grāmya*. Organic aspects are two-fold, [which are] working in a human being. Those human beings which are not elevated, which are ignorant, those organic actions[170] become *grāmya*, they are called "*grāmya*". *Grāmya* is just like the activity of those who are just like beasts, duffers, sheep, cows, bulls, and those human beings which are just like that. For instance, you see any beautiful young man and you want to have sex, that is *grāmya*, [because] you have become a beast; at that time, you are working just like a beast, just like a duffer. That is *grāmya*. *Grāma* is when you see some

170 "Organic action" refers to the way of your organs: *śabda*, *sparśa*, *rūpa*, *rasa*, and *gandha*, i.e, hearing, touching, seeing, tasting, and smelling.

beautiful person you will find the glory of God in him, and there will be no desire for sex there. That is *grāma*. There are two different aspects of mind in these organic activities. One is *grāma* and another is *grāmya*. *Grāmya* is the beast-like activity. *Grāma* is divine-like activity, when you find [that] everything is divine. You can kiss divinely also, you can have sex also divinely, but become divine. It is why in the beginning of the *Tantrāloka*, [Jayaratha] says:

Audio 5 (26:26)

śivaśaktyātmakaṁ rūpaṁ bhāvayecca parasparam /[171]

You must not think that you are mating with your wife or that you are mating with your husband–you should not think like that. You should think that, "My husband is Śiva and I am Pārvatī and we are mating like that. It is divine mating!"[172] That is what you should think. It will become *grāma* then. This activity will become *grāma*. Otherwise, it becomes *grāmya*. *Grāmya* is just beast-like.

That [*grāma*] is *abhaṅgi*, that is not destroyable, and that is not *grāmya*. [It is] *agrāmyam*, that is not *grāmya*, that is beyond this situation of *grāmya*. *Tat ekam upapattimat*, and [*grāma*] is to the point.[173] That is to the point, one hundred percent correct. Which point? *Tvayi karma phala-nyāsa kṛtām*

171 This is a quote from Jayaratha's commentary on the first verse of chapter one of Abhinavagupta's *Tantrāloka*.

172 Swamiji clarifies the culmination of this way of thinking with the following: "[When] the woman experiences that joy in her own brain, and the man experiences that joy in his own brain, that is double ecstasy, and as long as there is double union, double ecstasy, the act is not complete. But when this joy becomes only one in two, [then] the man experiences the female ecstasy and the female experiences the male ecstasy, these two ecstasies become one at that time when it is the complete act." Swami Lakshmanjoo, *Interview on Kashmir Shaivism*, with John Hughes (original audio recordings (1980), LJA archives, Los Angeles.

173 *Upapatti*, lit., proving right.

aiśvaryam, the glory which is obtained, which is attained, by those *sādhakas* while abandoning all actions in Your nature. *Karma phalanyāsaṁ*, all of those fruits of their actions, they surrender in Your nature. For those [*sādhakas*], all actions become *abhaṅgi*, and *agrāmya*, and *upapatti* (to the point).

JOHN: *Abhaṅgi* means?

SWAMIJI: *Abhaṅgi* means, it is not destroyed.

GANJOO: Indestructible.

SWAMIJI: Un-destructible . . . indestructible? Indestructible and *agrāmya*, not *grāmya*. You know "*grāmya*"?

ERNIE: Yes.

SWAMIJI: *Bas*.

JOHN: What does that mean, "not destructible"? I mean, because . . .

SWAMIJI: It is not destroyed! For instance, [when] you have sex, it is destroyed; in another moment, it is destroyed, it is nowhere. But when you adopt sex in the *grāma dharma*,[174] it will rise, rise, rise, rise always, because there will be the touch of divine consciousness there. Many people, while doing sex, many people have risen to God consciousness by the grace of Lord Śiva. This is the very nearest avenue to reach there! What?

DEVOTEES: Sex.

SWAMIJI: Yes, sex.

Audio 5 (28:58)

क्षमः कां नापदं हन्तुं कां दातुं संपदं न वा ।
योऽसौ स दयितोऽस्माकं देवदेवो वृषध्वजः ॥८८॥

kṣamaḥ kāṁ nāpadaṁ hantuṁ kāṁ dātuṁ saṁpadaṁ na vā /
yo'sau sa dayito'smākaṁ devadevo vṛṣadhvajaḥ //88//

That Being (*yaḥ*, that being)–in other words, that Lord Śiva–*kṣamaḥ kāṁ nāpadaṁ hantuṁ*, what is that *āpada*, . . .

174 The essential quality or character (*dharma*) of *grāma*.

Apada means, that torture; *āpada* is . . .

JOACHIM: Misfortune.

SWAMIJI: . . . misfortune. Yes, misfortune.

. . . [what is] that bad luck, which is not destroyed by Him? *Kṣamaḥ kāṁ nāpadam hantuṁ*, what misfortune, what bad luck, is not destroyed by that Being? And *kām dātum saṁpadaṁ na vā*, what kind of glory, what beautiful glory, is not released by Him, is not bestowed by that Being? Which Being?

DEVOTEES: Lord Śiva.

SWAMIJI: Lord Śiva. And that Lord Śiva, I will tell you in brief words, is my beloved; *sa dayito asmākaṁ*, He is my beloved, I love Him.[175] *Devadeva*, He is the Lord of lords. *Vṛṣa dhvajaḥ*, and He has got a flag of a bull, and He is my beloved who is capable of doing this. Capable of doing what? All misfortunes He destroys instantaneously, and all glories He bestows in one moment. He is capable of doing these two things. And He is the one who is loved by me, who is my friend. *Dayito asmākaṁ*, and He is the Lord of lords, and He has got a flag in His hand with a picture of a bull.[176]

Audio 5 (31:04)

मायामयमलान्धस्य दिव्यस्य ज्ञानचक्षुषः ।
निर्मलीकरणे नाथ त्वद्भक्तिः परमाञ्जनम् ॥८९॥

māyāmayamalāndhasya divyasya jñānacakṣuṣaḥ /
nirmalīkaraṇe nātha tvadbhaktiḥ paramāñjanam //89//

O Lord, I am really blind, *māyāmāyīmalāndhasya*, because the dust/impurity of *māyīyamala*, the impurity of the

175 "*Dayito asmākaṁ*, He is our daddy. *Dayito* means, lovable daddy, who is never rebuking you, who is always behaving with love-full words, love-full behavior." *Special Verses on Practice*, verse 41.

176 "The flag is the indicator of His absolute full knowledge and action." *Stava Cintāmaṇi* (1990).

ignorance of Your nature, has covered my eyesight, *māyā-māyīmala-andhasya*, and I have become blind altogether. Although *divyasya jñāna cakṣuṣaḥ*, although my sight is divine, filled with the knowledge of God, but even then my eyesight is made blind by putting that, by the covering of the impurity of, *māyā mala*. And there is only one way to destroy this, to remove this *mala* from my eyes; *nirmalī karaṇe*, to . . .

JOACHIM: Stainless or spotless.

GANJOO: For cleaning the eyes.

SWAMIJI: . . . clean the surface of the eyes, there is only one [medicinal] dust. *Añjana* is that *surmā*. What is that?

JOACHIM: Ointment . . .

GANJOO: Powder.

SWAMIJI: Powder. That *añjana*.

JOACHIM: Antimony.

GANJOO: Antimony powder.

SWAMIJI: The only antimony for clearance of my eyesight is just Thy *bhakti*, only Your devotion. That will make it clear. Give me that. I want That love which I must have for this [blindness].

Audio 5 (33:02)

निर्भयं यद्यदानन्द-मयमेकं यदव्ययम् ।
पदं देह्येहि मे देव तूर्णं तत्किं प्रतीक्षसे ॥९०॥

nirbhayaṁ yadyadānanda-mayamekaṁ yadavyayam /
padaṁ dehyehi me deva tūrṇaṁ tatkiṁ pratīkṣase //90//

Deva, O Lord, Your state, Your own state, which is *nirbhayaṁ* (without any fear, there is no fear of any kind), and That is *ānandamayam* (It is filled with joy), *ekam*, and that state of Yours is *ekam* (only one and unique), and *avyayam* (not perishable, it does not vanish at any cost), that state of Your Self, Your nature, I want to have. So, O Lord Śiva, *ehi*, come near me and give me That state, bestow me with That state, *tūrṇaṁ*, but immediately. Why do You wait? Why do You hesitate? Please do [it], and do it now.

This is what he says in this [verse].

Audio 5 (34:15)

अहो निसर्गगम्भीरो घोरःसंसारसागरः ।
अहो तत्तरणोपायः परः कोऽपि मकेश्वरः ॥९१॥

aho nisargagambhīro ghoraḥ saṁsārasāgaraḥ /
aho tattaraṇopāyaḥ paraḥ ko'pi maheśvaraḥ //91//

Aho, this is a great tragedy, this is a great torture for me to say that, *nisarga gambhīraḥ ghoraḥ saṁsāra sāgaraḥ*, this is the great ocean of the world, of repeated births and deaths. The cycle of repeated births and deaths is the greatest ocean, the biggest vast ocean of the world in which you are entangled by the cycle of repeated births and deaths. And it is *nisarga*, there is no beginning of this, there is no bottom. It is a bottomless ocean. There is no bottom, so it is endless. And it is *gaṁbhīra*, and very deep. And it is very terrifying, this *ghoraḥ saṁsāra sāgaraḥ*.[177]

JOHN: "Bottom" or "beginningless"? Because if . . .

SWAMIJI: There is no surface of that [ocean], on which this water is resting.

JOHN: In other words, the water didn't come from something else that was before that. It was always existing.

SWAMIJI: Yes. *Ghoraḥ saṁsāra sāgaraḥ*, this is a great tragedy for me to just see that, in front me, this is the position what I feel in this world, in this universe, this . . .

JOHN: Ocean of *saṁsāra*.

SWAMIJI: . . . ocean of *saṁsāra*. And, at the same time, this is a great joy to me, a joy to me to say, "*Aho*, . . ."

[This] "*aho*" is for joy. The first "*aho*" is for tragedy.[178]

177 The terrifying (*ghoraḥ*) ocean (*sāgaraḥ*) of repeated births and deaths (*saṁsāra*).

178 "*Aho*" is a particle which, in the first instance, implies painful astonishment, and in the second, joyful astonishment.

. . . this is a great tragedy to say that this is the position of *saṁsāra* in which I live. It is very deep, it is very fearful, and it is very threatening–this ocean of *saṁsāra*. And, at the same time, this is very joyful news here at the same time, that *tat taraṇopāyaḥ*, to make you cross this whole universe, this ocean of *saṁsāra*, there is one *taraṇopāya*,[179] that the Being who will make you cross this ocean is Lord Śiva. Lord Śiva is also existing here to make you, just to push you, on the other side of this universe.

Audio 5 (37:02)

नमः कृतकृतान्तान्त तुभ्यं मदनमर्दिने ।
मस्तकन्यस्तगङ्गाय यथायुक्तार्थकारिणे ॥९२॥

namaḥ kṛtakṛtāntānta tubhyaṁ madanamardine /
mastakanyastagaṅgāya yathāyuktārthakāriṇe //92//

O Lord Śiva, I bow to You. I want to prostrate before You because You have done very beautiful things for Your [own] person. You have done very beautiful things for Your [own] person, not for me. Who am I? I am just trodden down, I have nothing to say. But I have to say that You have been so much interested in Your own self![180]

DEVOTEES: (laughter)

SWAMIJI: *Kṛtakṛtānta*–the first thing You have done–*kṛtakṛtānta*, You have got rid of the lord of death, You have conquered the lord of death, so You will never die. For Your [own] person, You have done a great favor–for Your [own] person–that You have killed, conquered, the lord of death. And, at the same time, what have You done, what [is the] next good [thing] You have done for Your [own] person? That is *madana mardine*, You have conquered the lord of love also. He will never conquer You. Whenever You like to have sex, You will have sex, not by any . . . You won't be pressurized by the

179 The means (*upāya*) of salvation (*taraṇa*).
180 "That which suits You, You keep for Yourself, and You keep us full of gaps. I bow to You." *Stava Cintāmaṇi* (1990).

lord of love.[181] You have done this favor also for Yourself, *mastaka nyasta gaṅgāya*, . . .

> And, at the same time, we are always craving for water. You see [our] water supplies.[182] Sometimes it is with mud, sometimes it is not filtered, sometimes it is not chlorinated, and everything, it is always like that. We don't have good water, so we have to rush to Cheshmashahi.[183]
>
> **DENISE:** (laughs)

SWAMIJI:
. . . and for Your [own] person–what favor have You done for Yourself?–*mastaka*, You have put a water pipe, a fresh water pipe, on Your head!

DEVOTEES: (laughter)

SWAMIJI: (laughter) The Gaṅgā (the Ganges). *Yathā yukta ārtha kāriṇe*, You have done a great favor for Yourself, I must say it–*yathā yukta ārtha kāriṇe*.

Audio 5 (39:14)

ऐश्वर्यज्ञानवैराग्य-धर्मेभ्योऽप्युपरि सथितिम् ।
नाथ प्रार्थयमानानां त्वदृते का परा गतिः ॥९३॥

aiśvaryajñānavairāgya-dharmebhyo'pyupari sthitim /
nātha prārthayamānānāṁ tvadṛte kā parā gatiḥ //93//

There are four aspects, four great aspects, in this world, which are to be possessed by *sādhaka*s [aspirants]. There is *dharma*, *jñāna*, *vairāgya*, and *aiśvarya*. *Dharma* means, the aspects of good actions (you want to do good actions in this world). You want to [have] *jñāna* (knowledge), you want to

181 "You have nothing to do with a love affair and You have no such anxiety left." Ibid. See also verse 82.
182 Referring to the water supply in Srinagar.
183 A fresh-water spring in Srinagar where Swamiji use to collect drinking water.

realize the state of God consciousness (this is another good thing). You want to be detached from filthy things (*vairāgya*).[184] *Dharma*, *jñāna*, [*vairāgya*], and you want to possess *aiśvarya*, glory on all sides. These are the four aspects, which you want to have in this world.[185] *Upari sthitiṁ*, but above that is Your seat of nature. Above these, above these four great aspects in this world, is the position of Your seat on which You reside. So, You have *dharma*, You have *jñāna*, You have *vairāgya*, You have *aiśvarya*, You have all of these four aspects under Your command.[186] *Nātha prārthyamānānāṁ tvadṛte kā parā gatiḥ*, so, if we want to hanker after these four aspects, if you want to have these four aspects in this world, there is no way. The only one way is just to approach You. Only by approaching You, you can possess these four aspects.[187]

Have you understood it?

Audio 5 (41:10)

त्वय्यनिच्छति कः शंभो शक्तः कुब्जयितुं तृणम् ।
त्वदिच्छानुगृहीतस्तु वहेद्ब्राह्मीं धुरं न कः ॥९४॥

tvayyanicchati kaḥ śaṁbho śaktaḥ kubjayituṁ tṛṇam /
tvadicchānugṛhītastu vahedbrāhmīṁ dhuraṁ na kaḥ //94//

---

184 "Detachment from the world." Ibid.

185 "These four reside there in that kind of intellect, which is in *sukha*, which is in joy. You find joy in *dharma*, you find joy in *jñāna*, in *vairagya*, and *aiśvarya*. *Aiśvarya* is not limited *aiśvarya*. *Aiśvarya* is *svātantrya*. When you are absolutely independent to go inside your God consciousness, that is *aiśvarya*. *Aiśvarya* is not to construct a house–that is not *aiśvarya*, that is not glory. Glory is that state of being when you want to enter in God consciousness and you have that power to enter. That is *aiśvarya*. It is produced by that intellect which is residing in the cycle of *ānanda* (bliss)." *Parātrīśikā Vivaraṇa* (1982-85).

186 "For us, You have bestowed *adharma* (bad deeds), *rāga* (attachment), *ajñāna* (ignorance), and *anaiśvarya* (being a pauper) and wanting everything." *Stava Cintāmaṇi* (1990).

187 "O beloved God, if You do not come to our rescue, we will be grabbed by *māyā* and totally trodden down." Ibid.

Tvayyanicchati, if You don't like, if Y
anicchati, you don't wish), *kaḥ*, who is
Śambho, O Lord Śiva, *śaktaḥ*, can be cap
blade of grass? You can't bend one piece of a
you can't bend it, if You don't like that it should be be

---

188 "Once there was a dispute in heaven amongst the *deva*s (gods), Agni (fire), Vāyu (wind), and Indra (thunder); Indra is in the east, Agni is in the southeast, and Vāyu is in the northwest). All of them said, "We are great!" But they misunderstood that Lord Śiva had bestowed their greatness, and they thought they had acquired these powers themselves somewhere in heaven. At that time, sitting on some rock and witnessing this argument was an old Kashmiri pundit with a *tilak* on his forehead. Indra asked the others, "Who is this old man?" They told Vāyu to go blow that man away. Then Vāyu reached near him and asked the old man on the rock, "Who are you?" The old man said to Vāyu, "Who are you?" Vāyu said in response, "I am Vāyu." The old man said, "What is your power?" Vāyu said, "I could blow the whole Earth and the mountains [away] with my wind!" The old man cut one little piece of straw and challenged Vāyu to blow it away, but it did not move. The old man told Vāyu, "Get out, you rascal!" Indra asked Vāyu what happened and Vāyu said, "He is furious and he is so great. Please, I will not go back because I am afraid." Then Indra asked Agni to go and burn that old man saying, "The problem will be finished as he is interrupting our divine meeting." Agni went there and asked the man, "Who are you?" The old man asked, "Who are you?" "I am Agni, the god of fire. I can burn the whole world!" The old man showed him the piece of straw again, and with all his might, Agni tried to burn it but was unable. The old man kicked him out shouting, "You rascal!" After that, Indra said, "I will go myself. It is not in your power. He seems to be a very great personality, so wait here," but as soon as Indra reached the rock, both the pundit and the rock disappeared. Indra tried to find him and went into the ether to search for him, and after 300 years he was still searching. And after some time, an airplane came and in that plane was Pārvatī. Indra stopped that plane and said, "O Pārvatī, I want to know something from You, please wait." Pārvatī appeared through the window and She said, "O Indra, that was the supreme God, Lord Śiva, who gave you one drop of His glory and you became so powerful. That Brahmin was Lord Śiva Himself." Then, Agni, Vāyu, and Indra understood that Lord Śiva's glory has glorified them

DENISE: If He doesn't like it to be bent, it won't be bent.

SWAMIJI: It won't be bent even with great power! If you put all your power to bend it, it won't bend.

ERNIE: If Lord Śiva doesn't wish that.

SWAMIJI: *Tvad icchānugṛhīta*, [but] if You wish, a pauper can become Lord Śiva. A pauper can reside on the seat of Lord Śiva if there is desire in You, if You wish like that. *Tvad iccha-anugṛhītastu*, if You bless somebody with Your will, with Your sweet will, *vahed brahmīṁ*, who will not posses the state of Brahmā,[189] the state of God consciousness? Everybody will possess it. So, it is up to You! If You can make me rise, You can make me rise. If You don't wish, I will just fall. It is up to You. It is just only Your desire, just Your sweet desire, sweet will.

Audio 5 (43:00)

हरप्रणतिमाणिक्य-मुकुटोत्कटमस्तकाः ।
नमेयुः कं परं कं वा नमयेयुर्न धीधनाः ॥९५॥

harapraṇatimāṇikya-mukuṭotkaṭamastakāḥ /
nameyuḥ kaṁ paraṁ kaṁ vā namayeyurna dhīdhanāḥ //95

Those people who are intellectually advanced, who *hara-praṇa-timāṇikyamukuṭotkaṭa mastakāḥ*, who have got "fortunate foreheads," those persons who have got fortunate foreheads by bending, by doing prostrations, at the feet of Lord Śiva–those fortunate foreheads, so fortunate foreheads are those–and those who are intellectually advanced, those persons who are intellectually advanced, will never bow before You because there is no approach, [so] they won't prostrate before You, they will prostrate before those persons who have got those fortunate foreheads [by] prostrating [before] You. So, you must bow before those who bow [before] You.

---

and it was not their own power. Pārvatī told Indra, "Lord Śiva wanted to see you, so He disguised Himself as a Kashmiri pundit just to test your egos." *Stava Cintāmaṇi* (1990).

189 That is, Brahman (the Absolute).

Audio 5 (44:16)

सर्वविभ्रमनिर्मोक-निष्कम्पममृतह्रदम् ।
भवत्ज्ञानाम्बुधेर्मध्यमध्यासीयापि धूर्जटे ॥९६॥

sarvavibhramanirmoka-niṣkampamamṛtahradam /
bhavatjñānāmbudhermadhyam-adhyāsīyāpi dhūrjaṭe //96//

Dhūrjaṭe, O Lord Śiva . . .

(verse repeated)

. . . O Lord Śiva, let me [have] *bhavat jñānam budher*, from the ocean of Your knowledge, from the unlimited ocean of Your knowledge, please favor me [in that] You get out from the unlimited ocean of Your knowledge, You get out from that ocean, *sarva vibhrama nirmoka niṣkampam-amṛta-hradam*, the essence of nectar, [and bestow it to me].

Because, always in the ocean you will find nectar. It is our tradition, of [our] historical tradition, that nectar lies in the ocean. In that important ocean, there is nectar also. There is poison also, but there is nectar also. In Kṣīra-sāgara, there is nectar, which nectar was used by the gods and they became immortal.[190]

So, I don't want that nectar which made them immortal. I want from Your Ocean, from the ocean of Your knowledge, I want to have that nectar which is lying in the ocean of Your knowledge. Please get it out from Your ocean of knowledge, get it out and bestow it to me.

Audio 5 (46:20)

चित्रं यच्चित्रदृष्टोऽपि मनोरथगतोऽपि वा ।
परमार्थफलं नाथ परिपूर्णं प्रयच्छसि ॥९७॥

190 For more on the churning of the milky ocean (Kṣīrasāgara), see Kṣemarāja's introduction, verse 4, pages 2-7.

citraṁ yaccitradṛṣṭo'pi manorathagato'pi vā /
paramārthaphalaṁ nātha paripūrṇaṁ prayacchasi //97//

O Lord Śiva, this is a great wonder to me (*citram*, this is a great wonder to me) to say that, *yat citra dṛṣṭo'si*, if You are seen on a picture also, if Your image is seen on a picture (if Lord Śiva's image is seen on a picture), *manorathagato*, although You are beyond the imagination of one's mind (you cannot think of Lord Śiva), but the wonder is that if somebody sees Your figure on some picture, on some painting, *paramārtha phalaṁ nātha paripūrṇam*, the greatness is, the wonder is, that You bestow upon him the supreme fruit of God consciousness–to him also, who concentrates on a picture, a picture of You.[191]

Audio 5 (47:28)

को गुणैरधिकस्त्वत्तः त्वत्तः को निर्गुणोऽधिकः ।
इति नाथ नुमःकिं तवां (स्तुम् नुमः जुं त्वां)
किं निन्दामो न मन्महे ॥९८॥

ko guṇairadhikastvattaḥ tvattaḥ ko nirguṇo'dhikaḥ /
iti nātha numaḥ kiṁ tvāṁ (stum numaḥ kiṁ tvāṁ)[192]
kiṁ nindāmo na manmahe //98//

O Lord Śiva, who is more qualified than You in this world? You are the only person who is fully qualified. Who is beyond qualification in this world (*nirguṇa*, who is disqualified in this world) except for You?[193] You are the only person who is fully qualified and You are the only person who is fully dis-

---

191 Kṣemarāja quotes this verse in his commentary for verse 23, which Swamiji translated as follows: "If you see a photograph of Lord Śiva with great love, [by] just [observing] that Lord Śiva is very beautiful, by only that you will get liberation. This is the power of Lord Śiva." *Stava Cintāmaṇi* (1991).

192 Swamiji reworded this line of the verse and added "*stumaḥ*" to emphasize the act of bowing to Lord Śiva.

193 *Nirguṇa*, lit., worthless, [without any qualities].

qualified. In this way, I am confused what to do. Should I praise You or should I defame You? I can't understand what I should do. If You are fully qualified, I should praise You. If You are disqualified, I should defame You. What should I do? Tell me. You are fully qualified and You are fully disqualified (because You are *nirguṇa*). *Ko guṇair adhikaḥ tvattaḥ*, who is *guṇair adhikaḥ*, who is more qualified than You? No one except You are the only qualified being in this world. *Tvattaḥ ko nirguṇo adhikaḥ*, who is more disqualified in this world than You? *Iti*, in this way, *nātha*, O Lord, *numaḥ kiṁ tvāṁ*, should I praise You or *kim nindāmo*, should I defame You?[194] *Na manmahe*, I can't understand what I should do. I am confused. I have come to no conclusion because I want to praise You because You are qualified and I want to defame You because You are disqualified. What should I do?

Bas, 98th beginning.

JOHN: We've finished the 98th.

SWAMIJI: Ninety-eighth is finished. I think we will do it, we will finish it!

Audio 5 (49:36)

कीर्तनेऽप्यमृतौघस्य यत्प्रसक्तेः फलं तव ।
तत्पातुमपि कोऽन्योऽलं किमु दातुं जगत्पते ॥९९॥

kīrtane'pyamṛtaughasya yatprasatteḥ phalaṁ tava /
tatpātumapi ko'nyo'laṁ kimu dātuṁ jagatpate //99//

Just to explain the state of the joy of God consciousness, when the state of the joy of God consciousness is explained by somebody to some other person, that the joy of God consciousness is just like this and like that, *yatprasatteḥ phalam*, by explaining that, *yat phalam prasatteḥ*, whatever fruit is produced by explaining the state of the joy [of God consciousness], *ko'nyo'lam kimu dātum jagatpate*, O Lord, that fruit, that tasteful fruit, is so great and so [much] in a grand

194 "Should I love You for all of Your qualifications or hate You for all of Your disqualifications?" *Stava Cintāmaṇi* (1990).

scale–that fruit of my explaining, when I explain the joy of God consciousness, that, "I have experienced in this way the joy of God consciousness"–the nectar that oozes out in abundance, who can, . . . nobody can, after hearing also, nobody can just taste It. *Tat pātum api ko anya alaṁ*, nobody can taste That, nobody can taste the nectar of that Consciousness, that joy, although It is explained to him by the person who has experienced It. *Kimu dātum jagatpate*, so, this joy of God consciousness cannot be bestowed to anybody. Only It [can be] bestowed to him who has experienced It. You can't hand over this joy and . . .

JOHN: It's not transferable.

SWAMIJI: You can't share It.

DENISE: You can't give somebody That experience.

SWAMIJI: No, you can't share It. It is not shareable. It is so great that you can't share It.

Audio 5 (51:54)

निःशेषप्रार्थनीयार्थ-सार्थसिद्धिनिधानतः ।
त्वत्तस्त्वद्भक्तिमेवाप्तुं प्रार्थये नाथ सर्वथा ॥ १०० ॥

niḥśeṣaprārthanīyārtha-sārthasiddhinidhānataḥ /
tvattastvadbhaktimevāptuṁ prārthaye nātha sarvathā / / 100

O Lord, now, *niḥśeṣa prārthanīyārtha-sārtha-siddhi-nidhānataḥ*, You are the abode, You are the treasure (*nidhānataḥ* means, You are the treasure), of *niḥśeṣa prārthanīyārtha*, all achievements of great things. All achievements of great things are there. Where? In that treasure of Your God consciousness. Whatever you want to have, it will be bestowed from That store, That storage. Which storage? The treasure of God consciousness. If it is so, that one is capable to achieve anything from That treasure, but for me, if You ask me, *tvattas tvad bhaktimevāptuṁ prārthaye nātha sarvathā*, I ask from That treasure, I ask [You] just to give me that, bestow me that, devotion towards You. I don't want anything else. Although there are so many things existing in That treasure, from That treasure I ask only that You give me devotion for You, that is all. I want, *bas*, to develop Your devotion.

Audio 5 (53:36)

नमस्त्रैलोक्यनाथय तुभ्यं भव भवज्जुषाम् ।
त्रिलोकीनाथतादान-निर्विनायकशक्तये ॥ १०१ ॥

namastrailokyanāthaya tubhyaṁ bhava bhavajjuṣām /
trilokīnāthatādāna-nirvināyakaśaktaye //101//

O Lord, You are *nātha* (*nātha* means, the master of all of the three worlds). *Namaḥ trailokya nāthaya*, I bow to You who is the Master of all of the three worlds. O Lord, *bhavat juṣām trilokī nāthatādāna nirvināyaka śaktaye*, You have got the capacity (*śaktaye*, capacity; *nirvināyaka śaktaye*, without any hindrance), without any hindrance You possess the capacity of bestowing to Your devotees the kingdom of the three worlds, which You have already [in Your possession]. You are the King of the three worlds, and [with] that kingdom of the three worlds, You can bestow this, You have got the capacity to bestow the capacity of becoming the ruler of the three worlds. I bow to You.[195]

JOHN: He has the capacity of bestowing . . . ?

SWAMIJI: Bestowing everything! Whatever He possesses, He can give it to anybody. He is not just maintaining something for Himself. For instance, you have got one *lakh* of dollars.[196] You can't give away that one *lakh* of dollars. You will naturally keep something for your household expenditure and the remaining portion of that money you will give to people. But He does not [do that]. The nature of Lord Śiva is not like

195 "The whole kingdom, which You possess, You give it to any devotee . . . willingly. After that, You possess nothing and You are a beggar begging from door-to-door. There is no reason why You have given [away] Your whole kingdom, it is only [by] Your choice." *Stava Cintāmaṇi* (1990).
196 $100,000.

that. The nature of Lord Siva is, whatever He has, He gives it, and He again has more and more.

End of Audio 5 (55:40)

Start of Audio 6 (00:00)

निःशेषक्लेशहानस्य हेतुः क इति संशये ।
स्वामिन्सोऽसीति निश्चित्य कस्त्वां न शरणं गतः ॥ १०२ ॥

niḥśeṣakleśahānasya hetuḥ ka iti saṁśaye /
svāminso'sīti niścitya kastvāṁ na śaraṇaṁ gataḥ //102//

If there is a doubt in people, if you *iti saṁśaya*, if there is some doubt in some masters, a doubt in asking this question: "[For] removing all of the worries and troubles of the world, who has this capacity," when this question comes in some person, in some seeker's [mind], *svāminso'sīti niścitya kastvāṁ na śa-* . . . , [the answer is], You are That person only. And by this thinking, "*Kastvam na śaraṇaṁ*, in all of the three worlds, who is that person who has not taken Your refuge," [the answer is], everybody has taken Your refuge because You are the only person, You are the only Being, who can remove all of the worries and troubles and ups and downs of the world. Who has not come to Your refuge (*kastvāṁ na śaraṇam gataḥ*)?

Audio 6 (01:14)

भुक्त्वा भोगान्भवभ्रान्तिं हित्वा लप्स्ये परं पदम् ।
इत्याशंसेह शोभेत शंभौ भक्तिमतः परम् ॥ १०३ ॥

bhuktvā bhogānbhavabhrāntiṁ hitvā lapsye paraṁ padam /
ityāśaṁseha śobheta śaṁbhau bhaktimataḥ param //103//

Iti āśaṁśā, this kind of longing, this kind of desire, that, "I would like to *bhuktvā bhogān*, I would like to enjoy the pleasures of this universe, and after enjoying the pleasures of this universe; *bhava bhrāntiṁ hitvā*, I would like to remove all of the cycle of ignorance of this world (*ajñāna*); I don't want to remove my ignorance just for the sake of removing ignorance, I want to remove my ignorance after enjoyment of this world; I will enjoy this world, then remove the ignorance of this universe, and *lapsye param padam*, and then I will come under the seat of Your footrest," this kind of longing is seen only in Your devotees and none else–real devotees. Real devotees do this kind of longing, they have got these longings. What kind of longings?

JOACHIM: To be under the footrest of Lord Śiva.

SWAMIJI: No, not to only just directly go and remain at the footrest of Lord Śiva's feet. No.

DENISE: They want to enjoy the world.

SWAMIJI: They want to enjoy this world, and then remove all kinds of delusion, and then reach the abode of that God consciousness–the seat.

JOHN: Why is it held, why does he say, that real devotees . . .

SWAMIJI: This is Śaivism. [Śaivites] don't want to discard the enjoyment of the world. This is Śaivism, sir! After enjoying all of the pleasures of the world, I want to take refuge near You. That is a good idea (laughs)!

DEVOTEES: (laughter)

GANJOO: While enjoying!

SWAMIJI: While enjoying. *Na bhuktvār cana*? "*Ktvā-tosun-kasunaḥ*."[197] This is [what] the grammarian, Pāṇini, has told [us], that where there is *ktvā pratyaya*, the [suffix] "*ktvā*," *ktvā* means, e.g., "*bhuktvā gacchati*" [or] "*bhuktvā vrajati*"; *bhuktvā*,[198] he does this, and after doing this, he does that; after enjoying the good things of this universe, he takes the refuge of Lord Śiva. [He does] not only take refuge [of Lord Śiva] and discard the good things of the world. No, that is not the real way of Śaivism. The real way of Śaivism is, just while enjoyment . . .

GANJOO: *Kāṅkṣya*.

---

197 From Pāṇini's *Aṣṭādhyāyī*, 1.1.40.
198 Having enjoyed or eaten or possessed.

SWAMIJI: *Kāṅkṣya*[199] does not matter.

. . . while [enjoying], you must get entry in God consciousness–while enjoying this universe. And this kind of longing, only *śobheta* (*śobheta*, it is decorated), it gets decorated only in Your devotees.

Audio 6 (05:08)

नाथ स्वप्नेऽपि यत्कुर्यां ब्रूयां वा साध्वसाधु वा ।
त्वदधीनत्वदर्पेण सर्वत्रात्रास्मि निर्वृतः ॥१०४॥

nātha svapne'pi yatkuryāṁ brūyāṁ vā sādhvasādhu vā /
tvadadhīnatvadarpeṇa sarvatrātrāsmi nirvṛtaḥ //104//

Nātha, O my desired One (*nātha* means, O my desired One), O Lord Śiva, *svapne api*, whatever I do in my dreaming state, *brūyām vā sādhvasādhu vā*, whatever I speak, good or nonsense in this world, *tvadadhīnatvadarpeṇa sarvatra atrāsmi nirvṛta*, let me merge in Your nature of God consciousness everywhere, in each and every respect. Whatever I do, whatever I do in the dreaming state, whatever I say, whatever I speak, in this daily routine of life, whatever I say, good or bad, whatever I say, let that become divine, *tvad adhīnatva darpeṇa*, and let that be reflected in the mirror of God consciousness always. And *sarvatra atrāsmi nirvṛta*, let me merge in God consciousness in each and every respect of the daily routine of life, not only at the time of meditation.[200]

While feeding Viresh also, you must merge in that God consciousness. That is the real way of Śaivism. Do you know?

---

199 Desire.

200 "In these two cases of dreaming and wakefulness, I see there is no room for these opposite behaviors of good and bad because they are both residing in Your state of Parabhairava. So, in both ways I am rested in Parabhairava by these two different activities." *Stava Cintāmaṇi* (1990).

Audio 6 (06:47)

ज्योतिषामपि यज्ज्योतिस्तत्र त्वद्धाम्नि धावतः ।
चित्तस्येष तमःस्परशो मन्ये वन्ध्यात्मजानुजः ॥ १०५ ॥

jyotiṣāmapi yajjyotistatra tvaddhāmni dhāvataḥ /
cittasyeśa tamaḥsparśo manye vandhyātmajānujaḥ //105//

Jyotiṣāmapi yat jyoti, That Light which is the light of all lights (*jyotiṣāmapi jyoti*), *tatra tvad dhāmni*, and that is Your abode, that is Your place, that is Your residential abode. What?

JOACHIM: The Light of lights.

SWAMIJI: The Light of lights. And whenever *cittasya*, any mind, *tatra dhāvataḥ*, is directed towards That Light, any mind which is directed towards That Light–which light?–which is the Light of all lights and which is Your abode, and for that mind, if there is the apprehension of darkness–this kind of thinking that there may be apprehension of darkness sometime, on some occasion; [that on a] rare occasion, there will be some traces of darkness existing in that mind–this kind of thinking is as good as this thinking that a barren woman has a child (laughter).

DENISE: It's absurd.

SWAMIJI: It is absurd. It is absolutely impossible. The mind will always be shining for the whole life–then. So there is no possibility of that mind to get entry in any case in darkness then, if it is directed towards That . . .

JOHN: Light of lights.

SWAMIJI: . . . Light of lights.

Audio 6 (08:50)

मन्ये न्यस्तपदः सोऽपि क्षेम्ये मोक्षस्य वर्तमनि ।
मनोरथः स्थितो यस्य सेविष्ये शिवमित्ययम् ॥ १०६ ॥

manye nyastapadaḥ so'pi kṣemye mokṣasya vartmani /
manorathaḥ sthito yasya seviṣye śivamityayam //106//

From my thinking, this is my understanding (*manye* means, this is my understanding), *mokṣasya vartmani*, on the path of liberation, the path on which you are liberated from repeated births and deaths, and which is *kṣemye*, the great protector (that path is always protecting a man [person]), from my viewpoint, from my thinking, I believe (*manye*, I believe) that, *so'pi nyasta padaḥ*, he has also stepped on that path, he has also stepped on that path, . . .

Which path?

JOHN: Path of liberation.

SWAMIJI: Path of liberation.

. . . who *yasya manoratha sthitaḥ*, who have only longings, who have only longings: "When that time will come when I will meditate on God? When that time will come when I will merge in God?" This kind of [having] only longings, anybody who has only this kind of longing in his mind, from my viewpoint, he has also stepped on that path. Who? He who has only longings, who has not stepped [on the path] at all, but who has only longings that he would like to tread on that path. He is treading.

JOHN: Already.

SWAMIJI: He is treading already. He is on the path.[201]

---

201 On this point, Kṣemarāja references a verse by Abhinavagupta: "'Oh, it is too late! It is now 3:00 am.' If I am sleeping and the clock shows 3:00 am, I abruptly get up from bed and call all of my kith and kin to my bed and say, 'Leave your bed now! We will start meditating now and sing the glory of Parabhairava.' [Although] they sit only for five minutes and do nothing, and only by this longing that, 'I will get up and sit as it is time for meditation', only this longing takes them abruptly to the state of God consciousness. This is the greatness of Your Being. Longing carries them, not effort." *Stava Cintāmaṇi* (1990). The source text of this verse is unknown.

Audio 6 (10:46)

स्थित्युत्पत्तिलयैरलोकत्रयस्योपक्रियास्विह ।
एकैवेश भवच्छक्तिः स्वतन्त्रं तन्त्रमीक्षते ॥ १०७॥

sthityutpattilayairlokatrayasyopakriyāsviha /
ekaiveśa bhavacchaktiḥ svatantraṁ tantramīkṣate //107//

Sthiti utpatti layair loka trayasya upakriyāsu, the adjustment of these three worlds by its creation, by its protection, and by its destruction, this is how God adjusts this universe. God does not adjust this universe by creation only, [otherwise] everybody will get bored. They will never die and they will get bored (laughter).

GANJOO: Too much of population.

SWAMIJI: Not too much of . . . they will get bored with [having] only one body (laughter). So this is *upakāra*, it is a great favor He does for us, that, after creation, He destroys us. It is a great favor from Him that we receive. He protects us (this is also a favor). After protecting [us], He destroys us–it is a great favor from our Lord to us. Otherwise, we would remain always as one [the same person] and it would have been no fun (laughter). [If] always John was living for three thousand one hundred and so many years. What is there? We must [have] change. Everybody likes change. *Sthiti utpatti layair loka trayasya upakriyā*, so this is the great favor that God does to this threefold universe (*bhūḥ*, *bhuvaḥ*, and *svaḥ*).[202] *Ekaiveśa bhavat śaktiḥ svatantraṁ tantram-īkṣate*, there is one power, one great *śakti*, of Lord Śiva, who is capable of adjusting [life] in this way.[203]

Audio 6 (13:07)

त्रिलोक्यामिह कस्त्रातस्त्रिताप्या नोपतापितः ।
तस्मै नमोऽस्तु ते यस्त्वं तन्निर्वाणामृतह्रदः ॥ १०८॥

202 See verse 46, fn 85.
203 That is, Lord Śiva's *svātantrya śakti*. See Appendix 5.

trilokyāmiha kastrātastritāpyā nopatāpitaḥ /
tasmai namo'stu te yastvaṁ tannirvāṇāmṛtahradaḥ //108//

Trailokyām, in this cycle of the three worlds, *tritāpyā nopatāpitaḥ*, in this cycle of the three worlds, who is that person who is not put to great trouble by the threefold pains?

The three-fold pains you know? [They are], *ādhyātmika, ādhidaivika*, and *ādhibhautika.*[204] And *ādhyātmika* pain is of your mind, e.g., grief, sorrow, . . .

JOACHIM: Depressions and things.

SWAMIJI: . . . attachment, love, lust. This is also another pain. And *ādhidaivika* is [the pain that comes from] these thunders and earthquakes, etc. And *ādhibhautika* is [having] a headache, a toothache, a stomachache–everything. All of these three-fold pains are always existing in a being who is created in this universe.[205]

Tritāpya nopatāpitaḥ, who is that person who is not adjusted in these, who has not come in the grip of these threefold pains? And who is the protector who would relieve us from these threefold pains? *Trilokyāmiha kastrāta*, who is the protector from this, *tritāpyā nopatāpitaḥ*, who has not come in the grip of these threefold pains? *Tasmai namo'stu te yastvaṁ tat nirvāṇāmṛta hradaḥ*, I believe You are the only person, You are the only Being, who could rid us from this cycle of the three pains in this world and keep us, make us, rest in *nirvāṇa*

---

204 *Ādhyātmik*, concerning self or individual personality. *Ādhidaivika*, relating to or proceeding from gods or from spirits; proceeding from the influence of the atmosphere or planets, proceeding from divine or supernatural agencies. *Ādhibhautika*, belonging or relating to created beings; elementary, derived or produced from the primitive elements, material.

205 In his commentary, Kṣemarāja references a verse from Abhinavagupta's commentary of verse 40, chapter 18, of the Bhagavad Gītā: "Just from Brahmā to a mosquito, there is no one who is peaceful, and that uneasiness is found in everybody in this world." *Stava Cintāmaṇi* (1990).

amṛta hradaḥ (*amṛta hradaḥ* means, the lake of the nectar of God consciousness). And that nectar of God consciousness is just final liberation. You are the only Being to do that.[206]

Audio 6 (16:06)

कृत्रिमापि भवद्भक्तिरकृत्रिमफलोदया ।
निश्च्छद्मा चेद्भवेदेषा किंफलेति त्वयोच्यताम् ॥ १०९ ॥

kṛtrimāpi bhavadbhaktir-akṛtrimaphalodayā /
niścchadmā cedbhavedeṣā kiṁphaleti tvayocyatām / / 109 / /

I have got one doubt. O Lord, I have got one doubt, one question. I want to put that question before You, and that is, *kṛtimāpi bhavad bhaktir akṛtrima phalodayā*, it is a fact that if anybody who develops Your devotion, [which is] artificial devotion, not real devotion, . . .

> Artificial devotion is that kind of devotion when you devote [yourself to] Lord Śiva in the presence of people.
>
> **JOACHIM:** Showing off.
>
> **SWAMIJI:** Showing off. If anybody comes, you remain like this (Swamiji assumes a meditative posture)–this kind of devotion. He devotes, he devotes, internally he devotes at that moment, but for show. Let it be for show, but he devotes, he does something internally in the presence of people. That is the artificial way of Thy devotion.

. . . *kṛtrimāpi bhavad bhakti*, Your devotion[207] which is artificial, *akṛtrima phalodayā*, but the greatness of Your devotion is, because it is Your devotion, it will divert him towards that un-artificial devotion in the end. This is Your greatness. This is the greatness of Thy devotion. [Even] if that devotion is done artificially, it will divert one to its un-

206 "I bow to You, Lord Śiva, as You are the only one who can take people out of these threefold tortures." Ibid.
207 That is, devotion for Lord Śiva.

artificial state of devotion. This is a fact. Now, I have got one question to ask. That is, *niścchadma cet*, if anybody has got devotion, if anybody develops devotion for You, un-artificial [devotion] from the very beginning, what will come out of that? This is my doubt. I want to ask You, what happens to him in the end? The un-artificial devotion . . .

JOACHIM: Becomes un-artificial.

SWAMIJI: . . . becomes un-artificial. What will un-artificial devotion . . . where will un-artificial devotion be diverted? This is my question for You.

And no answer (laughter)

DEVOTEES: (laughter)

SWAMIJI: *Niścchadmā cedbhavedeṣā kiṁphaleti tvaya ucyatām*, let You explain it to me, the answer of this question.

Audio 6 (18:38)

तच्चक्षुरीक्ष्यसे येन सा गतिर्गम्यसे यया ।
फलं तदज जातं यत्त्वत्कथाकल्पपादपात् ॥ ११० ॥

taccakṣurīkṣyase yena sā gatirgamyase yayā /
phalaṁ tadaja jātaṁ yat-tvatkathākalpapādapāt //110//

That is an eye, that is a real eye, by which eye You are seen, You are observed. From my viewpoint, that is an eye. That is not an eye which does not observe Your state. That is a real eye, *yena īkṣyase*, by which eye You are seen. *Sā gatir*, that is stepping, that is stepping on, . . .

What is that stepping on? Walking.

. . . that is real walking, *yayā gamyate*, by which walking You are . . .

JOACHIM: Reached.

SWAMIJI: . . . You are reached. *Phalam tat*, and that is the fruit, *yat jātam*, which is created by the *Pādapa* Tree, by the fruit tree, of Your *kathā*, Your topics, the topics in connection with You.

The topics in connection with You, [Bhaṭṭa Nārāyaṇa] has made this the topics in connection with You, Your topics. Whenever you want to have gossip regarding what kind of [Being] is Lord Śiva, what is His action, what is His way of thinking–this kind of topic–and this kind of topic is a fruit tree. And whatever [comes] from this fruit tree, the fruit that comes, that is a fruit! It is not a fruit, this apple is not a fruit, which has created indigestion in me.

DEVOTEES: (laughter)

SWAMIJI: I took fruit yesterday and . . .

Tat cakṣurīkṣyase yena sā gatirgamyase yayā phalaṁ tat aja jātaṁ, O immortal Being (*aja* means, O immortal Being), that is [real] fruit which comes from the tree of Your gossip tree (*tvat kathā kalpa pādapā*).

JOHN: Which is the fruit? Any fruit. I mean, real fruit . . .

SWAMIJI: That is the real fruit, which comes out from the tree of Your discussions.[208]

Audio 6 (21:16)

श्रेयसा श्रेय एवैतदुपरि त्वयि या स्थितिः ।
तदन्तरायहृतये त्वमीश शरणं मम ॥ १११ ॥

śreyasā śreya evaitadupari tvayi yā sthitiḥ /
tadantarāyahṛtaye tvamīśa śaraṇaṁ mama //111//

Śreya is "the supreme state of joy."

JOACHIM: *Śreya*. From "*śrī*" or . . . ?

SWAMIJI: *Śrī–kalyāṇa*. That is the *kalyāṇa* of *kalyāṇa*, that is the 'joy of joys'. *Yā tvayi upari sthitiḥ*, that which is the state of Your existence, the state of Your God consciousness, is the state which is the joy of joys. *Tat antarāya hṛtaye*, and That state, I want to focus on That state, and while focusing on

208 "In the real sense, that is the fruit which has come out from reaching Your glory. That fruit is not from the *Pādapa* Tree in heaven in the real sense." *Stava Cintāmaṇi* (1990).

That state, I come across [and have to pass] through all kinds of obstacles in-between. Whenever I try to think of You, something comes in-between and distracts me from That point. That is *antarāya*.

Antarāya is *vighna*. What is "*vighna*"?

GANJOO: Obstruction.

SWAMIJI: Obstructions. Nothing else, *bas*.

JOACHIM: Hindrance.

SWAMIJI: Hindrance! And all of those hindrances should vanish from me. Those hindrances come while I meditate on You. *Tad antarāya hṛtaye*, for removing all of those hindrances, *tvamīśa śaraṇam*, I take refuge in Thee.[209]

Audio 6 (23:18)

अहो स्वादुतमः शर्व-सेवाशंसासुधारसः ।
कुत्र कालकामात्रे न यो नवनवायते ॥ ११२ ॥

aho svādutamaḥ śarva-sevāśaṁsāsudhārasaḥ /
kutra kālakalāmātre na yo navanavāyate / / 112 / /

Śarva sevāśaṁsā sudhārasaḥ (*śarva* means, Lord Śiva;[210] *sevā* means, just to think of Lord Śiva), *āśaṁsā*, and this thinking of Lord Śiva, this craving to think of Lord Śiva, . . .

> We are not capable of thinking of Lord Śiva, [but] we just crave that some time may come, by His grace, that we will have the capacity of thinking of Lord Śiva (that is *āśaṁsā*).[211]

. . . that craving is *sudhārasa*, that is the *rasa*, that is the

209 "The most precious seat of all is that seat by which one is seated in Your nature. I have come to this conclusion that Your seat is the real seat, but so many hindrances come and keep me away from Your abode. My only refuge is Your blessings. Otherwise, there is no hope for me to be seated there." Ibid.

210 *Śarva* is an appellation of Lord Śiva as Rudra, the destroyer.

211 Hope, expectation, desire.

nectar of supreme nectar, the taste of supreme nectar. And this taste of supreme nectar–this craving only!–it is *svādutama*, very sweet! *Aho svādutama*, it is very sweet, it is a wonderful point to put before [You] that, "It is very sweet." What is very sweet?

JOHN: This craving.

SWAMIJI: Only this craving!

DENISE: Craving to think about Lord Śiva.

SWAMIJI: The craving that, "I would like to think about Lord Śiva." *Kutra kālakalāmātre na yo nava*, and it is so sweet that, *kutra kālakalāmātre*, and where, on which point, does it not become afresh and afresh always? It is always giving you an injection of freshness if there is desire. If the desire is existing in you that you just want to think of Lord Śiva, this desire will always be [fresh], it won't be old, it will never become old. It will be freshened, it becomes [more] fresh, day-by-day, day-after-day.[212]

Audio 6 (25:28)

मुहुर्मुहुरविश्रान्तस्त्रैलोक्यं कल्पनाशतैः ।
कल्पयन्नपि कोऽप्येको निर्विकल्पो जयत्यजः ॥ ११३ ॥

muhurmuhuraviśrāntastrailokyaṁ kalpanāśataiḥ /
kalpayannapi ko'pyeko nirvikalpo jayatyajaḥ / / 113 / /

Aja means, He who is *ajanma*, He is without birth. It means, He is without birth, without death. *Aja* means, He who is not born, who does not die, that is, Lord Śiva. And He is *ko'pi* (*ko'pi* is, a very rare being–*ko'pi*). *Eka*, and He is only one. There are not such two beings. He is only one Lord Śiva, who is *muhur-muhur-aviśrā*, who is exhaustively *trailokyaṁ*,

---

212 "I would like to possess that taste of the nectar of Your meditation, which is sweeter than the sweetest thing in this world, and which does not get boring. On the contrary, as long as you taste that nectar, it gets sweeter as You taste more and more. The craving and desire of tasting it again becomes more than it was before. This is the greatness of the taste of Your nectar." *Stava Cintāmaṇi* (1990).

creating and manufacturing and developing the state of these three worlds along with its *prakṛti*, *kalpanāśataiḥ*, with so many unbelievable processes.

> You see, you will find in one blade of grass or you will find that fineness of *prakṛti* (nature),[213] how it is developed–in this one leaf of this tree. You will find the fineness of That [*prakṛti*] in that one leaf. What to think of all of these leaves?

Not only this–everywhere you will find the fineness of this manufacturing industry of Lord Śiva, who manufactures these three worlds with *kalpanā śataiḥ*, with so many hundreds and thousands of techniques. He puts those techniques in that. *Aviśrānta*, and He is not tired. Although He puts all of these techniques with great effort, but *ko'pi*, He is unique, and *nirvikalpa*, He is without *vikalpa*,[214] He has nothing to do, He has not to put any force in His understanding. Without understanding, He does all of this.[215]

JOHN: Effortlessly.

SWAMIJI: Effortlessly. Let He be glorified; *jayatyajaḥ*, let He be glorified, glory be to That.

Audio 6 (28:23)

मलतैलाक्तसंसार-वासनावर्तिदाहिना ।
ज्ञानदीपेन देव त्वां कदा नु स्यामुपस्थितः ॥ ११४ ॥

213 Here, Swamiji is speaking of *parā prakṛti*, viz., Lord Śiva's *svātantrya śakti*. "*Prakṛti* is explained in the *śāstras* (scriptures) in two ways. *Aparā prakṛti*, which is said to be eightfold, is the combination of the five great elements, along with mind, intellect, and ego. *Parā prakṛti* is that energy of Being which governs and contains all of the activities and conceptions of this universe." *Kashmir Shaivism–The Secret Supreme*, 95.

214 Differentiated thoughts, differentiated perceptions.

215 "He uses all tricks and powers to create this world but He Himself is method-less as there is no sign of exertion or planning in His Being." *Stava Cintāmaṇi* (1990).

malatailāktasaṁsāra-vāsanāvartidāhinā /
jñānadīpena deva tvāṁ kadā nu syāmupasthitaḥ / / 114 / /

There is one craving in me, O Lord. That craving is, I want a candle of knowledge. I want a candle of knowledge by which knowledge I would like to see You and come near You, remain before/at Your feet. *Jñāna dīpena*, by the candle of knowledge, *deva*, O Lord Śiva, *tvām kadā*, when shall I *syām* (become) *tvām upasthitaḥ*, in front of You? When shall I remain in front of You by the help of the candle of knowledge? Which candle of knowledge? *Malatailākta saṁsāra vāsanā varti dāhinā*, which has got a wick (*varti* means, wick), a wick which is soaked in *āṇavamala*, *māyīyamala*, and *kārmamala*–this is the oil.[216] *Āṇavamala*, *māyīyamala*, and *kārmamala*, these three *malas* have become, are taking the place of, oil. And it is soaked in that oil of *āṇavamala*–the three *malas*.[217] *Mala taila ākta saṁsāra vāsanā*, and the wick is the universal adjustment, the *saṁsāra*.[218] The whole of *saṁsāra* is the wick and this is soaked in that *āṇavamala*, *māyīyamala*, and *kārmamala*, and it is burnt, *jñāna dipena*, and that is the knowledge of the flame. By that knowledge of the flame, this is my desire that, by the light of the flame, I would like to remain at Your feet. When shall that time come?

JOHN: By the light of this flame of the burning of *saṁsāra*.

SWAMIJI: Yes.

JOHN: With the three *malas*.

SWAMIJI: Three *malas*.

---

216 See Appendix 8 for an explanation of the three *malas* (impurities).

217 *Āṇavamala* is the basis of the other two *malas*.

218 "The *malas* are in place of oil, and these impressions of all worldly habits, good and bad, and of kith and kin, are like a wick which we ignite and it goes on giving light to that place." *Stava Cintāmaṇi* (1990).

Audio 6 (30:40)

निमेषमपि यद्येकं क्षीणदोषे करिष्यसि ।
पदं चित्ते तदा शंभो किं न संपादयिष्यसि ॥ ११५

nimeṣamapi yadyekaṁ kṣīṇadoṣe kariṣyasi /
padaṁ citte tadā śaṁbho kiṁ na saṁpādayiṣyasi / / 115 / /

O Lord Śiva, there is one thing, [and] that one thing is–it is a very important one thing–*nimeṣamapi yadyekaṁ kṣīṇadoṣe kariṣyasi padaṁ citte*, if You keep my mind, if You make my mind, only for one moment, one second (*nimeṣamapi yadi ekaṁ*, *ekaṁ nimeṣam*; *nimeṣa* means, only for one twinkling of the eyes, that is, only for one second), if You make my mind *kṣīṇa doṣe*, without any blemishes, without any blemishes of the variety of thoughts, variety of foreign thoughts, except Your thought, . . .

You understand?

JOACHIM: Yes.

SWAMIJI: . . . if You do this favor to my mind only for one moment, *tadā kim na saṁpādayiṣyasi*, what shall I not achieve afterwards? I will achieve everything! You have only to do this favor only for one second with my mind. Do this in my mind for one second and I will show You.

JOHN: "I will show You" (laughs).

SWAMIJI: I will show You where is the speed-breaker (laughter).[219]

---

219 On this point, Kṣemarāja references a verse from the *Netra Tantra*: "If Parabhairava sits in my mind for one second, there and then, I will be seated there for eternal time. Ordinarily, when one goes into that state of Parabhairava, he goes in and is thrown out. But in this case he is not thrown out, he is established for good, just after one touch." *Stava Cintāmaṇi* (1990).
"If, in the period of one twinkling of the eye, You make some fortunate soul blissful by fixing him in the state of Parabhairava, *kim na saṁpādayiṣyasi*, then what more could You do? You have done everything for him. So, whatever is being done in one twinkling

Audio 6 (32:14)

धन्योऽस्मि कृतकृत्योऽस्मो महानस्मीति भावना ।
भवेत्सालम्बना तस्य यस्त्वदालम्बनः प्रभो ॥ ११६ ॥

dhanyo'smi kṛtakṛtyo'smi mahānasmīti bhāvanā /
bhavetsālambanā tasya yastvadālambanaḥ prabho //116//

Prabho, O Lord Śiva, O my Master, *iti bhāvana*, this kind of thinking that, "*Dhanyo'smi*, I am fortunate," "*Kṛtakṛtyo'smi*, I have done what was to be done in this world," "*Mahānasmi*, I am great, I have become great in this universe," this kind of thinking (*iti bhāvana*, this kind of thinking) becomes solid to that person, *bhavet sālambanā*, it becomes support-full, . . .

Sālambanā means . . .

JOHN: Substantial, solid.

SWAMIJI: Solid.

. . . substantial to that person, *yastvad ālambanaḥ prabho*, who has held Your Being, who has got a hold on Your nature.[220]

Audio 6 (33:18)

शुभाशुभस्य सर्वस्य स्वयं कर्ता भवानपि ।
भवद्भक्तिस्तु जननी शुभस्यैवेश केवलम् ॥ ११७ ॥

---

of an eye, that is all [that is needed], there is no [need] to insert effort. There, *tīvra tīvra śaktipāta* is found and that is under your control, not under the control of Parabhairava. That *tīvra tīvra śaktipāta* is under your own control! This is the Shaivite Philosophy. Because you *are* Parabhairava. You have to produce *śaktipāta* for yourself. When you don't like [it], then don't produce it–still you are great. When you don't like, as somebody does not like to have *śaktipāta*, what then? He [Parabhairava] is always there." *Bhagavad Gita–In the Light of Kashmir Shaivism*, 8.14 commentary.

220 "O Lord Śiva, he who is in search of You, and who has seen the treasure of Your treasury, he is already full, and he has nothing to long for." *Stava Cintāmaṇi* (1991).

śubhāśubhasya sarvasya svayaṁ kartā bhavānapi /
bhavadbhaktistu jananī śubhasyaiveśa kevalam / / 117 / /

O Lord Śiva, You have got power: You are the doer of all good and bad in this universe. This is a great thing that You have, that You've possessed. You possess the power of doing all good and all bad. Whatever good and whatever bad happens in this world is done by You. *Śubhāśubhasya sarvasya svayaṁ kartā bhavānapi*, but there is a greater thing in Your devotion! You are the creator of all good actions and bad actions, good things and bad things–You are the creator of these two things–but Your devotion[221] is more fine than Your nature [because] it creates only good things; *bhavad bhaktistu jananī śubhasyaiveśa*, it creates only good things, not bad things. What?

JOHN: Your devotion

SWAMIJI: Your devotion.[222]

Audio 6 (34:28)

प्रसन्ने मनसि स्वामिन्किं त्वं निविशसे किमु ।
त्वत्प्रवेशात्प्रसीदेत्तदिति दोलायते जनः ॥ ११८ ॥

prasanne manasi svāmin-kiṁ tvam niviśase kimu /
tvatpraveśātprasīdettad-iti dolāyate janaḥ / / 118 / /

O my Master (*svāmin*, O my master), there is one doubt in me. Is it a fact that, when one's mind is purified (*prasanne manasi*, when your mind is completely pure from all sides), You get entry in that [mind]? Is it so?

JOHN: He's talking about any person. When a person's mind becomes clear . . .

---

221 Devotion to/for God.

222 "This is the wonder that more greatness is seen in Your *bhakti* than in You." *Stava Cintāmaṇi* (1990). "O Lord Śiva, there is a difference between You and Your devotion. You are the creator of good and bad, but Your *bhakti* creates only good. So, Your *bhakti* is higher than You. I don't want You, I want Your devotion, love. I love Your love, I don't love You." *Stava Cintāmaṇi* (1991).

SWAMIJI: Huh?

JOHN: He's not talking about Lord Śiva's mind, he is talking about any person's mind.

SWAMIJI: Yes, any person's mind. O Lord Śiva, if any person's mind is completely pure, purified, do You get entry in that mind? Is this a fact? *Kimu*, or, *tvat praveśāt prasīdetta*, by Your entry that mind gets purified? What is the fact? Is it a fact that You get entry in a purified mind or [is it a fact that] by Your entry a mind becomes purified? What is the fact? What is the reality in these two?[223]

Audio 6 (35:44)

निश्चयः पुनरेषोऽत्र त्वदधिष्ठानमेव हि ।
प्रसादो मनसः स्वामिन् सा सिद्धिस्तत्परं पदम् ॥ ११९ ॥

niścayaḥ punareṣo'tra tvadadhiṣṭhānameva hi /
prasādo manasaḥ svāmin sā siddhistatparaṁ padam / / 119
(not recited)

Niścaya, but I have concluded, *niścayaḥ punareṣo'tra*, this is my conclusion on these two points. Which points?

JOHN: First you clear the mind, then Lord Śiva comes, or He clears Your mind.

GANJOO: You enter the pure mind or the mind gets pure by Your entry.

SWAMIJI: Yes. *Niścayaḥ punareṣo'tra tvad adhiṣṭhānam*, just Your getting entry in the mind is everything, is the purification of the mind, is the achievement of all powers, and is the supreme state of God consciousness–just Your entry. So I have nothing to do! You have to enter (laughs).

DENISE: (laughter)

GANJOO: Finished.

---

223 "This is the confusion in people. How can the mind be purified without You? And, if the mind is not purified, how can You enter?" *Stava Cintāmaṇi* (1990).

SWAMIJI: *Bas*, is it finished? We will finish it!

Audio 6 (36:37)

वचश्चेतश्च लार्यं च शरीरं मम यत्प्रभो ।
त्वत्प्रसादेन तद्भूयाद्भवद्भावैकभूषणम् ॥ १२० ॥

vacaścetaśca kāryaṁ ca śarīraṁ mama yatprabho /
tvatprasādena tadbhūyād-bhavadbhāvaikabhūṣaṇam //120

My *vacaḥ* (my word), *cetaḥ* (my mind), my activity (*kāryam ca*), and my body (*śarīra*), I have got these four [aspects]. I have got a body, I have got my language, and I have got a mind, and I have got actions. Whatever these four [aspects] I have got, *prabho*, O Lord Śiva, O my Master, *tvatprasādena*, by Your grace–I don't say it is due to me, I don't say that it is due, that You should do this–by Your grace, if this would happen, that *tvat prasādena*, by Your grace, *tat bhūyāt*, let these four [aspects] become *tvat bhavat bhāvaika bhūṣaṇam*, the ornaments of Your nature. Let my word sing only You, let my mind think only You, let my activity be diverted towards only Your action, let my *śarīra* (let my body) become just for Your sake. So, [these are] becoming the ornaments of Your nature, let [them] become the ornaments of Your nature.

Audio 6 (38:16)

स्तवचिन्तामणिं भुरिमनोरथफलप्रदम् ।
भक्तिलक्ष्म्यालयं शंभोर्भट्टनारायणो व्यधात् ॥ १२१ ॥

stavacintāmaṇiṁ bhūri-manorathaphalapradam /
bhaktilakṣmyālayaṁ śaṁbhor-bhaṭṭanārāyaṇo vyadhāt //121

So, this way, Bhaṭṭa Nārāyaṇa (Bhaṭṭa Nārāyaṇa is the author of these hymns), *vyadhāt*, he has written, "*Bhakti lakṣmī ālayam*"[224] [in] the *Stava Cintāmaṇi*. *Cintāmaṇi* is that jewel of the mind (that is the *cintāmaṇi ratna*). Whatever you desire from it, you will get it, you will achieve it. That is the *cintāmaṇi ratna*. The *cintāmaṇi ratna* actually exists in the heavens. Whatever you wish for, whatever you sing, whatever you think, you will get it. You just have to hold that *cintāmaṇi ratna* in your hand and you will get it. You will get anything, whatever you desire. This is the *Stava Cintāmaṇi*, this is that jewel of Your hymns, singing Your glories. *Bhūri manoratha phala pradam*, and it fulfills all kinds of your desires. And this is the abode of the glory of the wealth of devotion (*bhakti lakṣmī*), devotional wealth. And devotional wealth is for the sake of Lord Śiva (*śambhor*), and Bhaṭṭa Nārāyaṇa has put that before you.[225]

Finished!

End of Audio 6 (40:03)

| | Here ends the *Stava Cintāmaṇi* | |

Jai Guru Dev!

---

224 Devotion (*bhakti*) is the dwelling place (*ālayam*) of supreme wealth (*lakṣmī*).

225 *Stava Cintāmaṇi*, why have I named this *Stava Cintāmaṇi* (*stava* means, *stotra,* hymns, devotional songs)? Why are they *cintāmaṇi* (jewelry), [why] is it jewelry? *Manoratha-phala-pradam*, it is jewelry for everybody–one wants this jewel, one wants that jewel, one wants another jewel; one wants pink, one wants black, one wants white, one wants white-cum-black. *Manoratha phala pradam, bhakti lakṣmyālayaṁ*, this [*Stava Cintāmaṇi*], Śri Bhaṭṭa Nārāyaṇa's offering before Lord Śiva, is like Mahā Lakṣmī's (the goddess of wealth) *mishri kanda*, a small cone of sugar traditionally offered to Goddess Lakṣmī." *Stava Cintāmaṇi* (1991).

Stava Cintāmaṇi (1990)

Kṣemarāja's concluding Maṅgala Ślokas

[NOTE: there is no audio of these verses]

गुणादित्याज्जातो गुणगणगरिष्ठः शिवगुणैः
कृतामोदो बाल्यात्प्रमभृति गतसंगो जगति यः ।
स शुरादित्यो मां बहु बहुलभक्त्यार्थयत यत् ।
स्तुतौ तेनाकार्षं विवृतिमिह नारायणकृतौ ॥ १ ॥

guṇādityājjāto guṇagaṇagariṣṭhaḥ śivaguṇaiḥ
kṛtāmodo bālyātprabhṛti gatasaṃgo jagati yaḥ /
sa śūrādityo māṁ bahu bahulabhaktyārthayata yat
stutau tenākārṣaṁ vivṛtimiha nārāyaṇakṛtau //1//

Guṇāditya was a great philosopher. He was married and had a son named Śūrāditya who had all of the qualities of Śiva. Delightful from his very childhood, Śūrāditya was detached from worldly affairs and all of his attention was diverted toward Lord Śiva. As a warrior-son he had strong willpower, therefore, whatever he willed came true. As I [Kṣemarāja] was a direct disciple of Abhinavagupta he was also my admirer. He liked Śaivism, and though he had little intellectual knowledge, he understood the theory of the real

> Swami Lakshmanjoo said, "In that way Śūrāditya was like my master Swami Mahatab Kāk, because he too liked experiential knowledge and not book learning. My grandmaster, Swami Rām, liked both."

Śūrāditya kept requesting me to do something with the

hymns of Bhaṭṭa Nārāyaṇa so that he could understand their real meaning. So, at his request, I have made the effort of commentating on this book.

श्रीरामेण कृतात्र सद्विवृतिरित्येषा किमर्थेति मा
सन्तश्चेतसि कृध्वमास्ति विवृतौ कोऽपि प्रकर्षोऽत्र यत् ।
तेनार्थिप्रणयाद्दिनैस्त्रिचतुरैर्यां क्षेमराजो व्यधात् ।
क्षेत्रे श्रीविजयेश्वरस्य विमले सैषा शिवाराधनी ॥ २ ॥

śrīrāmeṇa kṛtātra sadvivṛtirityeṣā kimartheti mā
santaścetasi kṛdhvamasti vivṛtau ko'pi prakarṣo'tra yat /
tenārthipraṇayāddinaistricaturairyāṁ kṣemarājo vyadhāt
kṣetre śrīvijayeśvarasya vimale saiṣā śivārādhanī //2//

Bhaṭṭa Nārāyaṇa composed the *Stava Cintāmaṇi* and his immediate disciple, Rāma Kantha, made a commentary, but, as it was not liked by great Śaivites, no one cared to understand it, so in time that commentary faded away. So, at the heartfelt request of my admirers, I have written a commentary on these 120 *śloka*s, which I completed in just three to four days while residing in the ancient palace of the Kashmiri King, Lālitāditya, in Bījbihara.[1] It was necessary for me to shed more light and understanding on this important work of Bhaṭṭa Nārāyaṇa, so great souls should not blame me for doing this commentary.[2]

1 Bījbihara, also known as Vijeśvara, is one of the oldest cities in Kashmir.

2 Understanding that Rāma Kantha's previous commentary on the *Stava Cintāmaṇi* was not well received, Kṣemarāja asks for forgiveness from the great souls of his time, for embarking on yet another commentary of the same text. It would not be out of place to mention that Abhinavagupta's writings, and the numerous commentaries of his chief disciple Kṣemarāja, were often met with skepticism by the scholars of that period.

शंभोः प्रकाशवपुषः शक्तिरेका जयत्यसौ।
या स्फुरन्त्येव तनुते परामृतमयं जगत् ॥ ३ ॥

śaṁbhoḥ prakāśavapuṣaḥ śaktirekā jayatyasau /
yā sphurantyeva tanute parāmṛtamayaṁ jagat //3//

Lord Śiva is the embodiment of the Light of Parabhairava. His energy, which is the only energy glorified in this whole universe, appeared in my consciousness, so I exposed this supreme nectar of Parabhairava in just three to four days.

इति श्री महामाहेश्वराचार्या वर्य श्री भट्टनारायण
विरचितः स्तवचिन्तामणिः समाप्तः

iti śrī mahāmāheśvarācārya varya śrī bhaṭṭanārāyaṇa
viracitaḥ stavacintāmaṇiḥ samāptaḥ /

Here ends the *Stava Cintāmaṇi*, composed by the great Shaiva teacher *(mahāmaheśvarācārya)*, Śrī Bhaṭṭa Nārāyaṇa.

Appendix

1. Spanda System

The fourth system which comprises the Trika philosophy is called the Spanda System. The word *spanda* means "movement". The Spanda School recognizes that nothing can exist without movement. Where there is movement, there is life, and where there is no movement, that is lifelessness. They realize that there is movement in wakefulness, dreaming, deep sleep, and *turya*. Though some thinkers argue that there is no movement in deep sleep, the philosophers of the Spanda System realize that nothing can exist without movement. The teachings of the Spanda System, which is an important practical system, are found embodied in the *Vijñāna Bhairava Tantra*, the *Svacchanda Tantra*, and in the 6th chapter of the *Tantrāloka*.

Kashmir Shaivism–The Secret Supreme, ch 19, p134.

Spanda is nominated as *sphurattā* (vigor, life, life-giver, power of existence), *ūrmiḥ* (tide), *balam* (strength), *udyoga* (force), *hṛdayam* (heart), *sāram* (essence), and *mālinī* (supreme energy). These are nominations which are attributed to this *spanda* in the *śāstras* (scriptures).

The Mystery of Vibrationless-Vibration in Kashmir Shaivism, Vasugupta's *Spanda Kārikā and* Kṣemarāja's *Spanda Saṇdoha*, p116.

The one who is bent upon finding out the reality of *spanda* always (*satatam*)–not only in wakefulness, [but also] in the dreaming state also–he who is bent upon finding out the reality of God consciousness, does not lose [awareness of] even one hundredth part of his breath. Ibid., 1.21.

Spanda means "stable movement". It is that kind of movement which is stable, which is not in movement. You don't find It in movement but It is in movement–motionless movement. That is *spanda*, and from that *spanda*, this *jāgrata* (the cycle of wakefulness), the cycle of the dreaming state, and the cycle of the dreamless state (*suṣupti*), come out in manifestation, but it does not come out in manifestation after becoming disconnected from That *spanda tattva*, it is [always] connected with That *spanda tattva*. While being connected with That *spanda tattva*, it comes out. What? The state of wakefulness, the state of the dreaming state, and the state of the dreamless state (*suṣupti*). It comes into manifestation, but it holds within the state of That *spanda*. It is still one with *spanda*. It cannot remain, it can't exist, in the outside cycle of the world without *spanda*. *Spanda* is [always] adjusted with it because *spanda* is the life for this world. You can't ignore *spanda*! [Even] in the absence of *spanda*, *spanda*'s presence is a must. Ibid., 1.3, pp4-5.

This universe, which is a world of consciousness, is filled with, and is one with, the supreme state of God consciousness. God consciousness is *spanda*, a unique reality of supreme movement filled with nectar and an outpouring of the supreme bliss of independence.

Shiva Sutras–The Supreme Awakening, 1.9.

The element of *spanda* is that being of God consciousness in which this whole universe exists and from which this whole universe comes out. And [God consciousness] is not only the resting place of the universe, [He] is the *prasara sthana* also, the flowing energy. This universe comes out from That, it *has* to exist in God consciousness, and it is coming out from God consciousness *in* God consciousness, because there is no other space for the universe to exist.

Parātrīśikā Vivaraṇa, LJA archive.

2. *Vimarśa*

In the world of Shaivite philosophy, Lord Śiva is seen as being filled with light. But more than this, Lord Śiva is the embodiment of light and this light is different than the light of the sun, of the moon, or of fire. It is light (*prakāśa*) with consciousness (*vimarśa*); and this light with consciousness is the nature of that supreme consciousness, Lord Śiva. What is consciousness? The light of consciousness is not only pure consciousness, It is filled with the understanding that, "I am the creator, I am the protector, and I am the destroyer of everything." Just to know that, "I am the creator, I am the protector, and I am the destroyer," is consciousness. If consciousness was not attached to the light of consciousness, we would have to admit that the light of the sun or the light of the moon or the light of a fire is also Lord Śiva. But this is not the case.

The light of consciousness (*vimarśa*) is given various names. It is called *cit-caitanya*, which means, the strength of consciousness; *parā vāk,* the supreme word; *svātantrya*, perfect independence; *aiśvarya*, the predominant glory of supreme Śiva; *kartṛtva*, the power of acting; *sphurattā*, the power of existing; *sāra*, the complete essence of everything; *hṛdaya*, the universal heart; and *spanda*, universal movement. All these are names in the Tantras, which are attributed to this consciousness.

This I-consciousness, which is the reality of Lord Śiva, is a natural (*akṛtrima*), not a contrived, 'I'. It is not adjusted I-consciousness. Limited human beings have adjusted I-consciousness. Lord Śiva has natural or pure I-consciousness. There is a difference between adjusted consciousness and natural consciousness. Adjusted or artificial consciousness exists when this I-consciousness is attributed to your body, to your mind, to your intellect, and to your ego. Natural consciousness is that consciousness that is attributed to the reality of the Self, which is all-consciousness.

This universe, which is created in His consciousness, is dependent on That consciousness. It is always dependent on That consciousness. It cannot move outside of That con-

sciousness. It exists only when it is residing in His consciousness. This is the way the creation of His universe takes place.
Self Realization in Kashmir Shaivism, 3.56-57.

There are two positions of Śiva. One is *prakāśa* and another is *vimarśa*. When He feels this blissful state as His own nature, that is *prakāśa*. When He feels that, "The blissful state is My glory," that is *vimarśa*. When He feels that, "This blissful state is My being," that is Śiva. When He believes that, "This is My glory," that is Śakti. The cycle of glory is residing in Śakti and the cycle of *prakāśa* is residing in Śiva–both are in one. That is indicated by *visarga* in Śiva ('*aḥ*' or ':'). So, *vimarśa śakti* is supreme *parā parameśvarī* attributed to *svātantrya śakti*. It is the intensity of the independence (of the *svātantrya*) of Bhairava."
Parātrīśikā Vivaraṇa (LJA archives).

3. ***Upāyas***

The meaning of the Sanskrit word "*upāya*" is "means". The word "*upāya*" in Kashmir Śaivism is used to indicate the means to enter into Universal God Consciousness from individual consciousness. Our Śaivism proclaims that there are three means for entering into Universal God Consciousness: *śāmbhavopāya* (the supreme means), *śāktopāya* (the medium means), and *āṇavopāya* (the inferior means).

Āṇavopāya is the means found in the world of duality and is known as *bhedopāya*. The means which exists in the world of mono-duality, in the world where duality and non-duality exist together, is *śāktopāya*, and is called *bhedābhedopāya*. That means which exists in the world of pure monism (*abheda*) is *śāmbhavopāya* and is called *abhedopāya*.

Śāmbhavopāya is also called *icchopāya*, as it is the means which exists in *icchā śakti* (the energy of will). The means which exists in *jñāna śakti* (the energy of knowledge) is *śāktopāya* and is called *jñānopāya*. *Āṇavopāya* is called *kriyopāya* because it is the means which is found in *kriyā śakti* (the energy of action)."

The difference between *āṇavopāya*, *śāktopāya*, and *śāmbhavopāya*, is this: In *āṇavopāya*, the strength of your awareness is such that you have to take the support of everything as an aid to maintain and strengthen your awareness. In *śāktopāya*, your awareness is strengthened to the extent that only one point is needed as a support for your concentration and that point is the center. In *śāmbhavopaya*, the strength of your awareness is such that no support is needed. You are already residing in the meant (*upeya*). There is nowhere to go, just reside at your own point. The rest is automatic.

It is important to realize that, though there are different *upāyas*, all lead you to the state of one transcendental consciousness. The difference in these *upāyas* is that, *āṇavopāya* will carry you in a long way, *śāktopāya* in a shorter way, and *śāmbhavopāya* in the shortest way. Although the ways are different, the point to be achieved is one."

Paraphrase from *Kashmir Shaivism–The Secret Supreme*, chapter 5, pp33-40.

4. **The *praṇava mantra*, 'auṁ' ('oṁ')**

In Sanskrit, the word *akāra* means, the letter *'a'*; *ukāra* means, the letter *'u'*; and *makāra* means, the letter *'ma'*, which together form the *mantra*, *'auṁ'* (*'oṁ'*).

akāraśca ukāraśca makāro bindureva ca /
ardhacandro nirodhī ca nādo nādānta eva ca / /
śaktiśca vyāpinī caiva samanaikādaśī smṛtā /
unmanā ca tato 'tītā tadatītaṁ nirāmayam / /[1]

'A', *'u'*, and *'ma'*. *'A'* is the first ray of God, *'u'* is second, *'ma'* is third, *bindu* (*'ṁ'*) is fourth, *ardhacandra* is fifth, *nirodhī* is sixth, *nāda* is seventh, *nādānta* is eighth. *Bas*, this is the *āsana* (the seat). [Then] *śakti*, *vyāpinī*, and *samanā* are three

---

1 These verses from *Netra Tantra* (22.21-22) and *Svacchanda Tantra* (4.430-431), were often quoted by Swamiji while teaching various Śaiva texts.

other states of energies on that seat, on that corpse[2]–*śakti*, *vyāpinī*, and *samanā*. *Śakti* is *aparā*, *vyāpinī* is *parāparā* energy, *samanā* is *parā* energy."

Parātrīśikā Vivaraṇa (LJA archive).

"'*Oṁ*' is the combination of four letters: *a-kāra*, *u-kāra*, *ma-kāra*, and *bindu* ('*ṁ*'). These four letters will produce the sound of '*oṁ*'-*praṇava*. But actually, this *praṇava* is incorrect. After producing these four sounds, there are other sounds which are not spoken, which are not uttered. That is *akāraśca ukāraśca makāro bindurevaca*, these four letters are produced in the cycle of the utterance of '*oṁ*'. After uttering '*oṁ*', this *śabda* (sound), there is something else. That is, *ardhacandra-nirodhīka-nāda-nādānta-śakti-vyāpinī-samanā-unmanā*, these eight words are yet to be produced when you utter the *mantra* of '*oṁ*'. After '*oṁ*', you have to go in *ardhacandra*, then you have to get entry in *nirodhī*, then *nāda*, then *nādānta*, then *śakti*, then *vyāpinī*, then *samanā*, and then *unmanā*. So, there are twelve letters in the cycle of the reciting of the *praṇava* ('*oṁ*'). You have to get entry in *ardhacandra*, then *nirodhinī*, then *nāda*, *nādānta*, *śakti*, *vyāpinī*, *samanā*, and *unmanā*. Where *unmanā* is situated, there you find the actual position of God consciousness. That is *parā*."

Ibid.

The *unmanā* state is that state of *oṁ-kāra* where the mind is over, the functioning of the mind stops altogether–that is *unmanā*. When reciting this *oṁ-kāra*, you reach to the topmost point of *unmanā* (*unmanā* is not a state). After *unmanā*, you enter in the state of Śiva."

Vijñāna Bhairava–The Manual for Self Realization, Dhāraṇā 19, verse. 42

In his *Tantrāloka*, Abhinavagupta says:

---

2 *Mahāpreta* (the great corpse), or Sadāśiva in the pure transcendental state.

tasya nābhyutthitaṁ mūrdharandhratrayavinirgatam /
nādāntātma smarecchaktivyāpinīsamanojjvalam // TĀ 15.313

Swamiji translates:

Above that seat of *nādānta* (i.e., *brahmarandhra*)[3] is *parā śakti*. As long as the question of that body is concerned, Sadāśiva has no navel. In place of a navel, he has got *mūlādhāra*, and the point where *parā śakti* rises, that is *nabhi*, that is his navel. And this is the *nabhi* (navel) of Sadāśiva, that *preta* (corpse). Which *preta*? *Mahāpreta*, the great corpse. *Mūrdha* means, *brahmarandhra*; *randhra traya* means, three openings. From those three openings of *brahmarandhra* (that is the navel of Sadāśiva), and which is residing in *nādāntātma* (*nādānta, smaret*), the aspirant of the Trika system has to concentrate on three other energies: *śakti, vyāpinī*, and *samanā*. *Śakti* is ninth, *vyāpinī* is tenth, *samanā* is eleventh. These three energies are to be contemplated on the three openings of *brahmarandhra* of Sadāśiva. [There] it is called *ūrdhva dvadaśānta*. *Ūrdhva dvadaśānta* means, *brahmarandhra*. This is the surface of *brahmarandhra*, covered by all these three aspects–*śakti, vyāpinī*, and *samanā*."
Tantrāloka 15.313 (LJA archive)

tanmadhye tu parādevī dakṣine ca parāparā /
aparā vāmaśṛṅge tu madhyasṛṅgo'rdhvataḥ śṛṇu / /
yā sā saṁkarṣinī kālī parātītā vyavasthitā / /[4]

Parā devī is in the center (*tanmadhye tu parādevī*). *Dakṣine ca parāparā*, on the right side is the *parāparā* energy. On the left side is *aparā*. *Madhya sṛṅgo*, from supreme *parā* there is another spoke above: *yā sā śakti parā sūkṣma parātītā*

3 The top of the skull.
4 Jayaratha has quoted this verse twice in his commentary on the *Tantrāloka* (3.70 and 31.97). Swamiji considers it a very important verse, as it directly relates to the three supreme energies (the Goddesses) of the Trika.

vyavasthitā, that is, *kālākarṣinī*.[5] And above that is the position of Lord Śiva. This will all go and cover the seat (*āsana*) of Lord Śiva.

iti śakti-vyāpinī-samanāntaka-śṛṅgatrayam uktam /

Śakti, *vyāpinī*, and *samanā* are the three spokes explained there on that *āsana*.[6]

tatrāpi unmanasordhvakuṇḍalikāpada-paramadhāma-sitakamalatraya-rūpatayā nirūpitam

On that state of *śakti*, *vyāpinī*, and *samanā*, there are three white lotuses, which are one with that supreme *parā kuṇḍalinī śakti*. *Parā kuṇḍalinī śakti*, the greatest universal serpent power, is there. And *parama-dhāma*, that is the supreme state of God consciousness. There you find *sita-kāla-traya-rūpatayā*, three absolutely white lotuses, and there also you'll find *śakti*, *vyāpinī*, and *samanā*.
Parātrīśikā Vivaraṇa (LJA archive).

And those [three white] lotuses are residing in the cycle of the *unmanā* state. *Unmanā* means, above the cycle of the mind, above the cycle of thought. You can't concentrate on them. It is *aunmanasaṁ*.[7] That is why it is called *unmanā*.
Tantrāloka 15.313 (LJA archive)

5. ***Svātantrya***

All of these five energies of God consciousness are produced by His *svātantrya śakti* (of freedom), His free power. That is called *svātantrya śakti*. *Svātantrya śakti* produces these five energies of Lord Śiva. And *cit śakti* is actually based on His

5 This is Kālasaṁkarṣinī Kālī, the Supreme *paradevī* who draws all time into herself and dances on the lord of death (Mahākāla).
6 *Śakti*, *vyāpinī*, and *samanā* reside on the three spokes (prongs) of the *triśūla*. These three spokes are all in the same level.
7 Without mind.

nature, *ānanda śakti* is based on His Sakti (on His Pārvatī), *icchā śakti* is based in Sadāśiva, and *jñāna śakti* (the energy of knowledge) is based on Īśvara, and the energy of *kriyā* is based on Śuddhāvidya. All of these five pure states of Lord Śiva are one with Lord Śiva. *Cit śakti* indicates Lord Śiva's actual position, *ānanda śakti* indicates Lord Śiva's position of Śakti, and *icchā śakti* indicates Lord Śiva's position of Sadāśiva, and *jñāna śakti* indicates His position of Īśvara, and Śuddhavidyā is [His] fifth position [viz., *kriyā śakti*]. All of these five positions are filled with God consciousness. Below that is the scale of *māyā*, illusion. That will go from *māyā* to earth.

Special Verses on Practice, LJA archive.

The definition of *svātantrya* is "freedom in action and freedom in knowledge"; when you know with your freedom, when you act with your freedom. When you know and you don't succeed in that knowledge, there is not *svātantrya*. When there is not *svātantrya*, it is not really knowledge. When there is not *svātantrya*, it is not really action. The action of individuals is just like that. Individuals know, they know something–you can't say that they don't know anything–they know something, but that knowledge has not *svātantrya*. And they act also, they do something, but that doing also has not *svātantrya*. So, without *svātantrya*, doing and knowing has no value. When there is *svātantrya*, it is fully valued.

That essence of *svātantrya* is *anavacchinna*, beyond limitation, all-around beyond limitation. There is no such limit found in That state. *Vicchinna camatkāra maya viśrāntyā*, and this limited state of being is also found there. [Lord Śiva] is unlimited, but the limited cycle of God consciousness is also found there. So It is both limited and unlimited. That being who is limited only, he is not true. That being who is unlimited only, he is not true. Why? Because he is limited. The being who is unlimited is not true because he is unlimited only [and] not limited. That fullness of God consciousness is found [in one] who is limited and, at the same time, unlimited also. That is the fullness of God consciousness. The fullness of God consciousness is where nothing is excluded. Whatever is excluded, it is also one with That. That is the fullness of God consciousness.

Parātrīśikā Vivaraṇa, LJA archive.

Lord Śiva creates this external universe for the sake of realizing His own nature. That is why this external universe is called "Śakti", because it is the means to realize one's own nature. Therefore, in order to recognize His nature, He must first become ignorant of His nature. Only then can He recognize it.

Why should He want to recognize His nature in the first place? It is because of His freedom, His *svātantrya* (independence). This is the play of the universe. This universe was created solely for the fun and joy of this realization. It happens that when His fullness overflows, He wants to [become] incomplete. He wants to appear as being incomplete just so He can achieve completion. This is the play of His *svātantrya*: to depart from His own nature in order to enjoy it again. It is this *svātantrya* that has created this whole universe. This is the play of Śiva's *svātantrya*.

This kind of action cannot be accomplished by any power in this universe other than Lord Śiva. Only Lord Śiva can do this. Only Lord Śiva, by His own *svātantrya*, can totally ignore and mask His own nature. This is His *svātantrya*, His glory, His intelligence. Intelligence does not mean that in this super-drama called creation you will only play the part of a lady or a man. With this kind of [supreme] intelligence, you will also play the part of rocks, of trees, of all things. This kind of intelligence is found only in the state of Lord Śiva and nowhere else.

Self Realization in Kashmir Shaivism, chapter 1, "Fifteen Verses of Wisdom," Verses 5, 6 and 7, pp23-26.

Svātantrya śakti and *māyā* are one. *Svātantrya śakti* is that state of energy which can produce the power of going down and coming up again. And *māyā* is not like that. *Māyā* will give you the strength of coming down and then no ability of going up–then you cannot go up again. This is the state of *māyā*. And all these three *malas* (impurities) reside in *māyā śakti*, not *svātantrya śakti*, although *svātantrya śakti* and *māyā śakti* are one. *Māyā śakti* is that energy, universal energy, which is owned by the individual being, the individual soul. The same energy, when it is owned by the Universal Being, is called *svātantrya śakti*.

Svātantrya śakti is pure universal energy. Impure universal energy is *māyā*. It is only the formation that changes through a difference of vision. When you experience *svātantrya śakti* in a crooked way, it becomes *māyā śakti* for you. And when you realize that same *māyā śakti* in Reality, then that *māyā śakti* becomes *svātantrya śakti* for you. Therefore, *svātantrya śakti* and *māyā śakti* are actually only one and the three impurities (*malas*), which are to be explained here, reside in *māyā śakti*, not in *svātantrya śakti*.

Kashmir Shaivism–The Secret Supreme, 7.47.

6. **The Six-fold Proofs (*pramāṇas*)**

[*Pratyakṣa*]:[8] "*Ayam ghaṭṭa*, this is a pot", it is *pratyakṣa* because everybody can understand this, everybody can perceive this pot–when I say, "This is a pot." This is *pratyakṣa*. How this pot exists? It exists because of *pratyakṣa pramāṇa*, the proof is just obvious because it is seen, it is perceived, by everybody. That is one proof of [how to prove] a thing exists.[9]

[*Anumāna*]:[10] Another proof is *anumāna*. *Anumāna* is just imagination, calculation. For instance, on the top of the hill I see, I perceive, this smoke. I prove there [that] there is fire; on the top of the hill, there is fire. What is the proof? Because there is smoke. This is *anumāna*. Fire is not perceived, smoke is perceived. By [the perception of] smoke, we can conclude

8 Present before the eyes, visible, perceptible.

9 That is, of how to prove the validity of knowledge/perception. "[*Pratyakṣa*] is the topmost proof, which everyone agrees upon an undisputed fact." *Stava Cintāmaṇi*, (1990).

10 The act of inferring or drawing a conclusion from given premises; inference, consideration, reflection; guess, conjecture; one of the means of obtaining true knowledge.

that there is fire. That is *anumāna pramāṇa*. In *anumāna pramāṇa*, there are *pratijñā*, *hetu*, *udhāraṇa*, *upanaya*, and *nigamana*, these five-fold ascertainments.[11] This is *tarka*, this is logic. Logic has put five-fold ascertainments for this *anumāna*. *Paravato'yam vahnimāna*, on the top of the hill, there is a fire. Fire is not seen, smoke is seen. That is *pratijñā*. I ascertain that there is fire. That is *pratijñā*. *Hetu* is the cause: Why? How do you say that there is a fire? There is no fire. There is smoke, there is no fire. *Dhūmatvāt*, because there is smoke. This is *hetu*. *Hetu* is the cause. The cause of fire is because there is smoke. Now there is *udāharaṇa*: Is there any proof in other [examples] also for this [relationship]? *Yatra yatra dhūmastatra tatrāgni*, wherever you find smoke, there is fire. Go to the kitchen and see (*yathā mahānasaya*; *mahānasaya* means, kitchen). You can see that, perceive that, in a kitchen. In the kitchen, there is a fire; outside there is smoke. So, we calculate, ascertain, that there is fire.[12] It is *hetu* and *uddharaṇa* (*udāharaṇa* is "an example"). The example he has put of what?

DEVOTEES: Kitchen.

SWAMIJI: Kitchen. The kitchen is an example (*yatra yatra dhūmastatra tatra agni*). *Pratyakṣa* is done and *anumāna* [also]. *Anumāna* is imagination, proof through imagination; you imagine there is fire because of smoke.

[*Upamāna*]: And another third proof is *upamāna*. *Upamāna* is "similarity". [For example], "This wild yak is just like a cow."

ERNIE: The same shape.

SWAMIJI: Yes. A wild yak is just like a cow. You know a yak?

DENISE: Yes.

---

11 *Pratijñā* (the assertion or proposition to be proved), *hetu* (the reason for the inference), *udhāraṇa* (the example, instance), *upanaya* (application), *nigamana* (the summing up of the argument or conclusion of this five-fold deductive reasoning).

12 "I have seen the similarity in my kitchen when I light wood with fire. We see fire in the bottom, and that produces smoke." *Stava Cintāmaṇi* (1990).

SWAMIJI: It is just like a cow, but it is furious, very . . .

ERNIE: With horns.

SWAMIJI: Yes. *Sāsnādimatvāt*, it is because he has got this *sāsnā*.[13] *Sāsnā* is that hanging . . .

STEPHANIE: Skin.

SWAMIJI: . . . hanging skin here [below the yak's neck]; and horns, and all these things, udders, etc. This is *upamāna pramāṇa*, this is the proof of similarity.

[*Āgama*]: *Āgama pramāṇa*, e.g., "You must remember God otherwise you will go to hell."

DENISE: What?

SWAMIJI: "You must remember God otherwise you will go to hell. You will perceive the pain in hell if you don't remember God in this life." What is the proof of it? "It is said in the *śāstra*s (scriptures), it is explained in the *śāstra*s that you should remember God." *Śāstras* are also proofs. What *śāstra*s?

ERNIE: Vedas.

SWAMIJI: Whatever *śāstra*s, Vedas, Shaivism.

ERNIE: The Bible.

SWAMIJI: Now it is *āgama pramāṇa*, it is called *āgama pramāṇa*, *pramāṇa* (proof) through *śāstra*s. The *śāstras* say that you have to believe. You have to accept this theory of the *śāstra*s that, "You should remember God otherwise you will go to hell; otherwise you will suffer." But what is the proof of this? *Śāstra*. *Śāstra*s are the proof. It is called *āgama pramāṇa*.[14]

[*Arthāpatti*]:[15] And *arthāpatti*. *Arthāpatti* is just a kind of

---

13 Dewlap.

14 "For example, "Lord Śiva is existing", but where is the proof for that? There are three proofs: 1) Śiva *Śāstra*s, 2) the master's saying that Lord Śiva exists, and 3) the disciples experience. If all of these three agree, it is the best *śāstra* and it is true. If all of the three do not agree, then it is wrong." *Stava Cintāmaṇi* (1990).

15 Inference from circumstances, a disjunctive hypothetical syllogism.

conclusion. This is also a proof. "*Pīno devadatto divā na bhuṅkte*, this stout such and such person does not eat from morning to evening! From morning to night he does not eat, he does not drink! This stout person", *arthāpatti* says [the conclusion is], "he must be eating in the night time because he is stout." How could he be stout if he was not eating anything? He must be eating during the night. This is *arthāpatti*. *Arthāpatti* is, you conclude that he must be eating in the night.

ERNIE: So, it is also logic.

SWAMIJI: This is also logic. If this stout person does not eat, not even water from morning to evening, it is obvious that he must be eating during the night.

ERNIE: So, what is the difference between smoke and fire (number two with logic, the five rules) and this?

SWAMIJI: This is called *arthāpatti*. *Arthāpatti* is, e.g., because of stoutness. His stoutness carries you to this conclusion that he eats during the night. His being strong carries you to this conclusion that he must be eating at night.[16]

DENISE: Or else how could he be stout?

SWAMIJI: *Arthāpatti*.

[*Abhāva*]:[17] And *abhāva*, e.g., "There is no pot, the pot is not existing", "The *kongari*[18] is not existing", "The book is not existing here." This is also logic. It is called *abhāva*. *Abhāva* is, "Because the book is missing. Here, a book is missing." It is *abhāva pramāṇa*.

These are six, six-fold proofs. So, *pratyakṣa* is first, *anumāna* is second, *upamāna* (similarity) is third, *āgama* is the *śāstra*s (fourth), and *arthāpatti* [is the fifth]. *Arthāpatti* is, you [make] a conclusion, you conclude.

ERNIE: Yes, but don't you conclude with the smoke and the fire also? Aren't you concluding, making a . . . you don't see the

---

16 That is, if he does not eat during the day.

17 Non-being or non-existence.

18 A small fire pot, traditionally used in Kashmir to keep warm during the winter.

fire but you make a conclusion?

SWAMIJI: But we see smoke there.

ERNIE: I see, you don't see any food . . .

SWAMIJI: I don't see anything in that stout person, only stoutness. He does not eat [even] a little particle of rice or bread from morning to evening.

ERNIE: Smoke is a direct result.

SWAMIJI: Smoke is a direct result here. There is a difference between smoke (that proof; it is *anumāna pramāṇa*) and this is *arthāpatti*. *Arthāpatti*, we come to this conclusion because of his stoutness.

7. *Turya* and *Turyātīta*

When, by the grace of a master, this subjective body enters into Subjective consciousness with full awareness, and maintaining unbroken awareness becomes fully illumined in its own Self, this is called the fourth state, *turya*.

From the Trika Shaivite point of view, predominance is given to the three energies of Śiva: *parā śakti* (the supreme energy), *parāparā śakti* (medium energy), and *aparā śakti* (inferior energy). The kingdom of *aparā śakti*, the lowest energy, is found in wakefulness and dreaming. The kingdom of *parāparā śakti*, the medium energy, is established in the state of sound sleep. And lastly, the kingdom of *parā śakti*, the supreme energy, is found in the state of *turya*.

The state of *turya* is said to be the penetration of all energies simultaneously, not in succession. All of the energies are residing there but are not in manifestation. They are all together without distinction. *Turya* is called "*savyāpārā*"[19] because all of the energies get their power to function in that state. At the same time, this state is known as "*anāmaya*" because it remains 'un-agitated' by all of these energies.

Three names are attributed to this state by worldly people, by *yogin*s, and by illuminated humans (*jñāni*s). Worldly people

19 Lit., fully occupied, employed or engaged.

call it "*turya*", which means "the fourth." They use this name because they have no descriptive name for this state. They are unaware of this state and, not having experienced it, simply call it "the fourth state". *Yogin*s have attributed the name "*rūpātīta*"[20] to this condition because this state has surpassed the touch of one's self and is the establishment of one's Self. The touch of one's Self was found in sound sleep, however, the establishment of one's Self takes place in *turya*. For illuminated humans, *jñāni*s, the entire universal existence is found in this state of *turya* collectively, as undifferentiated, in the state of totality. There is no succession here. *Jñāni*s, therefore, call this state "*pracaya*,"[21] the undifferentiated totality of universal existence.

Turyātīta is that state which is the absolute fullness of Self. It is filled with all-consciousness and bliss. It is really the last and the supreme state of the Self. You not only find this state of *turyātīta* in *samādhi*, you also find it in each and every activity of the world. In this state, there is no possibility for the practice of *yoga*. If you can practice *yoga*, then you are not in *turyātīta*. In practicing *yoga*, there is the intention of going somewhere. Here, there is nowhere to go, nothing to achieve. As concentration does not exist here, the existence of the helping hand of *yoga* is not possible.

There are only two names actually attributed to this state of *turyātīta*, one given by worldly people and one by *jñāni*s. Worldly people, because they know nothing about the state, call it "*turyātītā*", which means "that state which is beyond the fourth". *Jñāni*s, on the other hand, also have a name for it. They call it "*mahāpracaya*," which means "the unlimited and unexplainable supreme totality". *Yogin*s do not actually attribute any name to this state because they have no knowledge of it. It is completely outside of their experience. *Yogin*s have though, through the use of their imagination and guesswork, imagined one name which might be appropriate for this state: "*satatoditam*," which means "that state which has no pause, no

20 Beyond limited-self-consciousness.
21 Lit., multitude, mass

break." It is a break-less and unitary state. In *samādhi*, It is there. When *samādhi* is absent, It is there. In the worldly state, It is there. In the dreaming state, It is there. And in the state of deep sleep, It is there. In each and every state of the individual subjective body, It is there.

Kashmir Shaivism–The Secret Supreme, 11.72-84.

The difference between *turya* and *turyātīta* is, in *turya*, you find in *samādhi* that this whole universe is existing there in the seed form, germ. The strength, the energy, of universal existence is existing there, but here he has [yet] to come out [into activity]. In *turyātīta*, he comes out in action and feels universal consciousness. This is the difference between *turya* and *turyātīta*.

Tantrāloka 10.288, LJA archive.

8. *Malas*

The three impurities are gross (*sthūla*), subtle (*sūkṣma*), and subtlest (*para*). The gross impurity is called *kārmamala*. It is connected with actions. It is that impurity which inserts impressions such as those which are expressed in the statements, "I am happy", "I am not well", "I have pain", "I am a great man", "I am really lucky", etc., in the consciousness of the individual being.

The next impurity is called *māyīyamala*. This impurity creates differentiation in one's own consciousness. It is the impurity of ignorance (*avidyā*), the subtle impurity. The thoughts, "This house is mine", "That house is not mine", "This man is my friend", "That man is my enemy", "She is my wife", "She is not my wife", are all created by *māyīyamala*. *Māyīyamala* creates duality.

The third impurity is called *āṇavamala*. It is the subtlest impurity.[22] *Āṇavamala* is the general internal impurity of the

---

22 "*Āṇavamala* is the root of the other two impurities. Which are those other two impurities? *Māyīyamala* and *kārmamala*." *Parātrīśikā Vivaraṇa*, LJA archive.

individual. Although he reaches the nearest state of the consciousness of Śiva, he has no ability to catch hold of That state. That inability is the creation of *āṇavamala*. For example, if you are conscious of your own nature and then that consciousness fades away, and fades away quickly, this fading is caused by *āṇavamala*.

Āṇavamala is *apūrṇatā*, non-fullness. It is the feeling of being incomplete. Due to this impurity, you feel incomplete in every way. Though you feel incomplete, knowing that there is some lack in you, yet you do not know what this lack really is. You want to hold everything, and yet no matter what you hold, you do not fill your sense of lacking, your gap. You cannot fill this lacking unless the master points it out to you and then carries you to that point.

Of these three impurities, *āṇavamala* and *māyīyamala* are not in action, they are only in perception, in experience. It is *kārmamala* which is in action.

Kashmir Shaivism–The Secret Supreme, 7.47-49.

This whole universal existence, which is admitted by other thinkers that it is ignorance, that it is *māyā* (illusion), that it is pain, it is torture–they explain it like that–but we Shaivites don't explain like that. We Shaivites explain that this [universe] is the expansion of your own nature. *Mala* is nothing, *mala* is only your free will of expanding your own nature.

So we have come to this conclusion that *mala* is not a real impurity [i.e., substance]. It is your own choice; it is the choice of Lord Śiva. The existence of impurity is just the choice of Lord Śiva, it is not some thing. It is *svarūpa svātantrya māṭraṁ*, it is just your will, just your independent glory.

If you realize that it is *svarūpa svātantrya māṭraṁ*, [that] it is your own play, then what will an impure thing do? An impure thing will only infuse purity in you, if you realize that impurity is not existing at all, it is just your own play, just your own independent expansion.

[So], *mala* is neither formless nor with form. It is just ignorance. It doesn't allow knowledge to function; knowledge is stopped. *Mala* is the absence of knowledge. *Mala* is not something substantial. So, this absence of knowledge takes place only by ignorance, otherwise there is no *mala*. In the real sense, *mala* does not exist, impurity does not exist.

Tantrāloka 9.79-83, LJA archives.

Bibliography

Published text with translation and commentary by Swami Lakshmanjoo:

The Mystery of Vibrationless–Vibration in Kashmir Shaivism, Vasugupta's *Spanda Kārikā and* Kṣemarāja's *Spanda Sandoha*, ed. John Hughes, (Lakshmanjoo Academy, Los Angeles, 2016).

Essence of the Supreme Reality–Abhinavagupta's Paramārthasāra, with the commentary of Yogarāja, original video recording, (Lakshmanjoo Academy Book Series, Los Angeles, 2015).

Bhagavad Gita–In the Light of Kashmir Shaivism (*with original video*), ed. John Hughes, (Lakshmanjoo Academy Book Series, Los Angeles, 2015).

Festival of Devotion and Praise–Shivastotrāvali, Hymns to Shiva by Utpaladeva, ed. John Hughes, (Lakshmanjoo Academy Book Series, Los Angeles, 2015).

Kashmir Shaivism–The Secret Supreme, ed. John Hughes (Lakshmanjoo Academy Book Series, Los Angeles, 2015).

Shiva Sutras–The Supreme Awakening, ed. John Hughes, (Lakshmanjoo Academy Book Series, Los Angeles, 2015).

Self Realization in Kashmir Shaivism–The Oral Teachings of Swami Lakshmanjoo, ed. John Hughes (State University of New York Press, Albany, 1995).

Light on Tantra in Kashmir Shaivism–Abhinavagupta's Tantrāloka, Chapter One, ed. John Hughes, (Lakshmanjoo Academy, Los Angeles, 2017).

Vijñāna Bhairava–The Manual for Self Realization, ed. John Hughes (Lakshmanjoo Academy Book Series, Los Angeles, 2015).

Unpublished text with translation and commentary by Swami Lakshmanjoo:

Bhagavad Gitartha Saṁgraha of Abhinavagupta, (original audio recording, LJA archives, Los Angeles, 1978).

Bhairava Stotra of Abhinavagupta, Universal Shaiva Fellowship, Sacred Verses for Worship, Los Angeles, 2010.

Dehasta-devata-cakra-stotram of Abhinavagupta (original audio recording, LJA archives, Los Angeles, 1980).

Interview on Kashmir Shaivism, Swami Lakshmanjoo a Scholar and John Hughes (original audio recordings, LJA archives, Los Angeles 1980).

Janmamaraṇavicāragranthaḥ, *Janma Maraṇa Vicāra of Bhaṭṭa Vāmadeva*, (original audio recording, LJA archives, Los Angeles, 1980).

Parātrīśikā Laghuvṛtti with the commentary of Abhinavagupta, (original audio recording, LJA archives, Los Angeles, 1982).

Parātrīśikā Vivaraṇa with the commentary of Abhinavagupta, (original audio recording, LJA archives, Los Angeles, 1982-85).

Special Verses on Practice, translation and commentary of selected verses from various texts (original audio/ video recording, LJA archives, Los Angeles, 1988).

Stava Cintāmaṇi of Bhaṭṭa Nārāyaṇa, (handwritten notes made by Denise Hughes, LJA archives, Nepal 1990).

Stava Cintāmaṇi of Bhaṭṭa Nārāyaṇa, (original audio recording, LJA archives, Los Angeles 1991).

The Tantrāloka of Abhinavagupta, Chapters 1 to 18, (original audio recording, LJA archives, Los Angeles, 1972-1981).

Additional sources - Books

Aṣṭādhyāyī of Pāṇini, Roman transliteration and English Translation by Sumitra M. Katre, first Indian Edition: Motilal Banarsidass, Delhi, 1989.

Śrī Sāmbapañcāśikā, A Hymn by Lord Kṛṣṇa's son Sāmba, Hindi translation by Swami Lakshmanjoo, (first publication 1944, republished by Ishwar Ashram Trust, India, 2009).

Kaṭha Upaniṣad, Sacred Books of The East, Translated by Various Oriental Scholars, Edited by Max Muller, Vol XI, p1, Clarendon Press, Oxford, 1884.

La Bhakti: *Le Stavacintāmaṇi de Bhaṭṭa Nārāyaṇa*, Silburn, Lilian, trans. Paris: De Boccard, 1964.

Netra Tantram, with commentary by Kṣemarāja. Edited by Pandit Madhusudan Kaul Shāstrī, *Vidyāvāridhi*, Superintendent of The research Department of The Kashmir State, (*KSTS*), Vol. XLVI, Srinagar, Kashmir, 1926.

Pratyabhijñāhṛdayam, *The Secret of Self-Recognition*, Sanskrit Text with English Translation, Notes and Introduction by Jaideva Singh (Motilal Banarsidass, Delhi, 1963-2011).

Samudra Manthana, chapter IX of The Viṣṇu Purāṇa, translated by Horace Hayman Wilson (1840).

Shiva Mahimna Stotra, by Puṣpadanta, Sanskrit verses published by Ishwar Ashram Trust in booklet form (1972).

Svacchandatantra, with commentary by Kṣemarāja. Edited with Notes by Paṇḍit Madhusudan Kaul Shāstri, Superintendent of The research Department of The Kashmir State, (*KSTS*), Vol. XXXI, Srinagar, Kashmir, 1921.

Tantrāloka of Abhinavagupta with the commentary of Rājānaka Jayaratha, Edited with notes by Mahāmahopādhyāya Paṇḍit Mukunda Rāma Śāstrī, Officer in Charge, Research Department, (*KSTS*) Vol XXIII, Allahabad, 1918.

The Stava Cintāmaṇi of Bhaṭṭa Nārāyaṇa, with commentary of Kṣemarāja. Edited with Notes by Paṇḍit Madhusudan Kaul Shāstri, Superintendent of The research Department of The Kashmir State, (*KSTS*), Vol. X, Srinagar, Kashmir, 1918.

INDEX

abhāva 160
Abhinavaguptaxi, xxiii, 4, 84, 126, 143
absolute knowledge 73
Absorption (samāveśa) 31
ādhyātmika, ādhidaivika, ādhibhautika 128
āgama 159
Agni 115
ahaṁkāra xxvi
aiśvarya 114
ajñāna 122
akāra 16
Ambikā 13
amṛta 41
ānanda 84
ānanda śakti 155
ānanda vṛndāya 49
ananyāpekṣayā 29
āṇavamala, māyīyamala, kārmamala 93, 135, 163
āṇavopāya, śāktopāya, śāmbhavopāya 12, 151
ancient log 16
aṇḍas 17
aṇimā 70
añjana 110
anugraha .... xvi, 91
anumāna 157
aparā (inferior) 28, 153
aparā śakti 161
ardhacandra 16, 151
ārtha (the highest goal)..... 36
arthāpatti 160
Ārtharva Veda 81
artificial devotion .... xvii, 129
āsuras 41
attachment 64, 66, 73
auṁ 151
auṁ (oṁ) 16, 151
auṣadha 35
avenue of Lord Śiva 48
avyayam 110
awareness 161
bauddha jñāna (intellectual knowledge) .... xii, xviii
begging 69
Bhagavad Gītā 92
Bhairava .... xv, xxiii, 2, 22
Bhairava Stotra .... xv, xxiii
Bhairava Tantras xii
bhakti. xxi, 38, 54, 66, 74, 110
bhakti cintāmaṇi 38
bhakti lakṣmī 141
bhakti rasa 80
bhārūpaḥ 105

Bhaṭṭa Nārāyaṇa ..... xi, xxiv–xxv, 3–4, 7, 15, 47, 70, 94–95, 131, 140, 144
bhāvana 137
bhūr, bhuvaḥ, svaḥ ... xiii, 57, 79, 94
Bījbihara 144
bindu 11–12, 16, 151–152
bindu (prakāśa) 12
bindureva 16
bliss 76
bodha (knowledge) 10
bodha dīpikā 73
boon-giving tree 70
boredom 56
bottomless ocean 111
bowing .... xxv, 36
Brahmā ... xix, 44, 46, 70, 76, 87, 91, 128
brahmāṇḍa 17
brahmarandhra 153
Bṛhaspāti 57
brown hair 48
buddhi xxvi
Buddhism 25
candle of bhakti 73
candle of devotion xxi
candle of knowledge .. xxi, 135
candle of Thy devotion 73
cetaḥ 140
cintāmaṇi .... xx, 4, 38, 141
cintāmaṇi jewel .. xxiii, 4, 38, 41
cit, ānanda, icchā, jñāna, kriyā 103
citram 118
cobra 34
cognitive cycle 48
concealing (tirodhāna) ... xviii
concentrate 53
consciousness 10, 61
craving 90, 133, 135
creation (sṛṣṭi) .... xviii, 127
creation, protection, destruction . 45, 79, 103, 127
crescent moon 66
crookedness 72
cycle of ignorance 122
darkness 73, 125
darśana 49
Dehastha-devatā-cakra-stotram xx
depression 89–90
desire 44, 66, 77, 116
destruction (saṁhāra) xviii
detachment 88, 90
devotion . xvii, xx–xxi, 10, 38, 43, 54–55, 66, 70, 73, 80, 103, 110, 120–121, 129, 138, 141
dharma 78
dharma, jñāna, vairāgya, aiśvarya 113
dhūrjaṭa 29
dhyāna 49
discipline 82
disease 34
divine mistress 81
doubt 122, 129–130, 138
drama 74

dreaming .... xxvi, 23, 46
drinking wine 61
duality 39
duḥkha 29, 37, 99
Durvasa Rishi xii
dvandva 68
eating meat 61
ecstasy .. 9–10, 23, 48–49, 107
energy of illusion 55
enjoyment 74, 77
essence of nectar 117
eternal log 33
eternal nectar 7
excitement 50
final liberation 36, 129
five circles (aṇḍas) 17
five gods 45–46
five lords 51
five prāṇas 98
furious ocean 92
gandha (smell) 69
Ganges 113
garimā 70
Gāyatri mantra xiii
Gāyatrī mantra .... xxii, 94
glāni 89
glory 93
glory of knowledge 88
God consciousness xix–xx, 2, 10, 13, 24, 47, 54–55, 63, 65, 73, 86, 116, 119–120, 123–124, 139, 155
god of love 99
goddesses xix
gods xix
good actions 80
goose-bumps 102
gossip 131
grace .. 59, 63, 67, 91, 140, 161
grāma 106
grāma dharma 108
grāmya 106
great swan 20
great torture 111
greed 64
grief 99
Guṇāditya 143
guṇas 29, 40, 58, 60
guṇātīta 29, 61, 67
guru 3, 59
haṁ-saḥ ('I am He') 72
haṁsaḥ 21, 71
Harvan xii
heart of devotees 81
heavenly abode 76
hetu 158
hindrance 121
hindrances 132
hypocrisy 72
icchā (will) 19
icchā śakti 155
ignorance 20, 35, 87
illusion 55
illusive magic 55
imagination .... xviii, 118
Indra 115
īśitva 70
Īśvara . xix, 45–46, 70, 78, 155
Jagatnātha 64
jāgrat 46, 49

jāgrat, svapna, suṣupti 58
jayanti 93
Jesus Christ 33
jīvan mukta 23, 57
jñāna (knowledge) 12, 19, 21, 110, 113–114, 117, 135
jñāna śakti 150, 155
joy 76
kalākalita 23
Kālasaṁkarṣinī Kālī 154
Kaliyuga xii
kalpa vṛkṣa (tree) 25, 69
Kāmadahanam 99
Kāmadeva 99–100
kapardine 53
kārmamala 135, 163
Kashmir 60
Kashmiri pundit 115
King Lālitāditya 144
knowledge 20, 39
knowledge of oneness 84
kriyā...... 12, 19, 103, 150, 155
kriyā śakti 155
Kṣemarāja.. xix, xxiii, 1–3, 5, 34, 46, 59, 83, 92, 104, 117–118, 126, 128, 136
Kṣīra-sāgara 4, 42, 117
kuṇḍalinī 154
laghimā 70
Lālitāditya 144
Laws of Manu 83
liberation ... xxi, 34, 118, 126, 129
liṅgoddhāra .... xiii, xv
logic 160
longing 88, 122–123, 126
Lord Buddha 90
Lord Kṛṣṇa 33
lord of death (Mahākāla) 112, 154
Lord Śiva xx, 9, 13–14, 16, 18, 22, 28, 34, 38, 44, 47, 50, 59, 63, 71–72, 75, 83, 99, 102, 104, 110, 115, 127, 132, 141, 145
Lord Śiva's image 118
Lord Viṣṇu xv
love xx, 14, 28, 55, 58–59, 66, 68, 73, 75, 101–102, 118–119
magic 55
Magician 56
Mahā Lakṣmī 141
Mahādev Mountain xii
Mahādeva 48
mahāpracaya 162
Mahāpreta (the great corpse) 152
mahāsamādhi xxxiv
mahātmās 102
mahimā 70
makāra 16
malas .... xiv, 93, 135, 157
manas xxvi
Mānasarovara lake 72
Mandara mountain 7
mantra xviii, 9, 14, 16, 30, 77, 94, 104
master 92
matted hair 39

māyā .. xiv, 20, 56, 78, 85, 87, 114, 155–156, 164
māyā is divine 86
māyā śakti 20
māyīyamala xxi, 109, 135, 163
medicine (auṣadham) 35
meditate 53, 126
meditation 56, 62, 89, 133
milk 20, 42
milky ocean 5, 41–42
Mīmāṁsā 25, 33
mind 50, 53, 139
mind, intellect, and ego ... 134
misfortune 109
misunderstanding xvii, 84, 87
moha xiv
Mohammed 33
mokṣa 59
moon 11
mortality 105
Mount Kailash 72
mūlādhāra 153
nabhi 153
nāda 11–12, 16, 151
nāda (visarga) 12
nādānta 17, 151
Naiyyāyika 33
namaḥ (bowing) xxv
namaskāra xxvi
Nārāyaṇa 6
nātha 121
nectar 3, 41, 77, 117, 129, 133
nectar of immortality (amṛta) 42
Netra tantra 136, 151
nimeṣa 136
nirdvanda 39
nirdvandvā 28
nirguṇa 40, 118
nirodhī 151
niścala 39
Nyāya 25
objective cycle 48
obstacles 132
ocean of consciousness 46
ocean of ecstasy 76
ocean of joy 76
ocean of milk 4
ocean of nectar 77
ocean of] milk 4
oṁ 94, 151
oṁ-kāra 16
one hundred and eighteen worlds 17, 51, 98
organic field 47
outcasts 64
pain 37, 70, 76
pañcakṛtya 45, 51
Pāṇini's Aṣṭādhyāyī 123
parā (supreme) 28, 153
parā śakti 19, 153, 161
Parabhairava... xxiv, 1, 4, 18, 70, 90, 124, 126, 136, 145
Parabhairavī 68
paramānanda 10
Paramārthasāra xv
Paramaśiva xviii
Parameśvara 15, 18, 50
parāparā (medium) 28, 153
parāparā śakti 161

Parātriśikā Vivaraṇa 114
Pārvatī13, 100, 102, 107, 115, 155
Patañjali xv
patri mālā 33
pauper 116
pauruṣa jñāna xviii
penance 89
perfect ecstasy 10
pervasion 16
pitiable condition 69
possession 121
power 28
pracaya 162
prākāmya 70
prakāśa 11–12, 150
prakāśa rūpa 105
prakāśamāne 1
prakṛti (nature) 134
pralāya 45
pralayākala 46
pramātṛ bhava 48
prāṇana 98
praṇava mantra 'oṁ' .. 16–17, 151–152
prāpti 70
pratijñā, hetu, udhāraṇa, upanaya, ... 158
Pratyabhijñā śāstras 84
pratyakṣa 157
prostrate 116
protection 127
protection (sthiti) xviii
Purāṇa 25
purification 139
purified mind 139
puruṣa jñāna (direct experience) xii
puryaṣṭaka xxvi
Puṣpadanta 26
rajoguṇa 40
Rāma Kantha 144
rasa 32, 69, 80, 132
rasāyana 7
repeated births and deaths 37, 111
revealing (anugraha-grace) ... xviii
Rudra . xix, 44, 46, 70, 76, 87, 132
rudra śakti samāveśa xvi
rules and regulations 83
rūpa 69
rūpātīta 162
śabda 69
śabda, sparśa, rūpa, rasa and gandha 106
Sadāśiva .. xix, 46, 70, 78, 84, 152, 155
sādhaka 81, 104, 108, 113
sādhana 82, 89
sadness 70
Śaiva gurus 59
Śaiva yoga 93
Śaivism 123
sakala 46
śakti 17–18, 127, 151
śaktipāta 38, 102
śāktopāya 12
sālambanā 137

samādhi 2, 70, 162–163
samanā 17, 151
samāveśa xxvi
śāmbhava samāveśa . xviii, 31
śāmbhavopāya 12
saṁkalpa 105
Sāṁkhya 25, 33
sampradāya .... xvi–xvii, xxv
saṁpūrṇāmṛta 14
saṁsāra .... xxiii, 38, 111
saṁśaya 122
Samudra manthana 6
Śaṅkara 11, 13
Śaṅkaropal (Shiva Rock) .. xii
śāntātīta kalā 96
śarīra 140
śāstras 52, 159
satatoditam 162
sattvaguṇa, rajoguṇa,
tamoguṇa . 29, 40, 59–60, 67
sāttvic life 60
satya saṁkalpa 106
Self-awareness 10
separation 15
seva 55
sex . 50, 99–100, 106, 108, 112
siddha xxxiii
Śiva Mahimna Stotra 26
Śivadṛṣṭi .... xi–xii, xiv, xxvi
Śivastotrāvali 103
slave of sex 101
sluggishness 58
smṛti 49
so'ham 21
soma 66
Somānanda .... xi, xiv
spanda 2, 9, 147
sparśa 14, 69
sparśana 49
sphurattā 149
Śrī Kaṇṭhanātha 104
srotaḥ sahasreṇa 32
Stava Cintāmaṇi 4, 145
stuti 49
subjective cycle 48
subtle 18
subtlest element 51
śuddhavidyā 10, 155
supreme knowledge 90
supreme mokṣaḥ 36
supreme nectar 133
Śūrāditya .... xxiv, 143
surrender 44
sūrya (sun) 11
suṣupti 49
Svacchanda tantra 151
svapna 49
svarūpa svātantrya 164
svatantra 75
svātantrya100–101, 149, 155–
156
svātantrya śakti ... 18, 78, 85–
86, 127, 134, 154
Swami Lakshmanjoo ..... xxv,
xxxiii
Swami Mahatab Kāk 143
Swami Rām 143
swans 72
tamoguṇa 29, 40
tanmātras xxvi

Tantrāloka 107, 163
tapāsya 89
tarka 158
taste 32
teacher-disciple (guru-śiṣya).. xvii
the real pathway 31
the threefold pains 128
three guṇas 58
three malas 93
three Vedās 81
three worlds 53, 57, 121
threefold universe 79
tilak 65
timira roga 35
tirodhāna .... xvi–xvii
tīvra śaktipāta 38
touch 14
trailokya nāṭakam 74
treasure 120
triguṇa 58
triśūla 19, 28, 154
turya ... xxii, 46, 49, 147, 161–163
turyātīta 46, 49, 162–163
udāharaṇa 158
udyoga 4
ukāra 16
Ūmā, Pārvatī 66
unlimited ocean 117
unmanā 16–17, 152
upadeśa 4
upādhi 69
upamāna 159
Upamanyu 42
upāya 12, 20, 112, 150–151
ūrdhva dvadaśānta 153
Utpaladeva 84
vacaḥ 140
vairāgya 89, 114
Vaiśeṣika 25
Vaiṣṇava 26, 33
Vāma mārga 26
vaśitva 70
Vasugupta xi
Vāsuki 6, 34
Vāyu 115
Vedānta 25, 87
Vedās 25, 33, 52, 64, 82
Vidyāpati 57
vighna 132
vijñānākala 46
vikalpa 134
vimarśa 11–12, 149–150
vimarśa śakti 10
Viṣṇu ... xix, 44, 46, 70, 76, 87
vyāpinī 17, 151
waking, dreaming, deep sleep 46, 74, 147, 161
weakness 32
women 65, 87
worship 36
wrong notions 84
yoga 162
Yoga Darśana 70
yogic powers 70
Your bhakti 70
Your trick 56

Teachings of Swami Lakshmanjoo published by The Lakshmanjoo Academy

Bhagavad Gita–In the Light of Kashmir Shaivism

Festival of Devotion & Praise, Hymns to Shiva
Shivastotrāvali by Utpaladeva

Vijñāna Bhairava–The Manual for Self Realization

Shiva Sutras–The Supreme Awakening

Kashmir Shaivism–The Secret Supreme

Self Realization in Kashmir Shaivism–The Oral Teachings of Swami Lakshmanjoo

Essence of the Supreme Reality,
Abhinavagupta's Paramārthasāra

The Mystery of Vibrationless-Vibration
in Kashmir Shaivism,
Vasugupta's Spanda Kārikā & Kṣemarāja's Spanda Sandoha

Light on Tantra in Kashmir Shaivism
Abhinavagupta's Tantrāloka
Chapter One

Lakshmanjoo ACADEMY

The teachings of Swami Lakshmanjoo are a response to the urgent need of our time: the transformation of consciousness and the evolution of a enlightened humanity.

The Universal Shaiva Fellowship was established under Swamiji's direct inspiration, for the purpose of realizing Swamiji's vision of making Kashmir Shaivism available to the whole world. It was Swamiji's wish that his teachings be made available without the restriction of caste, creed, color or gender. The Universal Shaiva Fellowship and the Lakshmanjoo Academy, along with the Kashmir Shaiva Institute (Ishwar Ashram Trust) in India, have preserved Swamiji's original teachings and are progressively making these teachings available in book, audio, and video formats.

For the sincere aspirant, this knowledge is extremely valuable and uplifting for all of humankind. It offers humanity a clear and certain vision in a time of uncertainty. It shows us the way Home and gives us the means for Its attainment.

For information on Kashmir Shaivism or to support the work of The Universal Shaiva Fellowship and the Lakshmanjoo Academy and Kashmir Shaiva Institute (Ishwar Ashram Trust) visit the Lakshmanjoo Academy website or email us at info@LakshmanjooAcademy.org.

www.UniversalShaivaFellowship.org

www.LakshmanjooAcademy.org

www.IshwarAshramTrust.com

Instructions to download audio files

1. Open the link below to download the free audio https://www.universalshaivafellowship.org/StavaCintamani

   You will be **directed** to **"The Magical Jewel of Devotion in Kashmir Shaivism - Bhaṭṭa Nārāyaṇa's Stava Cintamani - Audio"**

2. Select "**Add to basket** " which will send you to the next page.

3. Copy "**StavaCintamani**" into the "**Add Gift Certificate or Coupon"** box

4. Click "**Checkout**" and fill in your details to process the free downloads.

   If you have any difficulties please contact us at:
   www.LakshmanjooAcademy.org/contact